Doc

Orra A. Phelps, M.D.
Adirondack
Naturalist and Mountaineer

Doc

Orra A. Phelps, M.D.

Adirondack
Naturalist and Mountaineer

Mary Arakelian

North Country Books
Utica, New York

Doc

Orra A. Phelps, M.D.
Adirondack
Naturalist and Mountaineer

by
Mary Arakelian

ISBN 0-925168-78-5

Library of Congress Card Number: 00-107856

Published by
NORTH COUNTRY BOOKS, INC.
311 Turner Street
Utica, New York 13501

This book is dedicated to

Lili, Sherene, and Fred,
Eric and Karina,
and The Adirondack Mountain Club.

Contents

Acknowledgments

I am most grateful to my late Aunt Orra Phelps and to my grandmother, Mrs. Orra Parker Phelps, who had the foresight to preserve their forty years of correspondence, diaries, trip logs, personal papers, and photographs, all of which have made this book possible. The biography had its genesis in my receiving this treasure of material, too valuable and interesting to destroy.

Doc: Orra A. Phelps, M.D. Adirondack Naturalist and Mountaineer would never have been completed without the help and encouragement of several of Orra Phelps's friends and colleagues. I am very grateful to those who also wrote endorsements, including: Dr. Nancy G. Slack, Dr. Arthur Newkirk, Ruth Schottman, Dr. Neal Burdick, Dr. John Haines, and Laura and Guy Waterman. To each and all of them I am profoundly grateful.

Dr. Nancy G. Slack, Professor of Biology at Russell Sage College and author of the introduction for this book, closely edited the manuscript, especially for scientific terminology. She brought to my attention the importance of the long lineage of female botanists and naturalists from Mount Holyoke College under whom the Phelps women studied, and gave me much scholarly advice.

Dr. Edwin Ketchledge and Dr. Arthur Newkirk most generously provided historical data concerning the ADK Natural History Program and material from the early ADK archives and shared personal correspondence, photographs, insights, and anecdotes.

Ruth Schottman thoughtfully critiqued the manuscript, and shared personal photographs and memories of her Adirondack trips and seminars with Orra and the Thursday Naturalists events over a delicious gourmet dinner. I also thank her for introducing me to Mary Brennan, who interviewed Orra when she was able to recall many events. Ruth also introduced me to The Land Trust of the Saratoga Region, Inc. which now is custodian of The Phelps Nature Preserve in Wilton, New York. I also thank Bill Towne for information about Orra's mentoring high school science students in their Paludiological Society.

x *Acknowledgments*

Edith Pilcher, author of *The Constables, First Family of the Adirondacks* and *Up the Lake Road*, critiqued a middle version of this book and recommended a fully chronological presentation for the final form, and helped me with considerable technical advice. Both Warder Cadbury and Bill Healy, who also read the manuscript, gave insightful advice, and encouragement. The Adirondack Research Library staff is to be thanked for their insistence that this book be published, for sharing their archival material, and for arranging for me to join Paul Schaefer at his home for a viewing of the film, "The Land Nobody Knows" as well as for an interview. I thank Mr. Schaefer for his memories of Orra's interaction with him and his brother Vincent Schaefer.

Many former hiking companions and friends shared tales of their north country adventures. Among them I am grateful to James Goodwin for his memories of their separate January 1, 1933 Marcy climbs as well as his and Orra's shared part in the opening of the Adirondacks to the general public, which he said was both positive and negative.

Phyllis Brown, Elsa Jane Turmelle and her brother, Dick Putnam, and family brought laughs and tears with their humorous and touching recollections of hiking days and what Orra's mentoring meant to her scouts.

The late Douglas Ayres' eyes shone when he recalled times with Orra in Fort Plain and in the Adirondacks. His voice trembled when he said they both should have had careers where they could have felt the sun and the wind more often. I am indebted for his offer to include his poem, "Elk Lake Studded," in Orra's memory.

Wendy and Dick Best gave insights into Orra's relationship with her neighbors, her role as a mentor to their family, her inspiration for their becoming Forty-Sixers, and how she shared her broad wisdom, even as a senior.

Lorraine Westcott generously shared how Orra, in her last three decades, was involved with the community, especially the Wilton Heritage Society, with teenagers and their families, and with other nature lovers. She has also been a driving force behind the preservation of the Phelps Nature Preserve and, along with the new neighbors, Terry and Dr. Patricia Hale, watches over it faithfully. Lorraine kindly led me to Laura Meade, a naturalist who carries on Orra's love of teaching about the special Adirondack flora. When Gloria and Fred MacMaster kindly let me wander through the old Phelps home before many of the furnishings were changed with new owners, it was like visiting the past. They also shared memories of being neighbors with Orra for many years and the many interests they had in common.

Laura Snell told me of her nurturing Orra while Orra mentored her from the late seventies until Orra's death. Laura shared work on the Saratoga Environmental Committee's surveying and in Orra's vegetable garden, took her out botanizing from the nursing home, and comforted her when she broke her arm. I am grateful for their special relationship and Laura's sharing a different facet of Orra's aging.

I am most grateful to the Adirondack Mountain Club staff for information and photos. Several Forty-Sixers and ADK members generously shared their remembrances and photos of Orra. Among them are: Grace Hudowalski, the Forty-Sixers' historian, who showed me Orra's Forty-Sixers record during a most pleasant visit at her Boulders home in the mountains; Dr. Marion Biesemeyer, who told of Orra giving a slide show at her home and details of their joint hike up Algonquin with Chief Justice William O. Douglas; Adolph and Mary Dittmar together with Bill Endicott who laughed and recalled old ADK times around a delicious lunch; and Helen Menz, who generously provided old photographs and anecdotes dating back to the thirties. Landon Rockwell, Ralph Geiser, Lillian Hunt, and James Nye gave me photographs and more vivid memories and accounts. Their interviews and correspondence kept me enthused and encouraged.

The New York State Museum staff most generously shared their memories of Orra Phelps, her many accessions and service to the museum, and kindly gave permission to include their photo of Stanley Smith, Assistant State Botanist. Special help came from: Dr. Richard Mitchell, State Botanist; Dr. Eugene Ogden, former State Botanist; Dr. John Haines, State Mycologist; and Dr. Robert Funk, State Archaeologist, who kindly identified arrowheads from the Phelps farm.

The Adirondack Museum staff has been extremely helpful. Gerald Pepper, Librarian, expertly lead me to source material and microfilms where I read of the Kates brothers meeting and sharing information with Orra. I also thank the museum for permission to use the photograph of Orson Phelps, a distant relative of Orra Phelps, the text of Orra's 1937 Marcy Centennial speech, and other background information.

The Crandall Library, Glens Falls, the Keene Valley Library, the Lake Placid Library, the Saranac Lake Library, the Saratoga Springs Library, the State of New York Library at Albany, and the Memorial Hall Library of Andover, Massachusetts were all extremely helpful in locating source material, especially from their Adirondack collections and microfilms.

Mount Holyoke College, Johns Hopkins University, and the United States Military Academy at West Point have been very generous with archival material. Carleton Coulter, III kindly provided information, a photo, and memories of his father.

I also wish to thank Jeanne Marie Childe and Dr. Neal Burdick, who skillfully edited and helped polish various versions of the book. Sherene Aram, Orra's grandniece and my daughter, also read the full manuscript and gave insightful comments about Orra's religious statements, her needs for nurturing, her feelings as she aged, the mother-daughter tensions, and family dynamics, as well as addressed the balance of action versus narrative in the biography. I also thank my sisters, Phoebe Hunt, Dorothy Hanlon, and Rachel Kellogg, and my aunt, Mildred Shaw, for many overnight stays during my research, memories of Aunt Orra as they perceived her, family photos, and unflagging support. I thank my daughter Lili Mash for her insightful memories of Aunt Orra and of the University of New Hampshire setting where Orra first fell in love, for critiquing portions of the book, and for her enthusiastic support.

Last, but not least, I thank my husband Fred Arakelian for the many dinners he cooked, the driving and hiking he shared, the absences he endured, the dusty archives he helped move and sort, and his general good humor despite some hectic days.

To all of these people, I am deeply grateful for their kind assistance.

Introduction

This biography of an extraordinary woman whose life spanned most of the twentieth century, opens with a 1936 scene in which Orra Phelps traveled at night to Lake Colden in the Adirondack wilderness to treat a camper with a badly slashed leg. As someone on the scene wrote, "She is the only doctor I have ever known who made a house call to a lean-to." The opening scene of this biography introduces Dr. Phelps in her combined life roles as a physician, an Adirondack explorer, and a compassionate woman.

Orra Almira Phelps's life is closely interwoven with that of her family. Her father, an early professor of agriculture at what became the University of Connecticut, later became a farm manager and Farm Bureau agent. He was never able to hold a job very long, which was a source of many struggles in the lives of both Orra Phelps, the mother, and Orra Phelps, the daughter.

Mary Arakelian provides a fascinating study of the two Orra's which addresses today's hunger for knowledge of unique women's lives and increased interest in mother/daughter relationships. The meaning of the name Orra is "odd", in the sense of out-of-the-ordinary. Orra Parker Phelps, referred to in the book as "Mrs. Phelps," studied botany at Mount Holyoke College with well-known botanists, Lydia Shattuck and Henrietta Hooker, graduating in 1888. She made extensive plant collections, both in Connecticut and later in St. Lawrence County, New York, which were sold to many universities. The field work, identification, and mounting of these plants were part of young Orra's original botanical education and a lifelong bond between the two women.

Mrs. Phelps described herself as a "wild girl of the woods"; when the young mother of seven had a mental breakdown she was advised to take one day a week off to go botanizing.

Young Orra attended Mount Holyoke and chose to study geology and zoology with another generation of well-known women scientist professors. Thus commenced thirty-five years of letters between the two Orras, providing the author with wonderful material, the "mother-lode for this biography." Graduating in 1918, Orra returned as assistant in geology and later obtained a position as assistant and then instructor at New Hampshire College. Fossil hunting was another joint mother/daughter activity.

Orra's true ambition from her undergraduate days was to become a physician. Medical school was not financially possible until 1921 when she entered Johns Hopkins Medical School, among the very best in the country at that time. Its financiers were wealthy women who insisted that it both require a bachelor's degree for entrance and admit women.

This book is of interest to historians of medicine and of the lives of medical students in the early 1920s. Orra's struggles to complete the difficult studies while holding two outside jobs are poignantly told. Both her courses and her clinical experiences, in an era of changing medical science and practice, are described in her letters to her mother.

Those who remember Orra in her field pants and Bean boots will be surprised to read her description of a dance given for all the women medical students and "the best of the men." She bought a "black satin dress trimmed with blue satin and black braid," and wrote, "So tomorrow night I expect to go 'tripping.' "

There were a number of men in her life, including long-time suitor Captain Carleton Coulter, a man of admirable character. The negative elements of the mother/daughter relationship are evident in relation to him and to other possible husbands. Several factors probably contributed to Orra's single life, in spite of three offers of marriage.

It was very difficult to combine a professional career with marriage and childbearing in that era. Moreover, Orra was a close witness to her mother's frustrations as an overburdened mother of seven with "enormous stifled intellectual capacities," and to her unfortunate marriage to Orra's father, a poor provider who was both controlling of and dependent on her mother and, in later life, mentally unstable as well. Mrs. Phelps had many prejudices—against non-Protestants (Captain Coulter was a Catholic), poorly educated people, and immigrants. She was both encouraging to her children in their educational and professional ambitions and controlling in other aspects of their lives.

On the other hand, mother and daughter shared a very strong bond in their love of plants, birds, and wilderness. Neither really discovered the Adirondack High Peaks until 1924 when they made a joint ascent of Mt. Marcy. Mrs. Phelps was then fifty-seven. It was a different era, backpacking without light tents, modern sleeping bags, or camping stoves. They carried heavy blanket rolls and their belts were hung with canteens and citronella-drenched kerchiefs, even before the black fly-repelling Old Woodsman of my earlier Adirondack climbs.

Moreover, they carried a nearly extinct item, the vasculum or metal plant-collecting can, wherever they went. What a picture! They now shared a car with son, Leon. They made trips to places such as Heart Lake and Adirondac Loj, which required special lifts plus trolley, train, bus, ferry rides, and much walking on roads current climbers traverse by car.

Orra learned to identify birds and their songs from her mother. She later taught others, both students at Mount Holyoke and Girl Scouts, with whom she had long and mentoring relationships. Her mother's diary provides delightful descriptions of special Adirondack birds: "A winter wren . . . lit on the tin stove not eighteen inches from me. Beautiful tiny creature, how can he hold so much pure music?" Of the Arctic three-toed woodpecker, always a thrill for a birder to come upon unexpectedly on a spruce-fir forest trail, she wrote: "He looked regal in plain shining upper plumage, barred sides, and an yellow crown patch."

While in medical school, and even as late as 1945, Orra continued to learn botany from her mother, sending Mrs. Phelps specimens to check her identifications. Orra was well-respected in later years for her great botanical knowledge of the Adirondack flora. However, she referred to her mother as the "real botanist," which was undisputed due to Mrs. Phelps's training at Mount Holyoke and later extensive practice of collecting plants from largely unexplored sites in two states.

Much was made of Orra's graduation from Johns Hopkins Medical School in the Saratoga newspaper. This same paper had previously recounted a walk home of nearly three hundred fifty miles from Baltimore to Wilton, New York made by Orra and a friend in order to save the train fare after her second year of medical school.

Orra is perhaps best known for her full alternate career with the Adirondack Mountain Club. She first went to Adirondac Loj in 1926 and climbed her second High Peak during the summer she worked at Saratoga

Springs Hospital. She then, and in subsequent years, was able to do her own exploring and obtained first hand hiking information with "zeal and vision." In 1930, it was noted that she made medical rounds by day but gathered information and wrote the text for the new ADK guidebook by night. In 1934, the first edition of the *Guide to Adirondack Trails, Northeast Section* was presented to the Trails Committee; maps were made. Orra delivered the manuscript to Howard Carlson, President of the Adirondack Mountain Club, in New York by taking the night boat from Albany. The first copies were ready in September and they sold for seventy-five cents each. Her mother wrote, "Guide Book received and I'm proud of you. It is a real bit of work and deserves heaps of praise."

Many Adirondack characters and other well-known people appear in subsequent chapters of this book. Orra knew all of them. Many, like Paul Schaefer, were hiking companions and worked with her on early conservation issues. The famous Adirondack hermit, Noah John Rondeau, was a friend. Orra led a 1938 ADK backpacking trip to his teepee, and Rondeau led them all up four trailless peaks: Mt. Seymour, Donaldson, Emmons, and Couchsachraga. This experience inspired Orra to climb all forty-six peaks over 4,000 feet. A 1938 letter from the hermit to Orra sheds new light on how she was perceived during that period and also on Rondeau's activities and friends, including Adirondack historian, Grace Hudowalski.

World War II brought new challenges. Orra became a Navy physician in early 1944. She was active in the Women's Medical Association, where meetings on important wartime diseases such as typhus fever were the topic. She was excited to meet Eleanor Roosevelt.

After the war, Orra continued her public health medical career as a senior medical officer for the Veterans Administration in Albany. When not at medical work, she was engaged in working with the Adirondack Mountain Club. Orra had become a Forty-Sixer after climbing Allen in 1947, became a charter member of the Adirondack Forty-Sixers, and was elected a director in 1948.

I first met Orra in 1955, on a botanical trip in the Adirondacks, while I was a young graduate student at Cornell. I climbed my first Adirondack peak, Algonquin, on that trip. I met Orra again when I came to the capital region in the late 1950s and joined the newly formed Eastern New York Botanical Club. Most club members were academics and members of the New York State Museum botanical staff, but Orra was a charter member and later its president. Stanley Smith, a phenomenally knowledgeable field botanist and keeper of the state herbarium, became Orra's botanical mentor and friend.

After Orra's retirement from the Veteran's Administration, she started a new and important career for the Adirondack Mountain Club as Ranger-Naturalist at Heart Lake. She displayed many aspects of Adirondack plant and animal life, as well as minerals. Orra's first displays were done in a tent then, by 1966, in a real museum building. She taught both the young and old, through museum visits and field trips. Orra inspired many to discover the beauty and excitement of nature in the Adirondack High Peaks.

During her retirement years Orra made many trips, largely botanical, to exotic parts of the world from Alaska to Iceland and New Zealand. She often travelled with retired Syracuse University botany professor, Mildred Faust, who became her close friend especially after the passing of her mother and most of her family. Orra continued to participate in Adirondack Mountain Club botanical activities into her eighties. Jim Goodwin recalls an ascent of Mt. Seymour in her eighties. I vividly recall climbing Wright with her when she was over eighty. Ruth Schottman remembers the "glowing, excited, exultant Orra" when she finally completed all the portions of the Northville-Lake Placid Trail at eighty-three.

Both Orra Phelpses were remarkable women. The older Orra wrote an autobiographical account of her childhood when she was over eighty. Her diaries and letters, many of which the author used in this book, might well provide her own biography. The interactions between this mother and daughter greatly enhance this book. The author provides personal insights into the lives of her aunt and her grandmother, lives she shared even as a child, one among many inspired by Orra's and her mother's knowledge and love of the Adirondack wilderness.

Dr. Nancy G. Slack
Professor of Biology
Russell Sage College

House Call to an Adirondack Lean-to
1936

The steep Adirondack trail was slippery and her flashlight was little help in the massive darkness that enveloped Dr. Orra Phelps. Though every turn, every crossing of Marcy Brook was familiar to Orra as she crisscrossed the water and pushed further into the wilderness, the deepness of the night and the urgency of her errand lent a strangeness to the mountains she knew so well.

Walt Williams had rushed toward the big lean-to at Marcy Dam, calling for the doctor. "A hiker at Colden campsite has gashed his leg to the bone with an ax! He needs Dr. Phelps! Right away!"

As Orra wrote:

> Mother and I were almost asleep in the big lean-to when Walt Williams came out from Colden with word that a man had cut his leg badly and needed stitches. He continued out to Heart Lake to get my first aid kit with skin needles in it. I started to walk in to Colden alone.[1]

After a quick inventory of her medical bag and backpack, the doctor added extra batteries, a thermos of coffee, and equipment needed to transform a camping site into a surgical arena.

Even though it was only September 6, 1936, nights were cold, even frosty. Dr. Phelps, dressed in warm wool gabardine slacks, put on heavy wool socks, laced her sturdy boots, and added a wool jacket, hat, and gloves. Within minutes, she was on the trail headed for Lake Colden four miles away.

As she hiked, Orra thought of the details: John Russ and his wife, Sylvia, with fellow Intercollegiate Outing Club[2] members, had returned from hiking MacIntyre (later changed to Algonquin). He'd been chopping firewood when his ax hit a tough knot, flew back, tore through his pants, and slashed open his ankle. Sylvia Russ and nearby campers used clothing to tourniquet and pack the leg. With such a deep cut, it was obvious that John needed a doctor.[3]

She took the yellow trail, shining her flashlight from time to time on the yellow metal tree markers, past more camping sites, crisscrossing Marcy Brook, hiking farther into the wilderness. In another mile, she passed the Avalanche lean-to, the three-sided Adirondack log shelter, and then the trail junction to Lake Arnold and Feldspar Brook. The grade became steeper, up log stairs, over rocks and roots along "Misery Hill." As she hiked higher, the wind felt colder. Mindful of the danger of hypothermia, she paused briefly for energizing hot coffee, and then pushed on.

The foot of Misery Hill, part of the trail to Avalanche Lake and Lake Colden.

About one and one half miles above Marcy Dam, Orra came to a point on the trail where water sprayed off the cliff in wet times. Some flowed south toward the Hudson River and some north to the St. Lawrence and Canada. To Orra this was the Adirondacks' "International Falls."[4]

The going was so rough through Avalanche Pass that it took her nearly an hour to cover one and one-half miles. Orra listened for every sound, felt every vibration. No need to startle a bear eating some of the beechnuts she felt underfoot, but the crunch of dry leaves under her boots already warned nearby creatures. The rising moon now cast ghostly light on the treetops.

Orra's strong hands and arms pulled her over fallen trees and her muscular legs got her up the mud-caked, hand-hewn ladders where the trail was especially steep or wet. She muscled over boulders that blocked the way and swayed eerily across floating wooden "Hitch-up Matilda" bridges hugging the cliff's base as the full moon rose over Colden.[5]

Orra groped her way along the wet moss-covered walls, fingering the vertical carpet where the sheer rock dropped straight into the lake. When she finally reached the Opalescent lean-to south of Lake Colden, John Russ and the outing group were confidently awaiting her arrival.

Orra checked the wound and reassured Russ. Pulse and temperature were normal; he

Orra Phelps (left) and Phyllis Brown, Girl Scout, on a trail ladder similar to ones Orra climbed in September 1936. *1947 photo*

was holding up well. A cup of hot coffee cooled on a stump as Dr. Orra quickly took charge of her "medical team." She handed her instruments to be sterilized in the cooking kettle over the blazing wood fire. Her hands, instruments, Russ's left leg—all must be thoroughly cleaned and disinfected, despite being miles from a hospital.

In the glow of the now full moon and a few flashlights, she gently tweezed, tugged, and swabbed away the dirt, wood shreds, and dried blood from Russ's injured leg. Meticulously she inched down the gash. Russ recalled that his ankle was so numb he barely felt pain as she continued to cleanse the deep wound. By then Walt Williams had arrived with skin needles.

When she was finally satisfied, she scrubbed her own hands again, and laid out the sterilized needle and ligatures. He winced as her hot needle sutured his already bruised skin. After a final alcohol cleansing, she painted the surface with iodine, the best antiseptic available, and carefully wrapped the ankle with gauze. A round of applause broke the tension when Dr. Phelps finally finished the surgery. She made sure Russ was warm and as comfortable as possible in his bedroll. Then she asked for a little more warm coffee.

This story has been told and retold, with variation, by many admirers over the years. Bob Beebe, the Union College Outing Club chairman of that weekend, wrote:

Bill Walker stands on a "Hitch-up Matilda" log footbridge at Avalanche Lake. Walker measured some trails for Orra's 1934 *Guide to Adirondack Trails, Northeast Section.*

> I don't recall now whether the doctor stayed over, or whether she returned that night to her home—probably the latter. By the end of the week Russ's injury was healing nicely, but he had difficulty in walking and needed a couple of more days of rest. We had to leave, but we left him and his wife well supplied with food and firewood. I later learned that they had walked out a few days later with no problems other than a limp.
>
> Over the years since 1936 I have encountered Dr. Phelps only twice, both times on the trail to Marcy Dam, and both times conducting nature walks for groups in the vicinity of Heart Lake. I mentioned the 1936 incident to her on one of these meetings, and she modestly shrugged it off as not worth mentioning.
>
> This incident is an illustration of Dr. Orra Phelps's dedication and self-sacrifice to others by hiking in to Lake

Orra Phelps and Walt Williams enjoy a High Peaks Adirondack vista. More than 60 years later, the scenery remains largely unchanged.

Colden at night to provide prompt medical care to a stranger. She is the only doctor I have ever known who made house calls to a lean-to![6]

Who was this self-assured woman who dared hike four miles into the Adirondack Mountains in the middle of the night to stitch some unknown camper's leg? Orra Phelps's story of self-reliance, her love of the wilderness, and who she really was begins with her parents in rural Connecticut.

At age 80, John Russ reminisces with the author about his experience with Orra Phelps back in 1936. Orra sutured John's ankle by campfire at a remote Lake Colden campsite.

Orra's Parents

Orra Phelps's father, Charles Shepherd Phelps, was born in 1862 in Northampton, Massachusetts, to a farm family whose forebears arrived in Charlestown, Massachusetts in 1634. After graduating from Massachusetts Agricultural College of Amherst in 1885, he became the head of the Department of Agriculture at Storrs Agricultural College, now the University of Connecticut. He married Orra Almira Parker in 1891 and shared her love of birding, botanizing, and writing. At Storrs, he specialized in the study of fruit trees and would later prize his apple orchard at Wilton, New York.

Charles Shepherd Phelps, circa 1886.

After sixteen years at Storrs, Charles left teaching in 1901, probably because he was such a moody and difficult person. He was not compromising, could be harshly critical of others, and had difficulty relating to younger people. Even his letters to his adult children focused mainly on himself — or an overdue bill or plans for his trips.

Numerous jobs managing farms in Connecticut followed. His longest position was for ten years at Robert Scoville's Grasslands Farm in Salisbury, Connecticut. When he lost his job there in 1913, he became the first Farm Agent in St. Lawrence County, at Canton, New York, a difficult move three hundred miles north. There, he wrote a monthly newsletter covering diverse topics: oat smut control, improving drainage, selective breeding, and farm finances. He spoke at area meetings and gave advice to farmers.

For his far-flung work, he purchased the family's first car and, like many early drivers, had difficulties. His wife wrote in a letter to the younger Orra:

> Papa had a very narrow escape one night last week. He had a meeting at Brasie Corners and on one of the bad hills between there and Gouverneur the car began to skid. It turned once and a half around without tipping over, then Papa jammed it against the rocks on the upside of the road, breaking an axle and smashing one wheel all to bits. Then he and the two men with him walked seven miles to Gouverneur getting there at three in the morning.
>
> It was a case of not wanting to use chains and the brakes wouldn't work.[1]

In addition to personality shortcomings, Mr. Phelps was a bookish man, and did not relate well to local farmers. He lost his job again, even though the board had "great admiration for the way [Mr. Phelps had] accounts brought to date and the March paper out, one of the very best in the state."[2]

So, in March 1917, the Phelpses again moved—this time to Saratoga Springs, New York, where Charles was the Farm Agent until 1919, when he was again forced out. He then became the Justice of the Peace and ran his own marginal farm in Wilton, New York until 1941. He published *Rural Life in Litchfield County* in 1917,[3] wrote many articles for agricultural journals, was active in the Congregational Church, and was a fifty-year Grange member.

Orra's mother, Orra Parker Phelps, dated her lineage to the Mayflower with the arrival of four of her maternal ancestors in Plymouth, Massachusetts in 1620: John Tilley, Elizabeth Tilley, Richard Warren, and John Howland.

Several Revolutionary War soldiers were also in her background and the Parker's fifth great-grandfather, Reverend John Williams, the Parson of Old Deerfield, Massachusetts, and his two daughters were among the captives of the Native Americans forced to march to Canada in 1704, a tale retold in *Boy Captive of Old Deerfield*.[4]

The Parker-Phelps family treasures their fifteen-generation fan, maintained through years of careful record keeping and research, which details the names of their ancestors.

Born in 1867, just after the Civil War, Mrs. Phelps was raised among New England ministers, teachers, and landed farmers in South Coventry, Connecticut. When the employer of her daughter, Katharine, questioned her religion, Mrs. Phelps wrote:

> [Say] that we are descended from five Congregational ministers including John Mather and John Williams and that the piety which should have lasted for generations was all used up burning witches and converting Indians.[5]

Mr. and Mrs. Martin Parker, parents of Mrs. Orra Almira Parker Phelps. The use of wasp nests as wall decorations is clear evidence of the Parkers' interest in nature.   *1897 photo*

To meet college entrance requirements, Orra's mother had walked, twice each week, summer and winter, three miles to the village, to recite Latin and Algebra to the minister.[6] At Mount Holyoke Female Seminary, now Mount Holyoke College, Miss Orra Parker of the class of 1888 majored in botany and education.

The famous Mount Holyoke botany teachers Henrietta Hooker and Lydia Shattuck nurtured her natural drive to learn and teach and her life long love of botany. Mrs. Phelps remained particularly close to Dr. Hooker, and went to stay with her during one of Henrietta's illnesses. She also urged Orra, who would also attend Mount Holyoke, to visit with her elderly mentor whenever she could.

Years later, Mrs. Phelps nostalgically relived her college days through her eldest daughter, Orra.

Your letters are delightful: I can go with you to all the familiar places and can see the beauty of the hills. And I've gathered chestnuts under those old trees . . . I'm glad you have the chance and hope you will come to love Mount Holyoke even as I do.[7]

Miss Orra Almira Parker, circa 1884.

Orra Parker taught school in Sedalia, Missouri and in Coventry, Connecticut before she married Charles S. Phelps. They wed on June 10, 1891 at the 'Martin Box', her parents' squarish-looking country home, in South Coventry, Connecticut. Seven children were born in the next twelve years: Francis, Lawrence, Orra, Leon, Phoebe, Katharine, and Bessie.[8]

In 1903, Robert Scoville, the wealthy farm owner who employed Mr. Phelps, commissioned Mrs. Phelps to make a complete collection of local plants titled, "Flowering Plants and Ferns of Salisbury, Connecticut." The project took her six years, somehow sandwiched into the whirl of household duties.

Orra and her siblings learned botany at their mother's worktable as well as in the swamps, meadows, and mountains as they collected, pressed, mounted, and labeled over 1,200 different species of plants, including 136 "rare or occasional" species.[9]

In her well-worn *Connecticut Flora* and *Gray's Manual of Botany of the Northern United States,*[10] Mrs. Phelps recorded her finds. This collection was stored for over sixty years, in specially designed cases in the Scoville Library in Salisbury, Connecticut.

The Martin Box, home of Martin and Almira S. Hibbard Parker and sons, Hibbard and Lucian (Orra Phelps' maternal grandparents and uncles).   *1887 photo*

In 1975, her daughter, Orra, proudly transferred it to the University of Connecticut at Storrs.

Mrs. Phelps kept diaries and wrote several letters daily. To add to the family income, she sold numerous nature articles, photos, and poems. She was active in the Grange, in the Connecticut Botanical Society, and assisted in presenting the Connecticut State floral display at the World's Fair in Chicago in 1903. Among her friends were botanists, ornithologists, geologists, and physicians.

Changes in Mr. Phelps's employment meant moving several times, which frustrated Mrs. Phelps since she had no control over this aspect of their life. They moved from Storrs in 1901, first to Torrington, then in 1903 to Chapinville, and finally to Salisbury, Connecticut.

In March, 1904, the year after the birth of her seventh child, and following their trip to the Chicago Centennial, an exhausted Mrs. Phelps was hospitalized for five weeks with a nervous breakdown. Her physician, Dr. Mary Phylinda Dole of Greenfield, Massachusetts, a Mount Holyoke alumna referred by Mount Holyoke friends, shared Mrs. Phelps's love of their alma mater, nature, and writing. Charles wrote to his ill wife:

> I was sorry to learn you had another bad spell. You must not overdo. I have noticed that your 'glimmering turns' frequently follow a time of nervous excitement and probably your meeting so many new faces . . . excited your nerves, at a time when you were not physically strong. Does the $7.00 per week charge include your room and board and physician's visits? If so, it is reasonable. The children all miss you. We gave baby Bessie her first birthday gifts at breakfast, a rubber doll and a ball.[11]

Seeing a female physician restore her mother's health made a lasting impression on the young Orra, who later recalled one of Dr. Dole's unusual recommendations. This busy young mother, with enormous intellectual capacities stifled by her family life, was to take one day each week to go botanizing; something Mrs. Phelps desperately needed.

A wonderful old photo shows the rocking chair and mending basket left askew as Mrs. Phelps marches off to the hills.[12] Daughter Orra explained:

> My mother made it her priority to take one day a week for herself. She went anywhere she wanted to go. She'd pick the good days, take mountain trails, or sometimes bushwhack all over the hills and fields around Salisbury.[13]

Mrs. Orra Parker Phelps leaves porch and housework at Salisbury on a weekly "botanizing" trip.

Working on her botanical collection was the best medicine for Mrs. Phelps and, to scientists years later, it was a lasting contribution. *House Mother's Holidays*, an unpublished collection of essays, recounted many of Mrs. Phelps's interesting hikes on her days off.

In her diary, she poignantly voiced her dilemma:

> From my youth up to the time of my marriage I was a wild girl of the woods. Even the time when I was corralled in the most conservative of women's schools failed to tame me for I would flee to the mountains before and after taking lessons and discipline and confess to a greater love for said mountains than for the wise and reverend faculty.
>
> Being caught by the marriage lasso, I have behaved fairly well, even if I say it who shouldn't. I've seven children on the highway of life and I've patched and darned and baked and nursed these twenty years, taking for mine only such scraps of time as I could steal and taking them often with the ghost of an unblacked stove and a brimming stocking basket to dog my steps and whisper first on one side and then on the other—you didn't do it, you left me undone—hurry home—hurry home, you shirk, you shirk, until I did run home and darn again all the while in revolt at the indoor life when all the wide world was calling me to come and play with it.
>
> Once I went to smash and spent five weeks in a hospital and a summer on the porch patching up with my broken health—the hardest patch I ever put on. This has been a hard winter and I've been shut in until I'm as cross as any body can be. I've scolded the House Head and bullied the children and I am ashamed. Therefore—while I cannot order all things as I wish, I am resolved that for the next twelve months I will deliberately take one day each week for mine. I will seek the mountains, the brooks, and the fields, I'll sit on a stump if I want to and will not tell anyone, out loud, why I do it.
>
> Should any ghost of my duties undone attempt to accompany me I will say, 'Get thee behind me, Satan.'
>
> Where unto I set my hand and seal this All Fools Day of 1910. Let us hope we'll fool the world by keeping this resolution.[14]

In 1911, an epidemic of scarlet fever hit the Phelps family especially hard. Mrs. Phelps, Bessie, and Francis were hospitalized and

Bessie lost all her hair. Twenty-year-old Francis, who already had learning difficulties, suffered a high fever causing additional brain damage. His reading and writing deteriorated to that of a second grader and his moodiness increased. His handicap was something the family bore privately, a heartache, especially for Mrs. Phelps, that her first born would never become educated and independent. There are different kinds of sadness, but this was one for which there was no cure, no change—only lifelong endurance.

In 1912, Mrs. Phelps was again caught in a treadmill struggle, known to many mothers, torn between caring for her large family and devoting time and energy to her own intellectual pursuits. With nine people to feed and clothe, a body worn down, and the depressing reality of Francis's impairment, Mrs. Phelps then had to face another of Charles's job losses.

A second breakdown resulted, during which the family's pivotal figure was again hospitalized. At seventeen, young Orra became the surrogate mother to her siblings.

Remarkably, in her recovery, Mrs. Phelps became stronger than ever before. After the family's move to Canton, New York, on the edge of the Adirondacks, she became a paid traveling lecturer for the New York State Farmers' Institute, a job found through Connecticut Farmer's Institute friends.

Leaving Orra in charge of the family, she jounced by train and trolley all over the state. She lectured about gardening, home canning, moth control, and first aid. Her journals and letters to Orra and the rest of the family spoke of a remarkable cast of characters, the distant Adirondack Mountains, the wintry landscape, and the bogs that promised special flowers in June.

Through this job she regained her usual good mental health and, at forty-seven, had a career uncommon for women of her time. She again began collecting rare plants, this time to sell to various universities as well as to enrich the collection at the State of New York Museum at Albany.

One of Mrs. Phelps's special lectures was "The Flowers and Birds of Northern New York," given in Ogdensburg, New York at the request of Mrs. Frederic Remington. In a letter to Orra, she explained:

> Monday I went by one o'clock bus to Ogdensburg and
> direct to Mrs. Remington's home. Such a magnificent
> place it is, looking out across a little park to the river.
> The house was full of paintings and bronzes by her late
> husband [Frederic Remington]. The limousine came
> around presently to take us two blocks to the church
> where I was to speak. I had a large and interested audi-
> ence. After the meeting we motored back to their house
> and had tea, sandwiches, and cake, then they [Mrs. R.
> and her sister] took me back to Canton with a check for
> $10 in my pocket."[15]

From 1916, when Orra entered Mount Holyoke College, until
Mrs. Phelps's death in 1950, this remarkable mother and daughter exchanged over two thousand letters; all saved in neatly tied bundles. Some
even have additional information entered at later dates. Orra's naturalist
mother wrote of the plants she had found, some bearing her name,
Phelpsiae, and of the hundreds of botanical specimens she collected for
the herbaria at Harvard, Yale, Syracuse, Cornell, and the Brooklyn Botanical Garden. She told of her search for geological specimens and strata,
and of taking photographs for her friends, Dr. George Chadwick and
Dr. Harold Alling of Rochester, New York.[16]

This was a tremendously rich heritage—especially for her daughter,
Orra—absorbed over many years. Although nature enriched their lives,
the family fought debt continuously. When they left Canton, Mrs. Phelps
feared not being able to pay all the bills. She wore her clothing until thread-
bare and even then turned the collars and used parts of old dresses and
coats to make "new" garments.

She and Orra, in particular, exchanged clothing depending on the
occasion. Mrs. Phelps once stayed home for ten weeks in the winter because she denied herself decent winter clothing in order that Orra and her
siblings could have them. Orra learned not to fuss over clothing and not
to value possessions, except for family antiques, books, and special rock,
plant, or fossil specimens.

When Mrs. Phelps complained about their finances, Orra wrote her
mother, imploring her to be more cheerful. In an impassioned cry that
many wives and mothers of the time were too cowed to voice, Mrs. Phelps
wrote back:

As to your lecture on cheerfulness—I used to be a cheerful lady but twenty-five years [of] being told that my schemes ¦ . . . and ideas are of no use has almost convinced me that I am useless. If Papa only expressed more concern over our finances I should express less. He has more than once told me that the children could get along without college education or get it themselves. The one thing that opened my eyes more than anything else was the attitude he took when he lost his position at Scoville's when he said to me, 'You can keep boarders to support the family and I'll raise garden stuff and eggs so you won't have to buy.' I want to put each of you girls where you will not have to depend upon a man for a support — every penny of which you are held accountable for. That doesn't mean that I want four old maids in my family — far from it. I want each one to have a happy home and children, but I do want each to have money of her own and the ability to give her children more than I could give mine. I have many ambitions and faith enough in myself to think that I might have made more of myself than I have, but if it comes to its fullness in my children I shall be well content. If I didn't have you, I'd just give up the struggle. It may be that I am unjust to Papa — he may be more worried than I think.

One thing did amuse me. I told him I was to allow Kay $60 to run the house for the four of them during the first month I was away and he said, 'She cannot possibly do it!' Yet he expects me to keep eight people for less than twice that — this is a grumbly grouch but — as I shall feel better for having said it and I'm sure you will not lay it up against me, I will let it stand . . . Wish I might provide for more of those sorry needs [of yours] . . .

With much love, Mamma.[17]

When the Phelps family moved to Saratoga County, New York, Mrs. Phelps collected geological specimens to sell and with the financial backing of her son, Lawrence, launched a jam and jelly mail-order business, selling from Maine to Arizona.

In September 1921, at the age of fifty-four, when most women were in semi-retirement, Mrs. Phelps began teaching at Saratoga Springs High School, finding sanity and satisfaction in her work while her personal life was stressful. The graying braids twined around her head and some extra weight were all that marked this dynamo of energy and knowledge as anything but a woman in her prime.

During her twelve years of teaching biology, hundreds of students learned to love natural science through her enthusiastic example. With her school salary, Mr. Phelps's farm income, help from son Lawrence and daughter Orra, the Phelpses purchased a farm in Wilton, New York.

Orra's Childhood
1895 to 1913

Orra Almira Phelps was born September 10, 1895, in a white frame house on the corner of Green Street, adjoining Storrs Agricultural College, at Storrs, Connecticut. "Orra" and "Almira" were her mother's given names as well; the name Almira linked them both with Orra's maternal grandmother, Almira Stanley Hibbard and her great-grandmother, Almira J. Stanley.[1]

The Phelps home at the corner of Green Street in Storrs, Ct., where Orra Phelps was born and lived as a child. The home was built by Mrs. Phelps's father, Martin Parker. *1908 photo*

Young Orra practically grew up outdoors.

> I remember as a child playing in a sand pit where there were tiny garnets that were almost perfectly round, twelve sided, dodecahedrons. We sifted through the sand and collected a whole vial of these semi-precious stones. There was a great big garnet that had been split in half . . . in a big stone in our back wall.[2]

From this early age, Orra's fascination with rocks and minerals grew.

> I . . . started school in Storrs and [sometimes] visited my older brothers' class. Once I was followed [from school] by the town bully and was so scared of him [that] I ran into a women's dormitory for refuge.[3]

Being chased and frightened by the town bully may have affected Orra's childhood security, but she grew to be resilient and self-confident. A sturdy child, Orra recalled playing nurse and making doll dresses to amuse her little sisters when they were "sick abed on two chairs." Orra's early skill in bandaging cuts and removing splinters generated ideas of a nursing career.

With a creative flair, she and her brothers once designed a vegetable circus from their garden, including elephants, clowns, and chariots. Orra and Lawrence also delighted in decorating birthday cakes, making one cake half chocolate and half vanilla as a compromise. The many Phelps children, plus cousins when they visited, often played outdoor games such as Red Rover, hide-and-seek, and sailing paper boats on the brook.

As the eldest daughter, Orra shouldered the responsiblity for some of the endless housework, chopping vegetables and chicken for great batches of stew; boiling the laundry; hanging wet wash outdoors where it froze

The seven Phelps children, during the long black stocking era: (left to right) Francis, Lawrence, Orra, Leon, Phoebe, Kay, Bessie.   *Circa 1906*

board-stiff in winter; killing, plucking, and gutting chickens; sorting and cleaning wheelbarrow loads of onions and potatoes; canning hundreds of jars of fruit and vegetables; and keeping the wood fires going.

The relationship between Orra and her mother was very close. Whether it was nature or nurturing, Orra's mannerisms, interests—even her appearance grew to resemble her mother's. When young Orra puzzled over her unusual name, Mrs. Phelps responded that in Scottish tradition it meant odd. Smiling, she said to the younger Orra, "I'm odd and you're odd, too."[4] Others might have termed them unusual or extraordinary.

Orra worked alongside her mother in the kitchen, and heard her laments about the housework and her desire to steal time, as Mrs. Phelps put it, "to play with the outside world." They frequently hiked together and loved nature in the same intense way. Kay, five years younger, was jealous of Orra's favored place in her mother's eyes but preferred more traditionally feminine activities to the vigorous outdoor life that seemed inborn to the two Orras.

Orra, her siblings, and her father were faithful Congregationalists, filling an entire pew during services. This religious experience at a young age was the foundation for Orra's strong, life-long faith. From family letters, it seems that Mrs. Phelps did not attend with the rest of the family, preferring a Sunday morning alone at home for her own soul searching.

On their long Sunday afternoon walks, Orra's parents shared their love of birds, spotting them by their calls, habits, color, and size. As Orra watched hummingbirds feeding at the sapsuckers' holes and marsh wrens building nests lined with cattail fluff and soft grass, they became her friends. She fondly recalled sitting with Lawrence on a stone wall, learning to whistle for bobwhites. "We did bobwhite whistles on that wall. I haven't heard any bobwhites in ages now," she recalled at age eighty-two.[5]

Once Orra climbed thirty feet up a tree and held back the branches so the Phelps's ornithologist friend, Professor Herbert K. Job, could photograph a nest of baby sharp-shinned hawks at Bingham Pond on Bear Mountain in northwestern Connecticut. In *Birds of America*, for which Job was a contributing editor, Orra penciled in the margin, "I helped take this photo when I was 14."[6]

The senior Phelpses also shared with the children their interest in astronomy; Orra was thrilled to see Halley's Comet wax and wane, as it arched fourteen million miles from earth in May 1910. A lifetime later, as the 1986 return of the comet neared, Orra hoped she would be able to see it a second time. Sadly, her dimmed vision clouded her view.

From 1910 to 1913, Orra and her two brothers walked three miles to private high schools in Lakeville; Orra to the Taconic School and her brothers to Hotchkiss. They would take the shortest route, along the railroad tracks. Her life-long closeness with Lawrence grew from these shared days. In the winter, they sometimes whizzed over the snow in their horse-drawn sleigh. Orra recalled:

> My playmates were my two older brothers and I held the belief that whatever they could do I could do. I was called a tomboy but I am sure that my good health and strength started then.[7]

Care and concern for others was evident in Orra at an early age. While returning from school one day, she spotted a roof afire where hot ashes had dropped. She ran and alarmed the owners, saving their house.

Orra's early education was well-rounded and included the arts, sports, and nature. In high school, she danced and played basketball and tennis. She also recalled playing "Puck" in Shakespeare's *Mid-summer Night's Dream*, singing in a youth chorus, and winning spelling bees. In a 1914 college essay she wrote:

> At Taconic I took up manual training and discovered I had quite a taste for metal work. Besides this I had quite a liking for athletics . . . I thought I would like to take up physical training . . . . In my senior year I was made Editor-in-Chief of the school newspaper, which position, I fear was food for my vanity.

However, the scope of her out-of-school education was unique. She soaked in the natural sciences as she tramped over nearby cart paths, brooks, and ridges. In a letter to her mother's sister, Aunt Bessie Gammons, seventeen-year-old Orra told of her pleasure in birding and hiking:

> This morning when I went out bird hunting, I saw more birds than I could find in the bird book. I was watching an indigo bird on the edge of the swamp when I heard a crash. I saw a deer, not . . . twenty-five yards away. It watched me for a while and then it bounded over the field and across the road. This afternoon Mamma, Leon, and I walked more than two miles below Lakeville. We were gone from two to six.[8]

By helping with her mother's big Connecticut plant collection, Orra learned the equivalent of college botany, the English and Latin names of innumerable ferns and other plants, and the valuable skill of mentally marking the location of plants in the woods.

The shaping of Orra's character, her developing maturity, and her resilience were no doubt influenced by both of her mother's breakdowns and her three hospitalizations.

The fear of their mother's having more breakdowns shadowed the children for the rest of their lives. Orra washed, mended, and ironed the family's clothing and

The Phelps siblings in Salisbury, Connecticut in 1912: (front) Bessie; (middle, left to right) Phoebe, Orra, Leon, Lawrence, and Katharine; (rear) Francis.

"mothered" her siblings. She took charge in the kitchen, baking and slicing many loaves of bread each week.

Even when Orra was eighty, she still enjoyed the challenge of making hearty oatmeal bread and was proud of her neat slicing. One wonders who nurtured Orra during these demanding and frustrating times? From the Phelps letters, it appears that her brother, Lawrence, was especially understanding.

It was at this time that her occasional tendency to be authoritarian probably developed. From necessity, Orra learned early to trust her own judgment, to be forceful in giving directions, and to demand attention from those in her charge. Orra recalled in Mary Brennan's 1982 interview:

> Most of my teen years were spent on the large dairy farm
> my father ran for Mr. Robert Scoville in Salisbury. The
> 'show place' was about a mile through a beautiful pine
> woods from the farmhouse where we lived.

Her chosen words of "show place" and "farmhouse" lay bare the
disparity between the two families, again a compromise for the
well-educated Phelpses. Orra continued:

> In that woods there was a spring around which the ground
> was soggy and wet. If I could visit that spring again, I
> would see if *Mitella nuda* still grew there. *Mitella nuda* is
> a tiny plant, its blossom stalk less than six inches high. It
> is related to *Mitella diphylla* [Bishop's cap] but doesn't
> grow as tall. It has the same kind of blossom though, like
> a snowflake on a stalk. It is a northern plant liking the
> muck around the spring where my mother found it. It
> was almost at its southern limit in Chapinville, which is
> now known as Taconic.[9]

Mr. Phelps's work took the family to Canton, New York in February 1913. Orra and her family felt wrenched from the familiar fields
and hills of Connecticut, where even though they had moved quite a
few times, they had become close to their relatives, colleagues, friends,
and familiar botanical haunts. All the family furniture and belongings
together with books, plant presses and mounted plant specimens, family Bibles, and genealogical charts made their way to Canton.

While Mrs. Phelps nursed Lawrence through an emergency tonsillectomy and settled Francis in a farm job, eighteen-year-old Orra
shepherded Kay, Phoebe, Leon, and Bessie aboard the "Boab Boat" en
route to Albany. There they caught the northbound train for Orra's
first trip through New York State, north to the mysterious, rugged
Adirondack Mountains, destined to be her home.

In some places, forest fires along the tracks had swept vistas clear;
in others she could almost touch the pines, deep green then hazy blue
and purple as far as she could see. Joining Mr. Phelps in Canton, the
family rented a house on Chapel Street and later lived at 14 Elm Street.

In December 1913, Mrs. Phelps began her Farm Institute travels,
pioneering in her field and earning needed cash. The younger Phelps

girls attended grammar and high schools, leaving Orra to keep house, sew, wash, and iron. When the pipes froze after Papa would let the fires go out, Orra rekindled them and thawed the pipes.

At this time, Orra began attending St. Lawrence University, located just up the street from where they lived. She cooked meals for six on their wood stove while keeping up with her studies. To whom could she complain? Again it was brother Lawrence who answered, lending her emotional support:

> Dear Orra,
> I know it is awful hard to be housekeeper and student all in one and oh, how I wish that you didn't have to. And I also wish that Mamma didn't have to work so hard and she won't another year if I can see my way through Yale without her help. I have worked hard this year . . . waiting on tables . . . So please don't think too hard of me and try not to let the housework discourage you. I know that lots of times things are far from smooth when Mamma is away, but Papa means right although he doesn't always seem to. Try to go out for something in college if you possibly [can], for I know you could be big if you had time. And don't give up going to Mount Holyoke for I think you can go still if you want to. [10]

While Orra was in high school, her mother had planted the seeds of hope for a Mount Holyoke College degree in young Orra's mind. However, with Lawrence at Yale and Leon at Cornell, two boarding at college was all the family could afford at that time. When her mother was not on the lecture circuit, the two Orras searched for and collected specimens of rare plants, in the woods and along the Grass River. The Adirondack High Peaks beckoned, but a decade would pass before Orra and her family would climb them.

— 4 —

College Years
1913 to 1918

Orra studied earnestly during her two years at St. Lawrence University, once writing:

> Every moment adds or detracts something from my intellect, my health, or my character. I can be so wrapped up in what interests me that I am blind to those of others. But I have opened my eyes; now I can view both sides of a problem, but stick to my own opinion until I prove the need to change.[1]

In her favorite course, Geology, Orra absorbed much about the Adirondacks' unique geologic history. Often Orra and Mrs. Phelps hefted pack baskets and rock hammers and trekked to garnet mines, talus slopes, and rock cuts as personal guests of

One of seven boxes of Phelps letters dating from 1904.

her teacher, Professor George Chadwick, another family friend.

After Lawrence's graduation from Yale in 1916, Orra transferred to Mount Holyoke College as a junior, giving the two Orras a shared college experience, though thirty years apart. The flow of letters between the two women then began. Orra described her full schedule of Geology, Zoology, Bible Study, English, and History plus work in the dining hall and laboratory.

Although she would have excelled as a botany major, after years of botanical work with her mother, Orra hungered for other subjects. Majoring in the sciences was unusual for women at that time, but it intrigued Orra.

Orra's letters were like painted murals of her time outdoors.

>...Laura and I went through the gardens—to Cowles Lodge. Upstream from the bridge, the banks were beautiful with autumn foliage and further on the swamp was a blaze of color. The view from the top [of Prospect] of that meadow toward the mountains was almost indescribable. The mountains with various shades of blues and purples, with the deep shadows in the valleys that you see only near sunset, formed the background. In the middle distance were fields, meadows, and woodlands of various shades of green, and the foreground glowed with brilliant coloring and mellow autumn haze.
>
>By the way, we found some chestnuts, picked them out of their burrs and [took all] we could carry in a hand-

Dr. Henrietta Hooker (left) and Dr. Lydia Shattuck, both famous botanists on the faculty at Mount Holyoke, were among the mentors of Mrs. Phelps in the 1880s. Both Mrs. Phelps and her daughter would help to perpetuate their legacy at the college. *Photos courtesy of Mount Holyoke College Archives and Special Collections, South Hadley, Massachusetts.*

kerchief. At the end of quiet hour, 9 o'clock, we invited in some other girls and passed around roasted chestnuts and apples. My first college party![2]

On October 19, 1916, Mrs. Phelps wrote a prophetic letter:

Dear Orra,
    Did you know you are writing a book? Keep on as you have begun, taking pains to tell the details . . . and you will have something worthwhile some day. It may be twenty-five years, it may be sooner—if enough of interest comes in. [Your] white partridge berries I never saw before. Am sending them to Harvard as your collection. You might take one to Dr. Hooker to let her know you are following in my footsteps.
                                        Mamma[3]

The professional friends of the Phelps family gave Orra entreés that few twenty-one-year-old women enjoyed. Mrs. Phelps and Orra became part of a chain of noted female botanists and naturalists stretching back to Mount Holyoke's Lydia Shattuck and Dr. Henrietta Hooker. Orra was not surprised to receive this letter:

Gray Herbarium
Harvard University
Oct. 20, 1916

Dear Madam:
    Professor Fernald has referred your letter and specimen to me. White fruited Partridge Berry has been found a number of times before and in 1911 was described as *Mitchella repens L. forma leucarpa Bissell.* In his discussion in "*Rhodora*" Mr. Bissell records the plant in Canaan, CT. and from a number of other places.
    Harold St. John

Mrs. Phelps wrote, "Dr. Chadwick promises a folio of South Hadley geology which you mustn't use as a trot." Orra absorbed more geology as she tramped along New England streambeds and ridges, examining ripples in the sandstone, striation in the deposits, and esker's meanderings.

Orra even asked Mrs. Phelps to send specimens of the Saratoga County "stone cabbages,"[4] graphite ore, and fluorite, showing Orra's commitment to geology and to her college. Her topographical study course sharpened her talent for reading the lay of the land and would help her read topographic maps during future hiking, mountain climbing, and flora forays.[5]

At various points in her life Orra had gifted mentors, a boost many accomplished people likewise experienced. Recognizing Orra's love of science, Dr. Mignon Talbot, Head of the Mount Holyoke Geology Department, became one of Orra's supporters, telling her that "a woman could do anything," words Orra would vividly recall at age eighty-seven.[6] This confidence proved a pivotal one in Orra's life; for the first time she saw herself through a professional's eyes, as a gifted and mature student with the possibility of unlimited growth.

Orra took six zoology courses, many with Dr. Anna H. Morgan,

Dr. Anna H. Morgan (left) and Dr. Cornelia Clapp, both noted professors of zoology, were among Orra's mentors at Mount Holyoke College.

who enlivened the zoology lab with dissections of grasshoppers, mice, frogs, and cats. There was even a dancing cat skeleton suspended as a wired mobile. With enthusiasm, Orra wrote:

> Yesterday we worked on pond water with the compound microscope. How some of the girls jumped when those wiggly critters came into view. We had to draw diatoms and amoebae and I hated to stop when my two hours were up.[7]

Dr. Cornelia Clapp, Mount Holyoke's longtime zoology professor and a well-known scientist, taught Orra's Bible study class. By then, Dr. Clapp had retired from her position as Chair of the Zoology

Department, but she left a legacy of strong women scientists, inspired and trained by her. Orra had been in church youth groups, but never with such an enthusiastic and deeply stimulating woman. Everyone, including Orra, chanted and sang with Dr. Clapp as she danced down the chapel aisle on Sundays.

In December 1916, when Orra received a scholarship, her mother cheered with joy and relief.

> Dear Orra,
> Hurrah for you, Orra dear! I'm so glad you got the scholarship. It isn't often that first year students get such favors. I am relieved to know of your good fortune . . . and am so glad to be able to give you a chance at Holyoke —wish I could do more.
>
> Love, Mamma

Orra spent her holidays in nearby Springfield, Massachusetts with her Aunt Bessie, a sprightly, warm Holyoke alumna. Compared to the hectic Phelps farmhouse, the Gammons's home was gracious and calm. Like their father, William Gammons, Bessie's two step-children, Dwight and Josephine, were interested in business. Although they were close in age to her, Orra's love of nature was lost on them. A teacher with no children of her own, Aunt Bessie loved Orra as a daughter, lived both her triumphs and her sorrows, and did whatever she could to ease her niece's way.

It is not surprising that Orra's no-nonsense outlook colored her description of her "Prom Night."

> Dear People-
> My prom was a wonderful affair. The grand march was led by President Wooley, our class president, and her man. At first we marched as single couples [Orra was escorted by her brother, Lawrence], then double, then eight abreast. In this formation we had our picture taken. The photographer had lots of trouble firing his flash-light powder, furnishing much amusement. If I were a proper college girl describing my Prom I should say the music was "heavenly," the floor "wonderful," the gowns were "stunning" and the men were "just the nicest," but

somehow I can't bring myself to "rave" as everyone else does. I did have a splendid time and I enjoyed some of the dances and some of my dance partners very much.

Orra[8,9]

Most remarkable about Orra's prom, and her sense of priorities, was that she dashed from the dance, in gown and gloves, to the zoology lab, donned a lab coat, and dissected a chick embryo at a critical hour—and then returned to the dance.[10]

Orra's easy manner came with forgetting herself and being interested in sports, music, art, Christian fellowship, nature, and her many friends. She was a natural leader; sure of how she thought things should go. It amused her to know that her lung capacity equaled that of her basketball team coach.

Following her parents' model, Orra the ornithologist/naturalist further emerged. She wrote:

Saturday I gave a talk on birding, giving directions for seeing and identifying birds. Then I told some funny stories about how grackles sing, . . . how hummingbirds visit sapsucker holes, and how the marsh wren [builds a] cave-like nest.[11]

On March 27, 1917, she explained:

My bird talk gave me such a reputation that I can scarcely manage it. Three faculty members and no end of girls are in line for bird walks with me.

The Zoo department takes early morning bird walks and this morning Dr. Smith said before we started out, "Now, Miss Phelps, I'm not going to pilot you on any bird walk. You've got to lead a group." I had only four girls and we saw the phoebe and kingfisher for the first time and heard bluebirds, robins, grackles, meadowlarks, and song sparrows.

Orra's mother asked Orra to fill some botanical specimen orders:

I've got an order for twigs from Dr. Richards at Columbia but don't see how I can fill it. Write me at once if you can send him 48 good twigs of horse chestnut, 36 twigs of spice bush and 12 of flowering dogwood to show the buttony blossom buds . . . express collect to Botanical Dept. Barnard College, Columbia University, New York City.[12]

Astronomy was another of Orra's fascinations. In January 1917, she saw a meteor, "a flaming spot of green, with a long fiery trail of sparks," blaze down behind the mountains. Another time an aurora borealis, or northern lights, filled the sky with dancing curtains of light. She couldn't resist sharing nature at its finest and did what was forbidden: she rang the fire bell, awakening her sleeping dormmates. The women who ran outside, long nightgowns flapping in the cold wind, were awed by the sight. Such was the impact on both the disgruntled and the amazed that, at Orra's sixtieth reunion, the event was still being discussed.

Orra Phelps during her junior year at Mount Holyoke in 1917.

In l917, during Orra's junior year at Mount Holyoke, came another milestone in her life: the senior Phelpses made their last move. With Lawrence's help, they began paying for the one hundred acre "French place" in Wilton, New York. Although Orra Phelps's career and interests would take her worlds away, it was the Wilton land that Orra would always call home.

Orra's May 1917 yearbook, the *Llamarada*, pictured her with straight ash brown hair, softly pinned back in a bun, wisps framing her pretty face. Here is how her classmates described her:

Altho Orra only came to Mount Holyoke this year, she soon established a reputation. She knows the Latin names of innumerable ferns, even if she has never been a botanical devotee. (Gasps of admiration are in order at this point.) Nor is her knowledge of Botany the only pinnacle of fame to which Orra has attained. The convictions which she cherishes so stoutly, she never hesitates to express fearlessly.

Be Happy, Orra.

Orra looked forward to Mount Holyoke's traditional fall Mountain Day, so when the chapel bell rang signaling that classes were canceled, Orra jumped into her middy blouse, knickers, cotton stockings, and sturdy shoes. She then picked up a packed lunch and started out for the day's hiking and picnicking on Mt. Tom.

Since the inception of Mountain Day in 1839, the college administrators always chose a day glistening with blue skies, crisp air, and beautiful fall foliage. On their way uphill, one of the hikers lost her wristwatch, but coming home, Orra scrutinized the trailsides until she spotted it. She had a knack for locating things, often rock specimens or rare plants. The location of fragrant pink arbutus on Mt. Tom and in "The Notch" she shared with only a few botanical friends.

Orra Phelps, member of the class of 1918, on the day of her commencement ceremony at Mount Holyoke. She is fifth from the left, looking toward the camera in profile.

Years later, Orra was destined to bushwhack up trailless Adirondack peaks and locate rare plants she had previously found, miles from the road or trail.

For her American Cities class she observed the Springfield City Council in session. Surprised at how perfunctory the men were in their decisions, she wrote, "If women can't govern more wisely, then I am sorry for them. It makes me glad I can be a voting citizen."

Orra Phelps, honored as the Mary Lyons scholar in zoology, graduated from Mount Holyoke in 1918, when only a small percent of women graduated from college. In September, Orra returned as an assistant in geology and studied chemistry as well.

Just before news of the World War I armistice broke, Orra wrote, "I'm waiting to see what economic changes the end of the war brings. I think that farm is going to be the best investment the Phelpses ever made." Orra celebrated the war's end on November 11, 1918 and through that week with colleagues amidst bell ringing and parades.[13]

Orra discussed with Dr. Talbot and her family physician, Dr. Towne, her almost impossible hope of studying medicine, but did not discuss it with her family (except for Lawrence) because money was so tight. While Orra was trying to save for medical school, in February 1919 another family setback occurred, as her mother wrote:

> Papa's resignation was asked and given last Monday. He is all broken up about it. When one loses a position because of failure he can take the bitter pill, but when he's ousted because of petty malice of an envious person, that is hard to bear. Please tell the girls [Phoebe and Kay] my heart breaks for them. Urge Kay to take stenography this term and put out all the lines you can for summer work. Leon gave up Cornell for the present.
>
> Mamma[14]

From the Phelps letters it was clear that the twin ballasts for the Phelps family's ship were daughter Orra and son Lawrence. His executive ability and her common sense and optimism helped steady their course and overcome obstacles. The Phelps children had been taught to help their siblings and parents, to support and comfort their elders, trying to be all that the parents never could be; truly a heavy load, but one borne stoically and with compassion. As long as they were so bound, they were not free to live their own lives fully, especially Lawrence and Orra.

They worried that their father lacked the ability to earn a decent living from the farm, wasn't physically strong, and had poor business sense. Both feared that the option of taking in boarders might ruin Mamma's health. Lawrence was never free to marry and have his own family, being saddled with bills for all the other children's educations. Orra, too, was charged even at Mount Holyoke to watch over Kay and Phoebe and to help with their bills.

Orra weighed a healthy 145 pounds and stood 5 feet 7 inches tall. Her only physical limitation was a slight astigmatism in her left eye, which glasses would have corrected, but she did without them. Because she had the stamina and the will power, Orra earned extra cash through evening and weekend childcare, meals included, for the Hayes family of Holyoke.

Orra's interest in orthopedics may have begun when, by chance, she accompanied Mrs. Hayes and her son for his orthopedic appointment. She returned to the Holyoke Hospital for a full day's visit soon after, writing home in April of 1919:

> I am drawn between two desires, first, if I had all the necessary money, I'd like to study medicine and specialize in orthopedics. . . . I want to do something I know I can do wholeheartedly. I do not want to teach but I would if there were money enough concerned. My other desire is to get a YWCA Industrial Secretary position, which pays from $75 to $100 a month. I don't want to have any more money spent on me and I do want to help Phoebe and Kay through.

On April 25, 1919 she wrote from South Hadley, Massachusetts:

Dear Mamma,
    The orthopedic doctor is Dr. W. R. McAusland and he was very nice to me.
    . . . I went to find the head surgical nurse, who was getting the room and the instruments ready.

Dr. McAusland washed his hands and arms in a tub full of green soap suds for twenty minutes. I was introduced, then given a sterilized surgeon's gown. The patient was a twelve-year-old, freckle-faced, Irish lad, whose one arm was nothing but skin and bone and hung limp from the shoulder. He had no power to move, nor had ever been able to move it. The socket of the shoulder joint had been diseased, leaving the arm hanging. The operation was to tie the forearm to the shoulder blade so that the arm might be given the shoulder blade motion at least. To give maximum use, the flesh at the elbow was cut and then sewed up so that the elbow would always be bent instead of straight.

First the whole arm and shoulder was painted with iodine and then with alcohol. Then towels were pinned on close around where he was to operate. It was marvelous to see the speed with which he cut. The thing I marveled at most was not the operation but that the doctor could poke and sling his instruments around without the patient's feeling it at all.

Orra minded the heat and ether at first, but since she wanted to see everything, she persevered.

After he was all sewed up again half the body was wrapped in sheet wadding and then the plaster bandages were applied. My, but it was great to see the doctor slap that bandaging on. Four inch gauze bandaging is saturated with plaster of Paris and the whole thing is soaked. After he was all nicely done up, we left him on the operating table till the cast was hard and then the nurse rolled in the wagon and carried him to the ward where I saw him later.

Later Orra saw rickets, clubfeet deformities, and a congenital hip defect treated. The hip operation was especially difficult.

He went straight in to the hipbone, cleaned out the socket, took a slice off the top of the bone so that it would fit and slipped it in. About this time Dr. McAusland began to hurry. He was putting plaster on the foot. Addressing me, he said, 'Here, nurse, hold this, just so.' So I held it while he bandaged and I got my fingers all plaster. But I didn't care and smiled within myself as did the other nurses. Even after the bandaging was done, I was bid to hold it till the plaster was hard. Moreover, I was left with the child when she began to come out from the ether, and if it hadn't been for me she might have rolled off the table.

She wasn't the only one I fixed. The next one was a small boy who had to have one hip and leg bandaged. I had to hold both legs just so while the doctor plastered and when it was done I had to pull out the spiking board. I felt fine all the afternoon and could have watched several more operations. The head nurse showed me everything in the hospital.

Lastly, I saw Dr. McAusland and asked him what he would advise me to do who wanted to take up medicine but could not go to medical school next year. He thought I was a graduate nurse! So did all the other doctors. When he learned that this was the first operation I had ever seen, he was dumbfounded. He said that of real medical work, out-patient work was all I could do without training. He couldn't get over [the fact] that I had never seen operations before and yet before the day was over was working as hard as any of the nurses.

Orra was so impressed by the skill and excitement of the surgery that her hope of pursuing medicine became an obsession. When Orra wrote to her mother of her decision, Mrs. Phelps replied:

> As to your choice, if you are inclined to a profession do not stop to pick pebbles by the way. Take into consideration all your natural inclinations, love of the outdoors and the like. . . A person can climb higher in a profession than any other line of work. If surgery attracts you, go ahead—I won't ask you to do a thing for me—with three stout girls I can do very well. Fare thee well, Dr. Phelps—Mother loves you just the same whether you carve turkeys or feet.[15]

By the spring of 1919, Orra was earnestly searching for a job to save money toward her dream of medical school. Her mother, who was overwhelmed with the farm and housework and endless bills, counseled:

Dear Orra,

    If your plan is cracked see if you can find a better one . . . Prof. Chadwick once told me, 'When fences are put up —it doesn't pay to wear one's self out trying to jump over.' I suppose this is where he got his nickname, 'Hole in the fence.'

    Thank you for all you have done and been. I am glad that you wrote so plainly of your work. Absent ones are liable to fancy that the one away is having it easy. I shall do all I can to help you in your choice. I want you to persevere.

Mamma[16]

— 5 —

Science Teacher at New Hampshire College
1919 to 1921

To finance her medical school dream, Orra worked between 1919 and 1921 as assistant and later instructor in geology and zoology at New Hampshire College in Durham, New Hampshire. Working over sixty hours a week, she identified and prepared specimens, did research, and taught natural sciences.

In the process she added a strong post-graduate education, valuable in her later work as an Adirondack naturalist.

Teaching at New Hampshire College was an eye-opener for Orra after Mount Holyoke College. Many students were so poorly prepared, spelling "hart, tung, gulet, glans," that she put a permanent glossary on the board. She wrote Mrs. Phelps in October 1919:

> I never had such a good time studying as I've had preparing lectures. I came across two recent articles in *Professional Papers of the US Geological Survey*, relating to this region—one is the stratigraphy of the rocks and one on the glacial geology! I'm eagerly devouring them.

On October 9, 1919, she wrote:

> Yesterday I saw hundreds of black ducks flying high overhead, more than I have ever seen. There are thousands of things I want to do: collateral reading in both physiology and geology, work ahead in all lab work, study field geology, get topographic maps of this section, and clean the store room.

Her passion for botanizing continued as she learned the region's plants, impulsively identifying all of the natural things she could.

37

Her mother readily identified specimens and sketches, and wrote:

> The little purple aster is called *Aster linariifolius*—
> stiff [leaf] aster. It grew sparingly on sandy road banks of
> the hill near Grandma's as we went to Coventry. There is
> a big *polygala*, four to sixteen inches high in purple, green
> or white . . . quite common along the coast from Maine
> to Florida.
> The magenta flower, with spreading bracts, which
> you sketched I take to be one of the adored blossoms of
> my childhood, *Liatris scariosa*.[1]

For ten dollars a month Orra roomed with the Hendersons, her
adopted family. Dad Henderson, the purchasing agent for the college,
included Orra on trips around Durham, Great Bay, and along the Atlantic Coast. After a glimpse of geography from the car or train, Orra
would investigate on foot, thinking nothing of setting out alone for a
nine-mile trek in unfamiliar territory. Armed with her topo maps,
compass, and lunch, she searched for Spruce Hole. She explained in
her October 27, 1919 letter:

> When I reached that point in the road nearest it, I struck up
> a steep slope, heavily wooded with young pine and oak. I
> made one wrong guess but went back and thrashed through
> the brush till I found a cart path, then a faint trail. In a few
> moments I was on the brink of the big kettle hole. At the
> bottom, is a pond perhaps a hundred yards long and sixty
> wide. All the other requisites are there — sphagnum, cran-
> berry, snowberry, pitcher plant, spruces, cotton grass, and
> maybe sundew. After climbing out, I raced home because I
> wanted to go to the three o'clock football game. Those
> clothes were so dirty that at night I scrubbed for two hours,
> but got them clean and boiled and blued.

When Orra first saw the Atlantic Ocean on November 16, 1919,
she wrote her mother:

> Mr. Henderson took us down the coast—rockbound
> indeed. The tide was just coming in, but we found some
> shells and starfish amidst tons of seaweed washed up

from the terrific storms. This is the first time that I ever looked at the real ocean with nothing but water between me and Europe.

Hampton Beach was a beautiful crescent, [with] breakers rolling in. The sun had just set and the glow was reflected east in the water, pink and lavender, except where the breakers were crystal white and translucent green.

In May 1920, on one of her marine biology field trips, Orra and her students found plenty of treasures. She wrote home:

Yesterday our classes had a glorious trip to Cape Neddick, Nubble Light, and the beach. The tide was very low so we could walk across to Nubble Light where we found all kinds of marine life in the rocky pools—sponges, sea urchins by the thousands . . . and starfish, snails, mussels, limpets, sea anemones, crabs, shrimp, hermits, and even little condor eels. The colors were marvelous.

Orra Phelps's Zoology class from New Hampshire College at Nubble Lighthouse, York, Maine.   *1920 photo*

Orra corresponded with her mentor, Dr. Talbot, who wrote her in October 1919, "If any girl could do [a job], you could." Orra reflected in a letter to her mother, "That's quite flattering but still, it comes pretty near my motto. I'm that conceited!"[2]

Describing herself as conceited rather than truly capable and deserving of her mentor's praise showed that Orra, like other females of her era, was yet to feel comfortable in the role of capable, educated, independent woman.

She met many professional women through her work in the YWCA and church. These women became role models and friends, helping her gain self-confidence. After she went to a New York City women's convention in December 1919, she wrote:

> The meetings were quite interesting. I met with other faculty members, deans of women, and women representing advisory boards of students. We discussed, informally, the problems of education of girls, *i.e.* whether individualism should be encouraged or repressed and to what extent, self-government, discussion groups with girls or faculty as leaders and girls' ability to apply academic theories to practical life. Industrial group leaders in city associations emphasized industrial problems and their bearing on women's status. I felt pretty big! And the trip cost me only three dollars of my own money.

Orra first voted in Durham in November 1920, and wrote:

> Today I cast my first ballot, voting on seven amendments to the constitution of the State of New Hampshire. How did it feel to vote? Not half as hard as teaching.[3]

Another growing experience was her trip to the International Volunteer YWCA and YMCA Convention in Des Moines, Iowa from December 31, 1919 to January 4, 1920. Orra was thrilled to see Niagara Falls en route. On January 11, 1920 she wrote to Mrs. Phelps:

> It is beyond me to describe the falls. Most impressive were the billows of foam thrown almost as high as the falls themselves. The trees around there were all ice, from the ever drifting mist . . . I got off and trod on Canadian pavement at St. Thomas.

With all expenses paid, she attended the Des Moines meetings, where speakers focused on uplifting the moral tone of college life. She kept her poise as she chaperoned student delegates and answered their questions from her life experiences. She maintained propriety among the young men and women in her charge, commenting, "Maybe I'm not a perfect lady by inherent nature but I can rise to occasions." In the same letter she also wrote:

> I gave the delegates' report of the convention, trying to encourage missionary responsibility, not just to foreign fields, but as much as their hearts can give and to the nearest needy person.

Orra transferred her membership to the local Congregational church, sang in the choir, and sometimes substituted as Sunday school teacher. Living at a coed college meant more men in her life, both as students and as friends. They confided in her about religion, about frustrated love, about their war experiences, and about their studies.

As she put it, "They know that I try honestly to live up to what I believe, with no use for sham." Continuing on January 11, 1920, she wrote:

> You may think that apparent familiarity with the students will dangerously affect my faculty standing. It is permissible for a student and a faculty member to walk together and go to dances. No familiarities in this classroom—nor hint of them.

Being one of the few women on the faculty at New Hampshire College in 1919 impacted Orra's life in other ways. She did not get the $100 raise promised her until the end of her first year. Even then, she found male colleagues were paid up to twice her salary. She had to be careful not to cause gossip by her independent behavior, to choose proper companions for hiking, and to be careful of her dress.

In December 1919, Orra confided:

> I wish I had you here to take trips with me. For academic or physical reasons it's hard to find a woman to go with me. As yet I know few men that I feel free to ask and I mustn't ask the same one very much or there will be "talk". Tied hand and foot by conventions! I don't want to shock people too severely but gradually they'll learn that I'm rather independent and quite unconventional.

Mrs. Phelps may have begrudged Orra her income and independence, because the parents' life during that time was so different.

Through Mrs. Phelps's friend, Dean Ross, at Skidmore, came a trickle of much needed cash and company. Groups of diners came to the Phelps farmhouse for chicken dinners in 1919, including Miss Helen Filene of Boston and her friends. Mamma wrote on December 10, 1919:

> Saturday evening was minus 18 degrees, so Papa and Francis kept a pine fire in the north room all day. The girls came in big sleighs, well wrapped up, each with a big blanket and a hot brick . . . One girl confided to me that she wore three pairs of bloomers and four pairs of stockings! One girl called for a cup of tea . . . instanter, as she was chilling.
>
> After they had eaten, they cleared the floor, and sang for an hour, sitting on pillows around the fire. Then they danced the Virginia Reel.

Still, Orra's mother ached for a professional job. She wrote of her frustrations:

> I know I could earn enough money to keep the whole family better than we are being kept but can't find a job. And I just feel like a wild bird in a cage; you children have all your angles about denying yourself all sorts of things but you would do better and be better with more opportunity for self-expression and so would I.[4]

Parts of her parents' life must have grated on her, but despite letters such as this, Orra overlooked the petty irritants and saw her family as better than most. She wrote:

> I have learned something of family life and the advantage of having college-trained parents. The ignorance and backwards points of view here are astounding. So I'm thankful that you and Papa have been broad minded enough to give us what we have, which is more than most people have, and more than money can buy, but in the long run will buy us all that is worthwhile.[5]

In another letter, in the same vein, she wrote:

> I'm going to give you some statistics that ought to be comforting. Of every one hundred students entering school when we children did, only eighteen ever get through eighth grade, only six graduate from high school, and only one graduates from college. So far we've smashed records 'all holler.'[6]

Orra Phelps knew how to handle challenges and rose to the occasion. In early March 1920, scarlet fever broke out on their campus. Orra was singled out as the person most capable of nursing back to health three quarantined young men, with only one mother helping and the doctor visiting once a day. She knew what to do, laid down the law with compassion, and ran a tight ship until they recovered.

In March 1920, when Orra attended the Faculty Science Club's lecture, "The Mountain Clubs of America," she considered joining the Appalachian Mountain Club, depending on the cost. She wrote on May 13, 1920:

> I found out that anyone can use its trailside camps. A member gets the club bulletins and a guidebook giving maps of trails, distances, and points of interest.

Little did she guess that ideas germinated here would lead her back to the Adirondack Mountains and contribute to one of her outstanding achievements more than ten years hence, editing an Adirondack Mountain Club guidebook. Orra vividly described a New Hampshire mountain trip with the Hendersons in her October 26, 1920 letter:

> All the way we could see mountains coming up along the horizon. Mount Chocorua was the most distinctive peak [sketch of peak in letter]. The first one hundred feet of the peak is simply bare rock. It was not the highest one in sight, but the higher ones were no more impressive. This mountain rises abruptly from the shore of the lake. Where we came upon it, we had a sweeping view of the lake and the whole range of mountains [surrounding] Chocorua.

> We stopped the cars and built a fire, made coffee, and broiled steak. We ate, oh, how we ate. I noticed both black and white spruces and lots of balsam. We'll see this together someday.

Promising to take her mother traveling was typically generous of Orra. They would travel together a great deal, but Orra would explore and do more than her parents ever could. She would climb more mountains and find more wildflowers than any of her siblings as well.

Perhaps both she and her mother knew this. Each planned hike or outing gave them something to anticipate, savoring the resulting trips three times: first in their plans, second on the way, and third in the memories. In addition, through their emotional closeness and their hundreds of letters, they shared many experiences though miles apart.

Orra's interest in earthquakes began with one she experienced in Canton five years earlier and was, like other facets of her expanding scientific knowledge, strong and lifelong. Orra was fascinated by the Knickerbocker Press account of the January 20, 1920, Adirondack earthquake:

SHOCKS CAUSE EARTH CRACKS, DISHES
BROKEN — LAKE GEORGE, SARATOGA, AND
CORINTH ARE JARRED BY HEAVY TREMORS—
LONG FISSURE FOUND

> Earthquake shocks early yesterday shook the Adirondack section. Cracks in the earth's crust, ranging in width from an inch to a foot, and several feet deep were found near the center of disturbance, thought to be east of Corinth.[7]

In June 1920, Orra was appointed Instructor in geology and zoology at New Hampshire College with a resulting salary increase. She attended her Mount Holyoke College reunion, but sacrificed attending summer school in order to help her mother raise cash by preserving and selling over nine hundred jars of vegetables, fruit, and jam.

On a rare day off, the two Orras hunted fossil starfish, lingulas, dalmanellas, and crinoid stems at Snake Hill, on the southeast shore of Saratoga Lake.[8] When Mrs. Phelps took the Snake Hill fossils to Dr. Rudolf Ruedemann at the New York State Museum in Albany, he recalled fossils she had found at Pittsford with Professor Chadwick. As she wrote young Orra:

> He has requested they be named for me and wound up by saying, 'I will name one new fossil for her and I haf (sic).' Then he produced the manuscript in proof and I saw in a long list of fossils, *Hughmilleria phelpsae!*[9]

In September 1920, Orra cheered for her mother. It was a great honor to have the *Hughmilleria phelpsae* named for her.

Again placing family duty before her own financial security and personal freedom, in September 1920, Orra began supporting and chaperoning Bessie, her seventeen-year-old sister, as a New Hampshire College freshman. Enroute to Durham, they stopped to shop in Boston. They bought union suits - $1.08, girdle ribbon - $.45, stockings - $.50, and pins and thread - $.21.

When they arrived in Durham, the biggest news was that Captain Carleton Coulter, a handsome instructor in Military Science, was

Captain Carleton Coulter.
1921 photo courtesy of the Coulter family

now boarding in the room next to Orra's.[10] This was the beginning of a wonderfully happy period in her life.

At the Veterans of Foreign Wars dance, she danced the Mud Hole Flop and waltzed with Captain Coulter.

She wrote on October 16, 1920, "Captain is very careful to pass himself around. I had a very good time for he is a bit taller than I and it is easy for him to lead me." Mrs. Phelps was not surprised to learn that, by November, Captain Coulter was teaching Orra and her friend to shoot rifles; another skill Orra couldn't resist learning, as she wrote on November 22, 1920:

> Captain put up a target for each of us, got a blanket to kneel on and a bench to rest our rifles on. We had regular army rifles but not regular cartridges. Then he showed us how to set our sights and load. As nearly as we could count, I shot thirty-two times and the sum of shots on both targets was: four bull's eyes and twenty-two in next to center ring. If I get to be expert, I'm going bear hunting on Christmas vacation.

Later, Carleton taught Orra to shoot a revolver, enabling her to defend herself against man or beast, if necessary. Almost none of her acquaintances ever learned to shoot, much less carry a revolver, but Orra was an adventurer and a woman ahead of her times. Orra and the captain sometimes talked by the fire on winter evenings. Orra explained in her January 21, 1921 letter:

> Captain and I had coffee and doughnuts, while Dad Henderson sat as chaperone in the next room . . . Don't get worried as to my behavior. We talked about the Negro race problem and the probabilities of alliances in the next war.
>
> When we were wiping the dishes, Captain asked me if I ever did anything bad, and I didn't answer him. When we were going upstairs he reminded me that I didn't answer his last question. So I said, 'Yes, I'd been bad plenty of times.' 'When?' And I couldn't think of anything terrible that I'd done, so I said, 'I can't think of anything just now.' He just howled with laughter and skipped upstairs and dropped on the top stair weak with laughing! Is not that conclusive proof of how good I've been, up here, at least?

Sometimes Orra and Carleton went horseback riding, although she did not like galloping too fast. She learned to hold a Morgan when it danced at cars, gradually gaining confidence in her riding. They shared many long Sunday afternoon hikes, despite cold, snow, and mud, logging nearly one hundred miles. He confided that it was the one time of the week when he could cease to be a captain and just be human. She wrote on February 6, 1921:

> It's funny to have Captain describing maneuvers and tactics on the landscape, while I see upheavals, glaciers, and retreating glacial lakes. The Captain is a pleasure because he is so sane and safe, and we walk for the fun of walking, letting conversation take what turn it will. He comes home and writes his mother, brother, and 'girl'.

Orra's mother and aunt questioned Orra's friendship with the captain. Aunt Bessie wrote:

> Am glad you are enjoying your work and so many pleasures. The only thing I am sorry about is that you spoke of him as Catholic. If the friendship should grow, I fear that fact might prove unfortunate. I'm hoping that whatever the outcome, you will be the happiest woman ever, for I love you dearly.

Orra wrote back in May 1921 to explain her relationship with the Captain and to allay her family's worries, in a letter obviously prejudiced by the times, her upbringing, and her limited experience.

> A. Bessie's letter hinted that I'd better watch my step lest my acquaintance with Captain arrive at an unpleasant or unexpected end. I know that unexpected things happen and [I think] we are both in the 'Safety Zone'. He still thinks the world of Louise and I want him to keep on liking her best and as for myself, I am looking farther. I should never, never be satisfied with a Catholic, but I can say—as a guarantee of his manliness, that I'd like to have my pick of half a dozen Protestants with ideals and moral standards as high as his.

Whether Orra acknowledged it or not, the increased male attention moved her to buy new shoes, silk stockings, and gloves. She sewed new party clothes, including a white satin skirt, which Carleton said was the prettiest thing he had seen in Durham except for the dress she had worn to the Christmas formal.

Orra's life continued to be shadowed by the Phelps family difficulties, the endless farm bills, Papa's depression, and her mother's frustrations. On campus, Orra was concerned with Bessie's spells of fatigue, which later proved to be caused by a congenital heart condition, and part of the reason for Bessie's failure in some courses. While living through these experiences was no doubt difficult for Orra, one of her strengths was the ability to go on with her life in spite of obstacles and burdens.

By April 1921, Orra still worried about how to finance medical school, while her mother had a different concern. Mrs. Phelps knew Orra loved the out-of-doors and questioned, "Have you ever thought how confining is the life of a surgeon?"

Orra had trouble convincing her family that she had decided to enter medical school and that it was crucial she start that year. On May 6, 1921, she wrote of how she felt about marriage and her career, grappling with difficult decisions:

> If I am ever to do anything but mediocre teaching, I must change now and pull myself up a peg or two. I may never have put it in words to you before, but you must know I feel it, for otherwise I wouldn't be a woman. I'd rather be married to the right man than be a doctor, but I haven't got the say so about the first and I have about the second. And if I can't be married, nothing would make me so happy throughout life as being a doctor. And I must get my preparation now, if ever. You may rest assured—though it looks vulgar in writing—that I am going to look for the right man and if I meet him, I'm going to do all in my power to trap him. Only he must be the right man. I'm not going to borrow money and go into debt [for medical school], because then I can stop anywhere and not have obligations.
>
> With love that cannot be expressed.
>
> Orra

In May 1921, Orra's mother encouraged her:

> I want you to go on with your life as seems wise to you. I
> know you will do happily and cheerfully whatever comes.
> I do wish you might find the right man. Go your way and
> if you are to meet Mr. Right, he will come to you—if not
> you will bring comfort and health to many and have a circle
> of friends which will grow larger each year.

Orra was ecstatic when she received acceptance to Johns Hopkins
Medical School, even though it was conditional.

> May 23, 1921
> JHU Med. Dept.
> Office of the Dean
> Baltimore, MD
>
> Miss Orra Phelps,
> New Hampshire College
>
> Dear Miss Phelps,
>   Your application for admission to the Johns Hopkins
> Medical School is at hand. You fulfill all our require-
> ments except in Organic Chemistry and German. In
> [chemistry] you will require a minimum of 100 hrs. of
> laboratory and 60 hrs. of class work and in German, pass-
> ing a reading test.
>   If you notify me that you are taking the summer
> course in Org. Chem, formal notification of our action
> will be sent you by July 15th, of course with the under-
> standing that the work in Chemistry must be satisfacto-
> rily completed.
>   Yours very truly,
>   J. W. Williams, Dean

Then the unexpected happened. As Orra and Carleton hiked
through the flume at Franconia Notch with his relatives, he proposed
marriage to her. Up to this point, her letters showed she had thought
of him only as a good friend. How could she answer him? He was a
Catholic and she had vowed never to marry a Catholic. But wasn't
this almost any woman's dream, to marry the West Point-bound cap-

tain of the guard, a rangy, handsome, idealistic man? Now her life was in a whirlwind.

For days they tried to figure the best way. As if to lend permanence to their friendship, they carved their initials inside the rim of the campus bell, high in the bell tower. Finally, he encouraged her to fulfill her medical school dream while he advanced his military career. They agreed not to see each other while she was in medical school, except to meet his parents in Baltimore.

Full of turmoil, she left Durham and its days of her first romance to visit her family, and to prepare for the next chapter of her life, medical school.

— 6 —

Johns Hopkins Medical School
1921 and 1922

When Orra came home to Wilton in June 1921, she hugged her family, erasing months of separation. She savored the familiarity of her own bed, Mamma's hot Parker House rolls, the family banter, and Wilton's wildflower palette. She shared the family's work, joys, and cares. Sensing she might be away for months, maybe years, Orra banked the images of the people and home she loved in her memory, making this a bittersweet interim.

Her conditional acceptance to Johns Hopkins meant taking Organic Chemistry during July, yet Mamma asked Kay, "Why can't Orra help us another year?" Then she rationalized, "To get somewhere in this world, Orra has to be a little selfish." Already feeling the loss of her sensible head and strong hands, the homebound Phelpses said good-bye to Orra as she boarded the night train, leaving their world for a larger one of her own.

A stranger in Baltimore, this young woman faced many challenges. That first day Orra realized her Johns Hopkins payment was due by four-thirty or there'd be a fine, but she had locked her checks in her trunk, which the Phelpses shipped on the later baggage train.

With a spare key in hand, Orra went to the station and pleaded her case. They found her trunk and accepted her content list as proof of ownership. Clutching her checkbook, she dashed for trolleys across town to the treasurer's office. When she arrived, she discovered her name was not on the medical school list. Although the registrar promised her the very next vacancy, she feared medical school politics might be worse than passing Organic Chemistry and German.

Next, Orra discovered that the checks written in New Hampshire bounced when the college withheld her final salary check until

51

her meal bill was paid. She was livid, but borrowed $100, settled the forgotten bill, and waited for her bank account to clear.

Although Orra and Captain Coulter had agreed not to meet, he kept turning up. As if by ESP, two hours after Captain Coulter arrived in Baltimore, they met by chance in a pharmacy. Keeping that Durham promise, he invited her to a family dinner. Orra liked his father, finding him open and friendly like his son, but Mrs. Coulter was "so southern" Orra had trouble figuring her out. Later that evening, he treated her to her first roller coaster ride and then to dancing at a roof-top cafe.

As if to forestall criticism, Orra wrote her mother:

> We talked about . . . my chances at medical school. His only concerns are to see me succeed in what I have chosen and to give me an occasional good time.
> I do think a good deal of him, but only because I know he's a fine man and I wish him every success—and a loving wife and a happy home. There are lots of men in the world, and he happens to be the first I've met—a good beginning—but not the only one by a long shot. What you fear is natural, that I may not realize how much I think of him . . . till it's too late. I'm going to take your advice and have a good time—without cracking my heart. Plus, I'm making it a rule that work must not be slighted.[1]

Her letters also described Baltimore's well-scrubbed marble steps, the row houses, and famous markets piled with fresh produce, seafood, spices, and flowers. She noted all the churches and hospitals, the slums, and ethnic enclaves, but longed for the country and wished she had hiking companions.

With the help of Mrs. Coulter, Orra found a job as a $40 a month housekeeping supervisor at the Women's Hospital during July, August, and September. Battling roaches, bedbugs, and head lice did not stymie her but the humid heat did, so she and two other women slept outdoors on the roof.

Orra said she was glad she could still be shocked—first by a daytime robbery in the nurses' dorm, after which she instituted more security and hid her valuables;[2] and then when a Mount Holyoke

Mrs. Phelps (center), off "botanizing."

College graduate offered Orra a cigarette, which she refused. Orra gradually became savvier, further preparing herself for the rigors of medical school. She increased her independence when she opened her own bank account in Baltimore, bolstered by a friend's $500 loan.

Mrs. Phelps also decreased her dependence on Orra and Lawrence when she became a biology teacher at Saratoga High School in September 1921. Her salary of $1,400 increased the Phelpses' financial security and lifted Mamma's spirits.

By September 19, 1921, Orra still had no word of her acceptance and, upon inquiring, was told her Organic Chemistry grade had not been recorded. Again she had to fight her way, appealing directly to the dean. "He asked me what I'd done since graduation and about New Hampshire College. He [then] called the registrar and said, 'I think we can find a place for her.' About all I said was, 'That was worth waiting for!' "[3]

Finding only men in her first class, Orra recalled teaching mixed classes at New Hampshire College and wrote, "Men cannot phase [sic] me anymore; I marched in and sat down." Orra sensed that another woman, who came in late, was very glad to see her.

Orra's late September letters continued to chronicle her life at medical school.

This a.m. we met our anatomy class partners and our cadaver. There are fourteen men and two women, assigned alphabetically into groups of four. . . . Today we examined the cadavers and did very little cutting. Our instructor is a very sensible fellow who tells us not to race and to take time for ourselves after class.[4]

Orra was exuberant about her work, explaining, "Today in Histology we examined the blood from an embryo pig — stained while it was still warm with a vital stain. My slide was one of the best in the class."[5]

Orra Phelps in medical school at Johns Hopkins University.

A few weeks later, using clinical terms, she explained:

We have begun to research the interior of our subject and find him most interesting. He had peritonitis, an ulcer of the stomach, and worst of all, an enormous aneurysm on the aorta, a sac like enlargement due to weakening of the artery walls. All the class has been to "see the show."[6]

Orra studied histology and physiology weeknights, but on weekends concentrated on anatomy, toting her heaviest book only once a week. Humor crept into the most serious work:

In anatomy work, our table has a 'goat'. The Italian says he can't be bothered finding all the nerves so he misses most of them, and has a poor looking dissection. He is useful because it makes my dissection look much better [by comparison]. The Swiss instructor brings him to my side and says, 'See, thees iss as it should be!' The work is more fascinating than ever . . .

Orra Phelps's Johns Hopkins class. Row 1 (left to right): Schuman, Beard, Gilpen, Phelps; Row 2: Geharty, Sweeney, Fletcher, Miller, Stoll; Row 3: Eldridge, Ott, Pond, Hecht, Specht, Worden, Androvic, and Selinger.

My cadaver has lost its head and both arms, so that now I can work independently from the three men. When we found a ten inch long appendix that ran straight, from the usual 'point' up under his liver, one of the bright boys remarked that this man might have had a pain in his liver due to his appendix. Dr. Hughson says that it is just such cases where a case of appendicitis is mistaken for 'gall stones'.

Over at Women's Hospital the other day they removed a double vagina, cervix, and a two-lobed uterus with a communication between the lobes. This is very rare and the doctor saved the specimen as a choice treasure.[7]

By early March 1922, her letters showed how draining medical school plus outside work was. She wrote:

This is the first night since the first of February that I haven't felt driven. This a.m. we took the test in Physiology and although grades are not given out, Mr. Coy told me that I 'did very well in both courses, fulfilling our expectations.' Considering my outside work, I think that's pretty good. The work next term is to be no easier. We are

Orra's well-worn medical equipment.

beginning laboratory work in Physiology and lectures and lab in Bacteriology and lectures in Physiological Chemistry.

Orra wrote that one woman failed neurology and supposed there were men who also failed. Bacteriology was fascinating, but intensely challenging. For Orra, the best part of producing colonies in gelatin was identifying what had grown from common dust.

Orra drove herself through the rest of the term. Her one final, Bacteriology, was exhausting, with questions ranging from her knowledge of anaphylaxis, to diphtheria, typhoid, smallpox, and food poisoning. She feared she did not do well but hoped, by some miracle, her lab work would lift her grade. The news, though, was not good.

June 8, 1922
Johns Hopkins University
Medical Dept. Baltimore
Office of the Dean to Miss Orra Phelps, 1st Year Class,

My dear Miss Phelps:
I regret to inform you that at the meeting of the 1st and 2nd year Committee held this day, it was reported that you had failed Bacteriology. This being the case, you are conditioned in that subject and can come up for re-examination one year after the previous examination.

In other respects your work, I am glad to say, has been satisfactory.

Yours very truly,

J.W. Williams, Dean

This failure was especially bitter because hard-earned money was lost and because she had waited so long and sacrificed so much. How could Orra fail Bacteriology? Failure was not in her vocabulary.

But looking at her hectic schedule, it is easy to understand. She had undertaken not only the full load of Johns Hopkins Medical School, one of the most competitive in the world, but several other jobs.

First, through church friends, Orra became a nanny for Dr. and Mrs. Walter Hughson, head of the JHU Anatomy Department, caring for their two daughters, Letitia, (Tishie), three, and Marjorie, one, in exchange for her room. The Hughsons and Orra soon became fond of each other, and the women in

Marjorie and Letitia Hughson.

the remarkable family—especially the grandmothers—became forceful role models.

Speaking as if they were her own children, with weekly demands of time, ingenuity, and energy, Orra confided:

> Grandmamma Curtis adores the 'near spoilt' Letitia. On her birthday Tishie was showered with clothes and presents, but only one worries me, her doll carriage, which must go with us every time we go out to walk. Until she gets a little bigger and more skillful as a pilot, it will take all my wits to get baby carriage, Tish and doll carriage and self across a street. She even stops in the middle of a street to have me blow her nose or tie her shoe. But I 'spect I'll soon get used to it.

The babies are asleep and I am enjoying the first moments of peace since 5:30 a.m. Dr. and Mrs. Hughson left here yesterday afternoon for a two-day trip to the Harvard-Princeton game—and Grace the maid, and Mary the cook, and I have been holding fort.[8]

To support herself, Orra took a second job as head housekeeper for the Women's Association: planning, buying, and managing for forty women. It paid $50 a month plus room and board but started in mid-February. Though she continued to live with the Hughsons, she now took her meals across town, juggling her schedule, spending precious time traveling in an effort to pay all her own bills.

Orra found time for church, but little for relaxation. After a rare day outdoors, she wrote joyfully:

Sunday Miss Hoerner and I had a seven-mile hike. We saw skylarks, bluebirds, and song sparrows and I gathered alder tags and cocoons. At a willow farm, where a man grows willow for baskets, we watched them being cut, sorted into various lengths, and then bundled and placed cut ends down in a pool of water.[9]

Orra's shortage of money continually nagged her. By March, she wondered if she would have the same job next year, writing home how well she'd managed as housekeeper. She dropped into bed at 10:00 P.M., rising at 6:00 A.M. to study. She cut her childcare time to weekends, then sharing the simple joys of nature. She wrote:

After breakfast Saturday, I noticed that the polyphemus cocoon I collected had come out. The moth was still on its cocoon tho' I think it had been out several hours. Mrs. Hughson just raved about it and Tishie thought it was fine.[10]

Finding strength and peace in the church, Orra joined the Brown Memorial Presbyterian Church at Easter and took the sermons to heart. One of her favorites was on Micah 6:8, "He hath showed thee, O man, what is good; and what doth the Lord require of thee, but to do justly, and to love mercy and to walk humbly with thy God?"[11]

Orra's education was not confined to medical school. She joined Catholic friends on Holy Thursday to hear "Tenebrae," chanted by one hundred fifty men in two choirs. As she met more people, she became friends with Jews and European immigrants as well.

Seeing the play, "Little Lord Fauntleroy" starring Mary Pickford, and the Baltimore Opera as Dr. Hughson's guest, diverted Orra's attention from all she was attempting — to succeed at medical school, to support herself financially, and to have time and energy just to live.

Failing bacteriology was a big price to pay, but that year Orra learned, as her mother had tragically learned with her breakdowns, that even the strongest person has a stress limit. Hoping for a second chance a year later, she stoically left Baltimore in June 1922 to recuperate in the Adirondacks.

Silver Bay Summers
1922 and 1923

Just as driving the back roads brings unexpected rewards, so did Orra's forced detour from medical school to Silver Bay, a YMCA and YWCA Christian Conference Center, on Lake George, New York. The setting during the summers of 1922 and 1923 was ideal and brought her unexpected peace,[1] fresh mountain air, a spiritually healing environment, and plenty of vigorous outdoor activity.

With old friends and many interesting new ones, Orra philosophized and prayed, went birding, learned to swim, climbed over the mountain to Jabe Pond and explored sphagnum bogs. She even learned that one could camp all summer on New York State land in a pitched

Silver Bay attendees, 1923. Orra Phelps appears in the second row, seventh from the left. The YWCA Christian Conference Center on Lake George during the summers of 1922 and 1923 brought her a chance for spiritual renewal and a welcome break from the rigors of medical school at Johns Hopkins.

tent, as long as nothing more permanent is built. It was a fact she would later include in her Adirondack trail guide.

She frequently spent her off duty time assisting in the infirmary, gleaning all the medical information and practice she could. The letdown of failing Bacteriology, of having her ambitious plans derailed, was the first major setback of her own doing. She had deferred her own plans for the welfare of her parents and siblings, but never faced a defeat like this. Now she did not even have the money to take other courses while she waited for bacteriology to be given again, so she stoically worked another year. This seemed like another test of her drive and backbone.

Orra immersed herself in religion at Silver Bay, hearing the most prominent preachers and theologians. This experience had a lifelong affect on her — enhancing her giving nature and Christian ethics. Her Silver Bay summers at the southern edge of the Adirondacks moved her to say, "The lake and the whole

A Chinese group at Silver Bay, one of several foreign delegations with which Orra interacted. She learned to put aside her family's racial prejudices during her time as a librarian serving Silver Bay's international visitors.

region is beautiful, even enchanting. The power of the place and its spirit is indescribable. One can get beautiful religion here, simple, deep, and pure."[2]

The senior Phelpses were not only prejudiced against Catholics, but against immigrants and the uneducated. Orra further overcame family prejudice while working as a librarian among Silver Bay's international delegations.

At times she taught non-English students English and admired the persistence of people trying to read books, searching the dictionary after every few words.

Living at Silver Bay, besides providing religious inspiration, also increased Orra's familiarity with and appreciation of the Adirondack Park. Just as she and her family had become familiar with the (western) Canton side of the park in the 1913 to 1917 period, Orra now pored over the southeast quadrant USGS maps and piloted groups of friends up nearby mountains and around orchid-laden marshes. On August 1, 1922, Orra wrote to Mrs. Phelps:

> Eight of us climbed Indian Head Mountain [on the northwestern edge of Lake George] where we ate our lunch. Then we headed for Ice Gorge, where the going was very precipitous, till we struck a brook bed, which made it more gradual. This led us down to another stream running at right angles, which made the gorge at one end . . . about fifty feet wide, the bottom filled with blocks of rocks torn from sheer walls. Trees grew on the steep sides as well as on the floor — and all was densely wooded. In one place we dropped down between blocks of rocks and through a tunnel and up again.

On another hike to Ice Gorge, Orra and her group found ice from the previous winter and rare ferns, including Goldies, the giant wood-fern, and the feather-like silvery spleenwort. She was in her element. Her letter went on:

> We tramped through the gorge for two miles, finally coming out to a country road, past a famous split rock. This glacial remnant, stranded in a mowing lot had one neat split from top to bottom — about five feet apart at the top and two to three feet at the base, as if cleaved by a big knife.[3]

Orra used her topographical map reading skills to bushwhack for miles around Silver Bay. On August 14, 1922, she wrote,

> Dear Mamma,
> Sat. A. J. Stearns and I climbed Catamount Mountain with six others, on an easy trail three miles through some of the largest beeches, maples, and black birch I have ever seen, but for the last mile — the hard part of the climb — we had

to follow old blazes and tramp through underbrush. It took us just two hours to reach the top — a large flat erratic. From there we had a wonderful view — of all the central range, including Mount Marcy — and very faintly on the other side — the Green and White Mountains.

Coming down we started on a beeline, without a trail — for Jabe Pond, Stearns leading. Because the sun was hidden, we bore too far west, scrambled up another hill which according to the map we should not have met, then dropped down into a swamp, where I glimpsed the orchid — *H. orbiculata* and snowberries. Then seeing a second hill ahead of us — which shouldn't have been there either — I produced both map and compass and we all decided we were west of Jabe Pond — so we struck due east. Presently we came to a hunting camp and the trail home.

The High Peaks beckoned Orra. When her brothers, Leon and Lawrence, climbed Marcy in the summer of 1922, the old competitive spirit and determination to do whatever they did surfaced in Orra. She set another goal for herself; some day she would climb Marcy and other High Peaks, with or without her brothers.

Orra had rarely gone swimming with young men, other than her brothers, and was shy about practicing her kicks on the sand before her young male teacher. However, she was determined to conquer her fear of deep water and of submerging her face. Finally, she learned to swim and by September mastered diving to the bottom for stones and swam one-quarter mile with ease. Mastering a new physical activity and overcoming her fear boosted her morale.

Another healing incident occurred when Orra and another woman went rowing on Lake George and high winds came up. Orra continued rowing and "enjoyed discovering that I could manage a boat quite decently in a good strong wind. We shipped water once or twice, that is when a wave broke against the boat, but had a very pleasant trip."[4]

These experiences and others at Silver Bay in the Adirondacks empowered Orra with deeper faith and inner strength to overcome fears and vulnerability and gave her a lifelong spiritual home. During the next sixty years the Adirondacks were to be an integral part of Orra's multi-faceted life. In 1972, Orra would return to Silver Bay to teach botany at a National Wildlife Summit. The author and her family happily joined some of Orra's classes at that time as well as those of Wayne Trimm, noted wildlife artist.

In September 1922, Orra made another sacrifice for her family — she again deferred her return to medical school. With three younger sisters still in college, she felt they deserved priority. So she taught school and helped on the farm.

During this period, one of the family's major accomplishments at the Wilton farm was the hand-digging of a trench six feet deep and one-quarter mile long to bring gravity-fed spring water from the hillside woods into their home. The trench allowed them to bypass a stagnant attic coffin-like tank, which no doubt harbored untold germs. Lawrence engineered the project and frequently came from New York City to help. Working shoulder to shoulder with Leon, Francis, and Mr. Phelps, Orra helped dig the stony land until their hands were blistered. Horses hauled out stove-sized boulders that they could not lift and toted away stoneboat-loads of gravely soil and rocks.

As September 1923 approached, Orra ached to return to medical school but again faced a barrier; bacteriology was scheduled only during spring term of 1924. Disappointed but patient, she worked at home until March 17, 1924, then began the third trimester. She re-took Bacteriology along with Pathology, Medical Psychology, Physiological Chemistry, and Dr. Hughson's Applied Anatomy. After a week Orra confided to her mother, "I have recovered from any fear I had of starting again."

Everyone encouraged her return, but it was Lawrence who paid her bills. Slim and handsome, he never complained of wearing old suits to his AT&T executive job or of juggling his checkbook after sending money to the family. His social life was mainly the Brooklyn Boy Scouts and occasional hikes with friends such as A.T. Shorey, who would later become Orra's friend and sometime Adirondack hiking companion.

Lawrence was more than an older brother; he was a father figure and benefactor to the whole family. Except for Leon's bills, Lawrence paid a large part of all his siblings' education plus counseled and emotionally supported them, filling the role their father was unable to fill.

Captain Coulter also encouraged Orra as she returned to medical school:

Dear Orra,

I'm so glad you are back . . . let's hope you make it without another break and without working during the academic year. Hopkins is more than most can carry; if you try to do more, you attempt an impossibility.

After sharing his career advancements in the army, he continued:

Don't forget that if I can ever be of any help I am waiting for the chance . . . The fifty you repaid me or that last hundred is still waiting to go back to you or more if you need it. Best of luck and don't work yourself sick.

Sincerely, Carleton[5]

She plunged into her classwork, explaining:

In Physiological Chemistry we are separating milk into its constituents and analyzing each one in turn. I have my butterfat soaking in alcohol, the casein dried, the albumin and globulin drying and the lactase in solution.

In Bacteriology we are playing with *B. prodigious* which is a beautiful red in colonies and with *B. pyocyancous* which is a pretty green. The professors of this course are so different than the ones I had in my first year that it makes the work easier and more interesting.[6]

When Orra's Medical Psychology course required a family medical history, Mrs. Phelps responded on April 10, 1924:

My mother, Almira Stanley Hibbard, was active, very nervous, snappy, and ambitious. My father, Eliphaz Hibbard, was rather easy going and unambitious, but helpful and kindly. Mother's father was born in 1808, the son of a second wife born in his father's old age [sixty]. Grandfather Hibbard, a successful businessman, was very nervous, suffering a stroke of paralysis at sixty, leaving him unable to speak distinctly but able to get about. His wife, Almira J. Stanley, was extremely religious, came from a large family and was a dress maker and milliner. Grandfather Hibbard's great-great grandmother was the

Williams girl who, with her sister and father, Rev. John Williams, pastor of Old Deerfield, was forced by the Indians to march to Canada in 1704.

On Father's side, Grandpa Philo Parker was as solid as an ox. Grandmother Hulda Frost Parker was a great worker but worried all the time. I remember my great-grandmother Parker as a sprightly little old lady over ninety. Many of the Parkers were farmers and black smiths but great-grandfather Parker served in the war of '76 and his father was also a soldier.[7]

My grandmother Hibbard's mother, Nancy Nichols, 'lost her mind' due to a 'leakage' when, a watery bunch came between her shoulders and simultaneously she became childish. Mother always said she overworked, raising her family of twelve after her husband's death.

Oh, I forgot two immediate ancestors with problems. Your paternal grandmother, Nancy Leonard Phelps, died from poison, self administered, I fancy because she was tired of bearing children.[8] From things I have gathered Grandfather Solomon Phelps, aside from his drinking and tobacco habits, was not all he ought to be.

Through the conscientious care of her forebears, Orra had a family history far exceeding the requirements of her course—one that spoke of ambitious women with children, women who were often overworked caring for large families. The fact was not lost on Orra.

At Easter Sunday services, Orra met the nephew of Mary Garrett, the feminist benefactor who had given over three hundred thousand dollars from her Baltimore and Ohio Railroad inheritance to Johns Hopkins Medical School. The money was donated on the condition that women enter on equal terms with men and that all students should have, prior to admission, a degree of Bachelor of Arts or Science with training in physics, chemistry and biology, and possess a reading knowledge of French and German.

Orra recognized the importance of such women who paved the way for her and other early female physicians. In her mature years, Orra would also contribute to college funds to aid women and minorities.

Indicative of her priorities, Orra later wrote her mother, "Today has been a great day for me. I have seen not only my first autopsy, but my second and third. The most interesting one was an unusual case of brain tumors."[9]

After passing her dreaded bacteriology finals in May, Orra relished the class boat trip down the Chesapeake Bay, the fresh sea breezes ruffling her hair, like a bird released from a confining cage. Two medical arts students who shared Orra's appreciation of form, color, and light accompanied her. As they picnicked, they watched the changing water and sky and on the far distant shore a steel mill dumping red-hot slag into the water, sending up pillars of steam.

Years later, Orra would recall this pollution as she worked to protect the environment in the Adirondacks and in northeastern New York State. Botanizing by the bay, she found "white Johnny jump-ups spread in twenty-foot patches. The blossom looks like Canada violet but hasn't the coloring on the back of the petals."[10] Mrs. Phelps identified Orra's new plant as a wild field pansy, advising her to watch for the bird foot violet with bicolored petals.

Realizing how much she needed a change from the strain of medical school and being indoors so much, Orra declined a summer job caring for an invalid. She also needed to get over a nagging sore throat and regain her usual vigor, so she worked on the Phelps farm, often gardening and berrying. In July, she undertook something few women had done, something she dreamed of during her two Silver Bay summers; she climbed Mount Marcy.

The interweaving of her medical career and her Adirondack mountain climbing would last a lifetime.

— 8 —

Orra's First Mt. Marcy Ascent
July 1924

Author's note: *This chapter is taken in large part from Orra's first-person recollections of her first Marcy trip.*

Orra could hardly wait as they neared the Adirondacks. Today they were headed up Mt. Marcy, New York's highest peak. In mid-afternoon, the last week in July 1924, Orra, her mother, her brother Leon, and Lee Miller, her Silver Bay roommate, unloaded their duffel from their old Dodge at Lake Sanford.

They shouldered the knapsacks and blanket rolls and had ready Orra's camera and Mamma's vasculum, or botany can — a perforated, tubular metal container for storing plant specimens.

With belts hung with canteens and citronella-drenched kerchiefs, the group set off into the big woods. Before Leon had agreed to accompany the three women, Orra had considered packing her revolver. However, Lee had written, "As for the automatic, I would be more afraid of that than anything it might be used on."[1]

Orra and Mrs. Phelps, loaded with bedrolls and a botany can, are ready for their first ascent of Mt. Marcy in this 1924 photo.

When they crossed the log bridge at the end of the lake, they passed summer fishermen. Brushy second growth and huge decaying

68

stumps of the decimated mature forest surrounded them as they tramped along a woods road that had once carried horses, wagons, and lumbermen. Orra wrote:

> We passed the deserted Iron Works — the big sheds for crushing ore and empty miner's shacks — then the trail ahead of us disappeared into the deep, dark woods and we felt free.
>
> We hiked at a good pace, wanting to cover as many miles as possible before nightfall. The trail, soft and springy underfoot, was shaded with interlocking beech, maple, and birch. Where the trees parted enough to let in the sun, twisted stalk, meadow rue, and jewelweed grew tall. On mossy, damp banks, ferns flourished.
>
> Eagerly we pressed forward, sniffing the cool, clean air, keenly observing everything on this our first trip to Marcy. We listened for the whir of partridge, the scampering of squirrels, and the white throat's whistle. A stream babbled ahead, its bank, steep and rocky and its water swift and cold. Not trusting the rotting bridge, Leon hopped across boulders, dropped his duffel, and came back to help us. Trying to advise someone on the best way to cross a stream is akin to driving a car from the back seat — it doesn't work. We each chose our own route; each got a foot baptized.
>
> As we went through the deep woods, the sun's rays piercing low through the branches told us it was getting late, twilight coming more quickly in the shaded woods. We felt the weight of our packs but dared not mention it. Almost in silence we paced another mile, then stepped into the open sunshine, where reflections danced on the Opalescent River. Edged with blackberry briars and fallen logs, our path hugged the stream bank.
>
> The trail then left the stream and passed more of yesteryears' handiwork: a pile of cordwood, rotting, then more deserted cabins, a big open shed for sawing logs and a huge pile of decaying sawdust. We skimmed the best of the raspberries growing there, plant pioneers that took over after the lumbering stopped, and watched for those other berry lovers, the Adirondack black bears.
>
> Soon the trail dead-ended at another turn of the Opalescent, but with no bridge visible, no trail marker, no

stepping-stones. As we strained our eyes for a sign, Leon whispered, "Look!" A big buck stood motionless, head high, nose to the wind. We watched breathlessly for several moments and then, so suddenly it made me blink, he took one big bound and disappeared into the thicket.

The stream was still not crossed. Upstream it looked deeper and narrower, below wider between boulders. We decided to wade across, so shoes and stockings came off and we ventured cautiously over the cold, slippery-stoned bottom. Once across, Leon, Lee, and I dropped our packs and turned to help our fifty-seven-year-old mother. There she stood, knickers rolled above her stout knees, botany can swaying against her back, shoes with laces tied swinging around her neck, waving her arms for balance and deliberately pushing her feet forward like an Egyptian dancer. This scene was too much for us. We doubled up with laughter and howled until we couldn't see through our tears. Mother came ashore, slowly and with dignity, and scolded us — to no effect.

We dried our feet carefully. Then we donned our wool socks and shoes, and followed Leon's map, grateful for the easier level section. We hustled to a junction marked by a weathered sign, where the left fork turned north toward Lake Colden, but we continued straight. Finally reaching a good camping spot by the stream, we released the heavy packs and quickly made camp. Leon cut pegs, pitched the tent, and laid a leafy bed, then our blankets. Meanwhile Mother and Lee unpacked our "grub" and fetched water, while I gathered dead wood for the fire. By the time I had a good fire going, the soup pail was ready to hang and hash ready to fry. How good it all tasted — from soup to chocolate-covered peanuts for dessert.

Unnoticed, darkness fell as we gathered around the fire, warming ourselves and our dishwater. We could not see into the woods and became aware of the silence — broken only by the crackle of the fire. With no wind, the smoke rose straight up from our fire. [2]

Orra suddenly saw a pale flash of light . . . then thunder rumbled a warning. Mamma said, "Let's hope this thunderstorm isn't a bad one." Wind began whipping the trees . . . rain began to fall in huge drops. Orra wondered if it might be rainy all the way. Would they miss the view from the top? Orra recalled:

> We hastily rinsed the dishes . . . stowed our food and [tinder] and . . . all huddled, uncomfortably, in the tent until the storm subsided. . . . Then we prepared for bed, still wearing our hiking clothes. After arranging our camp "pillows": Mamma's her botany can and Lee, Leon, and I — our shoes, we folded ourselves into our blankets, found carefully dug "hip holes" then late night thoughts lingered: are the matches and tinder dry, the flashlight and glasses — until at last I began a series of catnaps and Mother snored softly.
>
> Awaking to a dim gray dawn, we all stretched the stiffness from our limbs and rubbed our hands in the cool mist, then built a little fire, and swung our coffee pot over it. After a hearty breakfast, we quenched the fire, took a last look for stray articles, and started along the trail. Before we'd gone two hundred yards we were

A balsam bed lines the floor of a tent with an Adirondack backpack placed outside. *1947 photo*

soaking wet from our knees down from the rain and dew-laden grasses but our bodies finally warmed.

The trail now began to climb steeply and steadily. Ahead of us we could see the corduroy road, made of logs placed like railroad ties only close together. On a steep, wet incline you can't be too careful, but we climbed as rapidly as the uncertain footing and our wind would let us.

One can walk miles in the woods without seeing the mountains, but at the top of this grade we looked back through the narrow trail opening to view the rolling expanse of green forest and distant mountain peaks rising out of a sea of clouds, our first view of the mountains since leaving the car. Beside us rose the rock walls of Cliff Mountain on the left and Redfield on the right.

Upward, we stepped lightly over the logs, past a deep gulch on the left and heard rushing water far below. The noise of Twin Brook grew louder as we climbed, then a turn in the trail led us to a corduroy bridge. Clear brown water coursed between boulders, from pool to foam-flecked pool. The bridge's log stringers were still in place but many of the cross logs had been torn out and were jammed together, criss-cross and on end, telling of the force of the spring torrents. We made a safe crossing, having come about four and a half miles from the car, then pushed on.

The trail now turned away from the stream, up a gentle grade, through mostly spruce and balsam firs. The rich mold of the forest floor was a seed bed of evergreens of every size, their new green tips flashing in occasional sunlight, interspersed with bunch berry, gold thread, and wood-sorrel in profusion. Our feet made no noise on the soft carpet of needles, nor did we speak, but marched on under the great spruces, thrilled by the beauty, the silence, the majesty — and we gave thanks.

Finally we came to Buckley's Clearing, another abandoned logging center, marked by a broken grindstone, dilapidated rusty stove, distorted bedsprings, and pile of charred timbers where a cabin once stood, all half hidden by rank growth of fireweed and raspberries. At the far end of the clearing we joined the other trail from Lake Colden and a little farther we came to the lean-to at the junction of Feldspar Brook. Here we unloaded our lunch, maps, and compass, stored these in our pockets and botany can, and cached our packs and bedrolls. Then we rested for fifteen minutes, flat on our backs on the balsam bed of the shelter, its interwoven sprigs forming a fragrant cushiony pallet. [*Balsam beds are no longer permitted.*]

By the map we were only two miles from our goal, the top of Mount Marcy, [first named by Native Americans as] Tahawus, The Cloud Splitter. Though we had been climbing all morning, we still had nearly two thousand feet to climb. The trail became a narrow path, wet, slippery, and steep, so we began to climb on all fours, pulling ourselves up from tree to tree. After twenty minutes of this, with many stops for breath, the trail leveled off and threaded its way through an old-growth forest of spruce, balsam, and white cedar, sheltered in the rocky gorge from the loggers' saws. The trail passed one of the largest white cedars I have ever seen. Leon said, "Let's try to join hands around one." At shoulder height we could barely touch each other's fingertips. Others immense in diameter stood nearby, not forty feet tall, but with their tops all twisted and gnarled by the elements.

At last we came to a long level stretch, to low growing spruces, alders, and water loving plants, then to a stream. Anticipation hurried us on, over sphagnum hummocks, until we glimpsed the smooth brown waters of Lake Tear of the Clouds, the highest pond source of the Hudson River, some 4,346 feet above sea level.[3]

Essentially unchanged since September 16, 1872, when Adirondack surveyor Verplanck Colvin and his guide, William Nye, first recorded seeing it,[4] Lake Tear of the Clouds was beautifully fringed by spruces and reflected blue sky and tumbling white clouds. Sheep laurel, leather leaf, and cassandra grew among the sphagnum. Orra continued:

We found some of our earliest spring flowers still blossoming here: gold thread, violets, blue and white, false Solomon's seal and *Clintonia* and this was the last week of July.

In the distance across the lake and beyond a dark band of spruces rose the gray anorthosite dome of

Tahawus, Mt. Marcy, 5,344 feet above sea level, the highest peak in New York State, but still three quarters of a
mile away. Our feet already wet, we splashed along the
trail until we came to the park shelter.

In a December 1924 letter, Lee Miller recounted her experience:

Dear Phelpsie,
    I will never forget that trip up Marcy. I can still see
in my mind the great open space where the State Reser-
vation camp was just before the final upward climb, the
part I couldn't make. Your mother and I sat there and
never said a word — just thinking, No, your mother was
'botany cruising'. It seemed thousands and thousands of
miles away from everywhere.
                                With love, Lee Miller[5]

While Mamma and Lee rested, Orra and Leon scouted ahead to
see Four Corners, another place she had read of but never seen, and
found trails heading north to Marcy, east to Panther Gorge and out to
Elk Lake, and south to Mt. Skylight.[6] Soon Mamma joined them.

On we three went, clambering between huge, gray
weather worn boulders, among low spruces, gnarled and
twisted, through a low tangle of Labrador tea, blueberry
bushes and dwarf alders, over beds of moss and mats of
Linnaea whose tiny pink bells poured forth a charming
fragrance. Over stretches of bare rock where all soil had
been washed out of the trail, we pushed and pulled each
other. All the time we felt the nearness of the peak as we
looked over stunted treetops. To our right we could see
the shoulder and bare crest of Haystack, New York's
fourth highest peak.
    Puffing and panting we arrived at the top of a bare
rocky prominence, with only low-growing vegetation at
our feet and nothing to obstruct our view to the south,
but to the north there was the bare dome of Tahawus
still five hundred feet above us. The spruces and alders
here were only knee-high. The thick springy carpet of
vegetation was full of rare plants, and to see these growing and to collect sparingly had been Mother's chief

ambition from the start. [*It is now illegal to pick alpine plants*.] Once rested she tramped on, deliberately gathering: twigs of northern willow, of crowberry and bearberry and sprigs of northern cranberry and rose bay. So we made progress slowly.

The keen wind made scrambling over that rock surface, with only cracks for foot and handholds seem like a steeplejack's stunt. The top at last! Bare of vegetation, strewn with rocks, it had weathered many storms. Perhaps direct lightning strikes had hit the copper bolt, placed in 1875 by the Colvin surveyors.

Four Corners lean-to, where the trails from Mt. Marcy and Heart Lake, Elk Lake, Colden-Lake Sanford, and Haystack meet.   *1937 photo*

Just over the edge, in every protected crevice, the sturdy alpine plants flourished. Though rocks crumbled, the winds and rains would not let any soil accumulate on top. These breathtaking winds forced us to seek the shelter of the boulders.

The view from Marcy is by no means the finest in the state but it is immense. We were lucky to have such a clear day, where others had climbed to face clouds or rain. For miles and miles, to the east, south and west rolled a tumultuous sea of mountain peaks, blending at the horizon with a sea of clouds. To the north the mountains fell away rapidly and in the distance we could see a few patches of cultivated land and a town or two. With map and compass we tried to name some of the lakes and mountains: Boreas Ponds, Upper Ausable Lake, Lake Sanford, Lake Placid, and the Saranacs. The mountains were easier: MacIntyre, Colden, Santanoni, Haystack, Redfield, the Gothics, Nippletop, Noonmark. . . .

Noon, it must be past noon and past our dinnertime. The sun, directly overhead, was warm where the wind did not blow. We ate our lunch of bread and cheese and chocolate in the highest and most exclusive dining room in the state.

No one wanted to leave, even daydreaming of watching sunset from the top, but going down a wet and slippery trail is not much easier than climbing and we were two miles from our duffel, three miles from our desired camp. We took a last long look around us, drew several deep breaths, and sighed a sigh of contentment. The labor of climbing had been forgotten in the glory of the reward. In the months and years that followed, the backaches and weary muscles cannot be recalled but the thrill that comes from first standing on top of Tahawus is unfading.[7]

— 9 —

Return to Medical School
1924 to 1927

Still exhilarated by her first Marcy ascent, Orra returned to Johns Hopkins in September 1924. After what she thought would be a routine physical examination, she found herself in the hospital. The doctor, after considering her history of sore throats and finding her appendix enlarged, advised an immediate appendectomy and tonsillectomy.

During two weeks' recuperation at the Women's Hospital, Orra received extra care from doting nurses she knew, but fell behind in her classes. Medical school was more of a struggle than ever. She would work six hours, sleep nine and nap as necessary, continuing school through sheer grit.

In November, Orra wrote home that her Pharmacology professor was "sure slim on botany."

Orra Phelps at Johns Hopkins Medical School, circa 1924.

Botany was Orra's forte, and her knowledge of its many home remedies such as dandelion greens for iron poor blood made her wish she had a mess of these nutritious greens. It was in this class that two of Orra's classmates, jealous of her botanical knowledge, tried to trick her by splicing together two plants and then asking her to identify the fake. Suspecting a trick, she found the insertion of one tubular stem into a different kind and identified both sections.[1]

Once Orra finished translating the ninety page German text required by Johns Hopkins, she was free to recuperate over Christmas break. This year she was more realistic, guarding both her strength and her resources by staying in Baltimore. She was particularly delighted with Lawrence's gift, a used $60 microscope, which she would continue to use in her eighties. Orra sent her mother Longstreth's, *The Adirondacks*, which had further whetted Orra's appetite for climbing MacIntyre and the other High Peaks.

Lawrence Phelps purchased this microscope in 1921 for $60. Orra used her brother's gift throughout medical school.

Another Christmas treat was a visit by Captain Coulter, where they caught up on months of each other's work, supported their mutual desire to achieve, and continued their friendship.

Her second semester included clinical work with patients. "Last week we had a convalescent from encephalitis, sleeping sickness. Because this is not common, the doctors illustrated it while they had a good case."

Though most people recoil at the word autopsy, Orra Phelps didn't as she stood her ground, focusing on the learning opportunity.

> This morning my group of six girls was called [to analyze] an autopsy before the whole class. Embarrassing? No, only when you think it is. I have a powerful lot of nerve and it comes in handy. Diagnosis was acute general peritonitis, salpingitis, endometritis, slight bronchial pneumonia, and cholecystolithiasis.[2]

Orra's struggle to keep going while ill during the first term compromised her standing and worried her. Each step of her journey seemed to test her determination. In March 1925, she received a notice from the assistant dean that her average was somewhat below their expectations and that improvement was advised. Orra buckled down even more, putting in long days.

April 1925

Dear Mamma,

Thursday I was at Hopkins from 9 a.m. until 11:20 p.m. I stayed for a faculty conference on microscopic slides.

Another day we went to Bay View, the city charity hospital, and had tuberculosis chests to thump and listen to. Two of us agreed about the front, then turned the patient around, whereupon the third year man percussed up both sides of the spine and pronounced the areas alike. I percussed and pronounced the right side 'dull' changing to 'flatness' in the upper part. He held his view and I wouldn't change mine. Then the instructor came, asked what we had found and then percussed, agreeing with me. So I felt pretty fine all the rest of the day.

The best part of the morning though was Dr. Finney's lecture about our moral obligations to patients.[3]

Orra knew she would be a conscientious physician, seeking her patients' well-being first, and her own gratification second. Her medical training was not the only opportunity to serve others; she continued to give time and energy to church youth groups, to settlement house work, and to the Girl Scouts. Orra's interest in scouting was so infectious that Mrs. Hughson became a District Director of Girl Scouts and consulted Orra about suitable service projects. Orra helped plan church youth conferences, including one of the first at her church with female speakers. When Mrs. Hughson's mother, Mrs. Curtis, had an operation, Orra visited her daily, bringing books and flowers. This year, however, she did not over-exert herself.

Orra still squeezed in some long walks in the country, usually on a Sunday afternoon with her new friend, Mary McGehee, an archeology graduate student. Orra longed for more time outdoors, once catching the end of a partial eclipse in January, the third in her lifetime. She wrote Mamma of the spring flowers and birds, especially all the mockingbirds.

As time permitted, she would correspond with friends, especially with Gardiner Littell, a colleague from Silver Bay. He wanted to convert Orra from Christianity to atheism and wrote:

> Dear Orra,
>   I believe absolutely nothing could change your faith. But we agree in one thing: we both want to work for others. I hope you will every so often remind me of this, because I don't hear it often enough in my environment.[4]

By the end of May 1925, Orra wrote her mother:

> I'm over half of my medical training and I don't feel all puffed up; I feel rather flat and empty. The final exam seemed easy... perhaps too easy...so it makes one fear a trick. I don't really expect failure but I haven't as much in my favor as some other girls. I'm not going to worry about it on the trip.

Orra's "trip" was, incredibly, to *walk* the 350 miles home from Baltimore to Wilton, New York, across three states with her friend, Mary McGehee. A month before, Orra had broached the subject with her mother, saying, "Mary McGehee and I want to walk home after school closes, using the money we'd save not coming home by train."

From Baltimore, they planned to hike north through the Susquehanna River Valley, past

Orra (left) and Mary McGehee, with bedrolls, while on their 1925 "trip" of 350 miles from Baltimore, Md. to Wilton, N.Y.

York and Scranton, Pennsylvania, taking long trolley rides across cities, then continuing north through the Catskill Mountains, crossing the Mohawk River at Hoffman Ferry, west of Schenectady, New York and finally home to Wilton.

Orra continued, "Mary's hiking and camping experience in Colorado and Wyoming was pretty thorough and being a good shot, she promises to carry my revolver. What do you say?"[5]

Trusting her adventurous daughter, Mrs. Phelps answered, "Dear Orra, I know the chief fun of a vacation is doing as one wants to, so if you want to walk home, do so . . . only watch your heels."[6] Orra had continuing tenderness in her heels, causing more than her share of blisters.

> Dear Mamma,
>   From 'topo' maps we have camping places decided, starting Tuesday, going into the country by trolley before we start hiking. You can reach us by mail: first—Hazelton, PA Thursday, June 4, second—Horton, NY which we should pass through on Monday and third—Gilboa, NY on Wednesday. We plan to get home Saturday by way of Lake Desolation, Porters Corners, and the King Station Road so you'll know where to send the State Constabulary if you want us in a hurry.[7]

On May 31, 1925 Orra wrote:

> With the new moon favoring us on our trip, don't worry for we know what dangers to avoid—*i.e.* autos—and we go well armed, with a bowie knife, the ax, and my revolver—as neat a one as you could hope to see! We will not try to carry much 'grub' but restock as we go along. The ax will probably break up dead wood and dig fish worms.[8]

Just before leaving Orra received good news; she passed all her courses, completing her second year at Hopkins. Tired but exhilarated, she and Mary left on Thursday, June 4, 1925, facing record heat, shouldering their knapsacks and blanket rolls, and dangling canteens and extra shoes.

Along the way, Orra photographed and noted flowers, rocks, and birds — everything in nature to share with her mother.

As the heat wave persisted, they swam in out-of-the way streams during midday, cooling themselves and especially their feet, soothing reddened toes and heels. After one week, Orra's first pair of shoes died and another was pressed into service.

On June 11, gale force winds sent limbs crashing and brought heavy rain and a thirty-degree temperature drop.[9] Fearing flash flooding as they hiked through Grand Gorge in the heart of the Catskill Mountains, they tented high above the river and hunkered down. After the storm, they climbed over and under blowdown, making every mile seem like five.

Part of the trip's success was due to Mary's teaching Orra to laugh at herself — in sweat-soaked clothes and battle-scarred shoes, at heaving limbs off their trail, and at 'tooting' from eating beans, beans, beans.

Once they crossed the Mohawk River at Hoffman Ferry, Orra knew the area, having collected fossils and plants near Middle Grove and Lake Desolation, west of Saratoga Springs. After nine nights and eleven days' hiking, the two footsore and weary women arrived at the Phelps's farm, much to everyone's relief.

The *Saratogian* of June 17, 1925 carried the news:

WILTON GIRL HOME AFTER LONG HIKE FROM BALTIMORE

Miss Orra Phelps, a junior at Johns Hopkins Medical School and Miss Mary McGehee, of Colorado, arrived yesterday at the home of Miss Phelps's parents in Wilton, having made [most of] the trip from Baltimore on foot. They started from school on June 5 [error- actually June 4], carrying packs and blankets, scout knives and an ax and camped each night en route. Owing to the excessive heat during the early days of the trip, they could not make as good time as would ordinarily have been the case, and were forced to stop during the hot part of the day. The two women were eleven days and nine nights on the road, having many interesting and exciting experiences to relate.[10] [Courtesy of *The Saratogian*.]

Orra's junior year at Johns Hopkins Medical School was one of her best, free from health problems, and freer with a $400 Presbyterian Fund loan. Though Orra longed for country hikes, she dug into classes in gynecology, surgical dispensary, and neurology.

Orra feared being overcome while giving ether, as this letter relates:

> Last Thursday I gave anesthesia. I came down off the 'audience rack' and sat on a stool with my head under a canopy, and dropped ether . . . drop by drop on the mask. But I was there long enough to find out that I could do it and not 'flop' from the ether.

Another time when Orra had to give ether to a dog for three hours during surgical practice, she made a point of walking home to 'clear her lungs.'[11] When Mrs. Phelps wrote that she feared going under anesthesia for dental work, Orra wrote:

> As for having anesthesia, remember that the Docs know what they are doing when they give it, and [you should] think about coming out all right and being better off afterward. I marvel sometimes, at the heroism of some of the people here who go under for unknown results.
>
> In Surgical Dispensary yesterday I observed three babies . . . the oldest fifteen months, the youngest one month. The youngest had a 'wrist drop,' a palsy from birth injury, the next a 'green stick' fracture of both bones in the forearm . . . 'green stick' means bent and incomplete break . . . and the third was a true fracture of the femur in a Negro baby with rickets. Three of us in the fluoroscope room had the dickens of a time setting the fracture and putting on a plaster cast.[12]

On October 29, 1925, Orra sent a well-typed letter:

> Dear Mamma,
>   Monday for the first time I was assigned to the Wassermann Laboratory. Our only job is to draw the

blood for the reaction, not to do the tests. I think I punctured 7 veins and drew blood correctly in all cases. The man who was working with me missed two out of the same number. We had one girl who howled because she thought it was going to hurt so much, but who went away smiling, while another absolutely refused.

Orra's life was not entirely taken up with class work. In a letter now frayed from age with birdseed caught in dust webs and partially mouse-eaten, she told how she 'came out in society.'

Dear Mamma,
At that meeting Sunday, I 'came out' in society. Mr. Weatherspoon, a returned Rhodes scholar, Leo Glenn, [another Silver Bay friend] and several others were there . . . from the Alexandria Theological group, at a most palatial residence, with wonderful paneling, high ceilings, beautiful chandeliers, and more or less grand portraits. We met in the parlor and I could hardly keep from laughing at the contrast at seeing Leo Glenn perched uncomfortably on a gilt chair and recalling him reclining in the hay on our barn floor last summer. The discussion went till 5:30 when we were summoned to a very elegant supper with silver tea and coffee service, silver platters and frail china. Glenn introduced me. At the end of the evening, I WAS INVITED TO RIDE HOME IN ONE OF THE BIG CARS.[13]

Orra even gave a dinner party at her shared apartment.

I invited Mr. Campbell and Mr. Baker, the Rhodes Scholar additions to our class. Using the prettier sitting room, we had a roast pork dinner and sat over the coffee a long time, traveling through France, Germany, and Italy. Altogether it was a successful party.
I have been busy this week trying to find a dress to wear to a dance . . . surprised? given by a woman who had been very interested in women medical students . . . who was one herself years back. All the women are invited and the best of the men. I have bought a black satin dress trimmed with blue satin

and black braid, with a flaring skirt and a long straight V in the front. So tomorrow night I expect to go 'tripping.'[14]

Orra's exposure to people of other faiths and cultures continued as she explained on January 16, 1926:

> I had a patient in neurology, a German Jew — 72 years old, much bewhiskered — who had facial neuralgia. I don't know whether he will find relief through medicine or not. The doctor gave him a prescription. 'Twas funny — having every word translated back and forth.

When students complained that they could not see in the surgical arena, Orra, the problem solver, and another person returned between classes to rearrange the chairs. The array of eight across and nine rows deep on only one side became long rows of twelve on each side facing the doctor and patient, providing twenty-four front row seats and only three rows deep.

In February 1926, Orra's sister Bessie, working as a dietitian at the Mossop School in Harrison, Tennessee, collapsed with the flu. Orra borrowed bus money and traveled 625 miles to bring her back to Johns Hopkins for evaluation. She nursed Bessie back to health, but Mamma feared a recurrence of Bessie's earlier heart trouble. Orra assured her mother the weakness was from the flu.

Orra's next letter combined her excitement over caring for newborns along with a talk with a fellow Adirondack hiker.

> Obstetrics finished with a flourish. I was given an opportunity to 'scrub up,' get sterile and assist with the baby after delivery. I clamped the cord, cut, and tied it. Then I gave the oil bath, put the silver nitrate in the eyes, bandaged the cord stump, and put on the flannel band. A greasy baby and greasy rubber gloves make a difficult job of it. One boy weighed nearly ten pounds, another was premature, but living and doing well. Because I couldn't get to classes I have many lecture notes to copy.
>
> At present I am homesick for the hills — fresh air and an open road . . . with Leon at the wheel and you on the back seat and a knapsack of grub at our feet.

Last Friday I walked home from the hospital with Mr. Weatherspoon, who has spent several summers at Westport on Lake Champlain. He asked me if I had ever been in the Adirondacks and I said, "Yes, I spent most of last summer there." He said, "I mean have you ever been on the high ranges?" [Orra answered], "I've been on top of Mt. Marcy twice, once in the rain and once on a beautifully clear day." He has been on MacIntyre, too, and thinks it is better in every respect.[15]

When April came, Orra again took off for the local hills with a friend to Lake Roland, where "cardinals sang and hepaticas, blood root, spring beauties, and cowslip are in bloom. From the trolley we saw magnolias, forsythias, plums, pears, and pink ornamental cherries." She said the chronic grouches complained of the heat, but she saw it as Baltimore's spring. In May, she enjoyed going to Washington, seeing the capitol for the first time graced with flowering trees in soft pastels.

In the spring of 1926, Captain Coulter wrote from the Panama Canal Zone about his army maneuvers and life, then added,

Dear Orra,

I am glad you still think medicine your chosen field. Don't get discouraged. You have all the punch in the world and that is what you need to get through. Here's looking forward to your graduation next year. You'll be the class of 1927, just ten years after mine. I would like to get back for my reunion next year and if I do, I will arrive there in time to see you get your degree. I am glad you are coming out of your shell in the social life. You know without being told that social life is a big part of the medical profession, one of the best ways for getting ahead.

You were right in imagining that Dad has become a Catholic. He was baptized on Christmas Eve two years ago.

Sincerely, Carleton

It was thus that Orra learned that Mrs. Coulter was a Catholic and that Mr. Coulter had converted. Their Catholicism still cast a shadow over the relationship, but more from Orra's parents' point of view than Orra's. However, she was not at a point of disagreeing with the senior Phelpses in this matter.

As friends helped Orra, she mentored others in turn. A former patient wrote:

> Dearest Miss Phelps,
> Today I became a student nurse at St. Mark's Hospital. I shall never forget my first trip to NYC and how you and I walked into St. Mark's together, you introducing me as a patient. I shall never forget your encouraging smile before I took ether. You wrote me encouraging letters when I thought further education was impossible and pushed me right into school.
> You told me I may be refused in hospitals time and again, but to keep on trying. I was refused twice but tried again and was accepted . . . I am so very happy and I owe it all to you.
> Ever thine pupil, Florence[16]

Fortunately, Orra found the ideal summer job at Saratoga Springs Hospital. She didn't ask her family physician for a reference because, as she wrote, "He does not believe women should be medical doctors, only teachers." A major turning point in Orra's financial struggle came when Mrs. Lena Curtis, Mrs. Hughson's mother, paid $1000 for the final year at Johns Hopkins. In November 1926, Orra was accepted for internship at Albany City Hospital, a highly respected medical center, close to home and to the Adirondacks. She then realized with mixed feelings that her medical school years were ending, but she could hardly wait to graduate.

At about this time Mrs. Phelps confided in Orra that she did not approve of Leon's and Bessie's companions. Orra admonished her saying:

> When you pray for [their] safety, you put the matter in God's care, and you need not worry further. To pray and then to continue to worry is not real prayer. We

('we' being the nation as well as our family) have so gotten out of the habit of trusting God, [thinking] we've got
to run the world and our affairs. We have to work a day
at a time but we should not make the sorrows of yesterday or the problems of tomorrow a burden to us.

All this outburst of philosophy is not sudden. I have
long had the idea that tho' we've been given the most
joyful religion in the world, we don't allow ourselves to
get enough of it to make us really happy. Philosophy and
religion are both going to make strides ahead in the next
twenty years because people are getting brave enough to
sift the facts in spite of convention and tradition. Mistakes are made, but so were they in Luther's day, in the
time of the Puritans, in your own mother's time, even as
now. Yet truth goes forward and all else falls by the way-
side.[17]

After Thanksgiving, Orra received paintings of Mt. MacIntyre
and Avalanche Lake by Andy Rossman and a box with pine, bittersweet, and ground pine to share with friends. Orra sent Christmas gift
boxes of greens and homemade candy to Captain Coulter and Mrs.
Curtis. She personally delivered one to the Hughsons, grateful for their
financial help, encouragement, and mutual affection.

In the last half of her senior year, Orra studied the virulence of
dental infection. She sampled root infections from twelve patients,
working with the School of Hygiene bacteriologist, two dentists, and
a graduate student. Orra's teachers were impressed with her comprehensive study. Her academic standing improved as they realized her
skill in addressing a common medical problem.

She thoroughly enjoyed gynecology and shared the news of the
new Women's Clinic operating room.

The news is the opening of the new JHU operating room
on the 6th floor of the "Women's Clinic." The whole
top floor is given over to GYN with the doctors' offices,
two ether rooms, sterilizing room, supply room, two
operating rooms, and a large conference room. For the
past few years it has been necessary to wheel patients
three blocks from the women's clinic to the operating

room. Now they are only taken from the 2nd, 3rd, or 4th floor up to the 6th.[18]

As a near-physician, Orra was called on by her family for every sort of advice and consultation, including her cousin's diabetes and osteomyelitis, which she assured her mother was not from poor character, her father's brother's suicide, Mamma's aching legs, her brother Francis's handicaps, or her father's depression. She wrote encouraging letters and in her diary mentioned special prayers for them.

Orra rarely got angry. However, discrimination against women, something she hoped to leave behind in medical school, did incense Orra. Her group of eight was requested to meet Sunday at 10:00 A.M. across town for a special course in pediatric diseases. After she and two other women took an hour and a half to get there, they found that the professor had rescheduled the class and told only the men. She was still fuming a week later.

Even during her hectic final term, Orra had time for scouting. After Mrs. Hughson invited her to sit at the head table of the scout rally, Orra designed a huge diorama depicting the habitats of fifty-one species of birds to be used as the backdrop. The painting of the diorama was entrusted to an artistic scout. Orra enjoyed the project, sharing her interest and talent for nature education.

Late in her senior year, Gardiner Littell visited her en route to Washington and they toured Baltimore. She said, "Gardiner is an amiable person, but his standards of intelligence are too exalted for me." Orra's commencement invitation list included Mrs. Curtis, Miss Mignon Talbot, and Dr. Anna Morgan, both from Mount Holyoke, Aunt Bessie Gammons, and Captain Carleton Coulter. Orra wrote, "This is my week of 'Lasts'—last clinic, last ward rounds, last dispensary, last patient on the ward, but not last at all—only a respite . . . and transference of activity to another field."

DOCTOR'S DEGREE IN MEDICINE FOR SARATOGA GIRL
Miss Orra A. Phelps Graduated Today From Johns Hopkins University, June 14, 1927

Miss Orra A. Phelps, daughter of Mr. and Mrs. Charles S. Phelps, has the distinction of being one of the few Saratoga Springs young women to receive a degree of Doctor of Medicine from Johns Hopkins University, Baltimore, Maryland. The JHU School of Medicine is considered one of the finest in the country.[19] [Courtesy of *The Saratogian*.]

In their spring letters, Orra and her mother planned long hikes in the Adirondacks after Orra's graduation. They envisioned tramping through Indian Pass, celebrating Orra's achievement by doing the second thing she loved most, being in the Adirondack woods. In a visionary letter, Orra wrote her mother:

I've had a big hunch about camping — or rather on a possibility of making camping profitable — that is to collect odds and ends, yarns and poetry about the Adirondack Park region, add some history that is interesting and pictures . . . not much of the famous scenes as of the things familiar to campers, such as "Hitch-Up-Matilda" and corduroy roads, the trail markers, the waterways, and the typical forest growth, etc. and make it all into a scrapbook — not the scissors and paste kind, but velour paper and printed kind.[20]

Orra had completed another major segment of her life's journey. She had earned her coveted medical degree, which she believed to be her passport to recognition and financial security as a woman and a way to serve her fellow man. She did not yet recognize the depth of her love of nature and, especially, the Adirondacks. Her dedication to her medical career and this love of nature would form the foundation for her lifelong dual careers: doctor and naturalist.

— 10 —

Orra Joins the Adirondack Mountain Club
1926 to 1928

Author's note: *The account of Orra's second Marcy ascent is based largely on Mrs. Phelps's diaries and is fleshed out in a manner consistent with Phelps records.*

As mentioned in Chapter Nine, Orra, her mother, and Leon again climbed Mt. Marcy in the summer of 1925, just prior to Orra's third year at Johns Hopkins. Mrs. Phelps recorded their second trip,[1] noting signs of glaciation in the bogs and the "shattered and shelved" mountains of the Adirondack region. This time they hiked the longer route, north past the abandoned Adirondack Village blast furnaces

Old Adirondack Village buildings at Tahawus (the Native American name for Mt. Marcy), abandoned when the mining operation closed in the early 1900s.

and the private Tahawus Club to Flowed Lands, via the Calamity Brook Trail.

This brook and trail, Calamity Mountain, and Calamity lean-to were all named in memory of David Henderson, who accidentally shot himself near there on September 3, 1845. His untimely death, the loss of his dynamic leadership and money, and the company's transportation problems were main causes for the closing of Adirondack Iron Works.[2]

When the Phelpses came to a rickety bridge marked "Unsafe — Take Lower Trail," they risked a dunking rather than hunt for the lower trail in the gathering twilight. Their destination had been the lean-to at Flowed Lands, but Mamma tired after three miles. Leon and Orra prepared their camp and Mamma crawled in and fell asleep, exhausted. They cooked and ate, then hung perishables in a tightly covered pail placed in the cold brook. Under a starry canopy they shared career hopes and frustrations.

In the eerie dawn light, while the younger two broke camp, Mamma, a slower-paced hiker, started ahead. She found a view of Flowed Lands and mist rising from a hidden ravine, making the arduous hike worthwhile. Had Orra known and forewarned her mother that she would have to descend a steep bank on a wobbly twenty-foot sapling ladder, Mamma might not have taken that route. The lean-to was occupied when they arrived, so the three backpackers ate breakfast on the gravelly sandbar, broiling bacon on forked green sticks over their fire.

After hiking a mile, they came to Opalescent Lean-to, where Mamma noted, "We joyfully left our backpacks and bedrolls and took only our lunches, canteens, and botany can." On they hiked, past the narrow walled flume where the Opalescent River thundered deep in the chasm, past intriguing trailside flowers and ferns to be collected on their return.

Finally, they rested at the Feldspar Lean-to, the same camping spot chosen the previous year, when they had come via the Twin Brook trail. Next came the stiff climb over great boulders and gnarled roots, edged with matted moss, balsam seedlings, and bunchberry carpets. When they reached Lake Tear of the Clouds the whole area, including

The Feldspar lean-to, a favorite of Orra's.   *1959 photo*

Marcy, was wrapped in dense clouds. No breathtaking views of the High Peaks of Essex would reward their efforts this time. They laughed when they recalled Lawrence's story of his scouts spitting across Lake Tear's outlet so that when they returned to Brooklyn they could say they had spit across the Hudson River.

They saw that the Roosevelt lean-to flew a white banner, indicating it was occupied. The public lean-to was so named because Vice President Theodore Roosevelt, an ardent Adirondack hiker and birder, received word while there on September 13, 1901, that President McKinley, who had been shot on September 6, was near death. Roosevelt and his party dashed back down the mountain and took a treacherous forty-mile ride in the dark to North Creek station where, at 4:39 a.m., he was informed that he was the new president of the United States.[3]

Orra found that the lean-to's occupants knew Lawrence. After sharing hot lemon tea, chocolate peanuts, and crackers, the Phelpses pressed on, eager to again see the rare arctic-alpine plants. Their eyes feasted on cushions of *diapensia*, the Lapland rose bay, blueberry bushes, mountain cinquefoil, dainty mountain sandwort, and a two-inch-high goldenrod. Busy exploring the alpine flora and tucking specimens into her botany can, Mrs. Phelps asked Orra, "Are we on top yet?" With heavy fog shrouding nearby rocks, Mrs. Phelps did not realize they had climbed the peak-like cobble on Marcy's flank, not the summit itself.

Orra's fear of losing sight of the rock cairns that marked the trail in the thick mist, the danger of hypothermia, and Mamma's limitations caused her to stretch the truth and tell her mother they were on top and should head back. Orra recalled years later, when she confessed her fib to her mother and her amazement that Mamma agreed to turn back, that being near the top of Marcy, swirled by wind and clouds, was a scary, never-to-be-forgotten experience.

Their return hike was a series of slips and slides, in drizzling rain. Other hikers asked their luck in seeing the view and consoled them with, "Better luck next time."

Back at the lean-to where they left their duffel, the fire cooked their evening meal as well as heated small stones, which they popped into their shoes to speed overnight drying. They slept that night on a balsam bed, floating on its cushion of springy balsam tips smelling like Christmas.

In the morning's early light, a voice said, "Did you hear the mouse on the roof?" "Did I?" echoed Orra. "It ran over my face."

They donned dry socks and semi-dry shoes, breakfasted, then used the camp's rusty pitcher to douse the fire, as Mrs. Phelps put it, "offering a libation to the gods of the mountains" before heading home.

Orra returned to Johns Hopkins, not free for further mountain climbing until August 1926, after she worked at Saratoga Springs Hospital. Lawrence advised her to buy or make a featherweight tent, so she and her mother "could be independent of the lean-tos and hike as far as their strength permitted each day."[4]

On Tuesday, August 24, 1926, Mrs. Phelps, Lawrence, and Orra took trolleys and the train from Wilton to Westport, New York, where they stayed overnight.

After a bus ride to Keene and a five-mile lift northwest along the highway, they started to hike west, searching for the trailhead of the South Meadows Trail. They bushwhacked in that general direction and finally found South Meadow Brook and a bit of trail. Mrs. Phelps recorded in her diary:

> We came out in sedgy meadow, wet underfoot when it began to rain. Beavers had dammed the stream and flooded the meadow so there was no hope of following the trail. I began to panic. "Are we lost?" I asked.
>
> Orra calmly replied, "Don't worry, we're heading in the right direction and we'll be on the trail in no time."
>
> We left the meadow for high ground to the left [south]. L. cut poles and pitched a lean-to using his floor cloth and Orra's new pup tent for sides. He made a roaring fire to dry everything. Orra and I cut balsam and dried it for beds. I gave my little right finger a most bloody gash which made me feel a bit faint. After a hot supper we dried out as much as possible and then crawled in. Rain stopped about five but Lawrence cut more dead trees to keep the fire all night and did a bit of scouting for the trail, to no avail.
>
> After breakfast Lawrence again went scouting. We waited hoping he wasn't lost and separated from us. An hour went by. Finally he came back and led us across an open field . . . to a grand wood road. Two miles of this and we came to our destination, Adirondak Loj, where Lawrence

The two-stall lean-to at Heart Lake where Orra and Mrs. Phelps camped in 1926 when they visited the lake for the first time.

introduced us to Jed Rossman,[5] the beloved Adirondak Loj caretaker, and engaged a shelter. Then we ate a bite of supper and Lawrence left to get back to NYC. Later Mr. Rossman transferred us to a smaller two-roomed shelter, a bit more secluded, where we set up housekeeping. We spent the early evening locating trails and getting a supply of berries.

So it was that Orra Phelps first came to Heart Lake on Thursday, August 26, 1926. She would come to know this tract intimately over the next half century. Jed Rossman and the succession of caretakers of the Loj became her friends, each learning from the other.

Jed Rossman, caretaker at Adirondack Loj. *1931 photo*

The next morning they left at seven for the top of MacIntyre. The summit was wrapped in clouds, with a cold wind whirling the season's early snowflakes. They stayed only long enough to glimpse some of the alpine plants, then returned to the safety of camp.

On Saturday, they hiked a short way into Indian Pass, but were disappointed with the section they had seen. It wasn't until a year later that Orra and her mother would see the rugged, breathtaking middle part of Indian Pass. The following day they hiked for the first time through Avalanche Pass to Avalanche Lake.

Mamma wrote, "Most wonderful," and in

Mr. and Mrs. Phelps with Orra at Heart Lake Trading Post in the early thirties.

Andy Rossman's words, "It's heavenly!" On their return to camp, Jed made them laugh with his homespun yarn:

> Seems a city feller arrived at the Loj with a companion after dark for his first sleep in an open shelter. He came to Jed's shack to ask if there were wild animals about at night. On being told that once Jed went out early in the morning and found two bears in a trap and eight patiently waiting to get into the trap, the novice went to his shelter for a sleepless night, only to recount his experience in the morning with gratitude to a kindly Providence who had guarded him through what seemed endless hours of darkness.[6]

Soon after Orra graduated from Johns Hopkins, she returned to the Adirondacks to take their long-anticipated hike through Indian Pass from the southern end. On July 20, 1927, Orra hiked with Leon and Mrs. Phelps from the end of the road to the Henderson lean-to. Leon stayed overnight, enjoying their beefsteak supper and balsam bed, but left the next day.

Mrs. Phelps recorded in her diary that she and Orra hiked alone to Preston and Hunter Ponds, where they found holly fern and *Habenaria dilatata*, the white bog orchids. Mrs. Phelps wrote:

> The view of Indian Pass from Lake Henderson was exquisite. At Summit Rock, which isn't a summit at all, we rested. There is the most awe-inspiring landscape one can imagine . . . the towering cliffs, sheer as a wall on Wallface Mountain, the great gulch filled with huge rock fragments and a feeling of immensity. In the afternoon we carried part of our duffel to the foot of the climb at Indian Pass. The next morning was pleasant but the punky flies, or biting midgies as some call them, were so fearful that we fled from our camp in great haste. Orra fished along Indian Pass Brook landing four nice trout. The climb was frightful. Orra went over it three times as I couldn't carry a very heavy pack. We didn't stop for a noon meal but ate raisins, an orange, and bar of chocolate. We arrived at Scott's Clearing on the northern end of the pass in time to cook our trout before the rain began.

Both women found great satisfaction in sharing their finds with the state botanists, a contribution to science that Orra would continue for more than fifty years. On this particular Saturday, August 23, 1927, Orra and Mrs. Phelps were searching for arnica, which Dr. Homer D. House, the New York State Botanist, had said they might find in that area. They thought they

Mr. and Mrs. Phelps start out from the Avalanche Lake lean-to with camping gear during a trip they made in the early thirties.

found some, though not in bloom, together with mountain sandwort growing in the brook bed. They saved specimens, then hiked in the rain to Heart Lake.[7]

Leon and Mr. Phelps joined them, bringing mail, and shared lunch before Leon returned home. While Mr. Phelps was healthy for a man of sixty-five and enjoyed country living, it was Mrs. Phelps who craved being in the mountains. During the next three days, Orra and her parents hiked to the Avalanche shelter, through Avalanche Pass to Lake Colden, on to the Flowed Lands shelter, across the new bridge over the Opalescent, and finally out to Lake Sanford, where Leon met them with his car.

In September, near her thirty-second birthday, Orra began her internship at Albany City Hospital, where she was one of only three women on the staff. Her September 14, 1927 letter described some of her work and showed her realistic acceptance of death.

> We had a death on the ward, a patient known to have tuberculosis and a bad heart. The end was very sudden and quiet. He could never have been better, so it was just as well for everybody. It seems that we have to be registered in City Hall before we can sign death certificates and we get $.25 apiece for all we sign! In order to

Interns at Albany Hospital in 1927. Orra Phelps is in the front row, third from the right.

claim our quarters, Dr. Knott and I went down to register.

The patients on the Contagious Ward are changing. Three of the infantile paralysis cases have been moved to the Children's Hospital and we have a new scarlet fever and a new diphtheria case. We are keeping the two diphtheria carriers 'till they have their tonsils out and get well.

Orra was only thirty-five miles away in Albany and frequently went home, but Mamma's letters kept her in almost daily touch with her family. The heartache of his mother's tragic suicide revisited Papa again when his brother, Ed Phelps, killed himself. On October 2, 1927, Mrs. Phelps wrote:

Dad went to Ed Phelps's funeral . . . Ed finally succeeded in making away with himself in spite of the fact that he was in an asylum where such things are guarded against. Dad was pretty well used up . . . and hasn't wholly gotten over the effects yet. Last week was very trying for him . . . what with the primary contest and the funeral. Moreover, he starts jury duty tomorrow and because he was away couldn't make collections for things sold, hence he could not meet very important bills. I do hope he settles down for with both Francis and Dad on edge I get tired out. Have felt very tired all week.

The best news of the week is that the farm loan has been granted. We've got to raise a lot of extra cash to meet all their requirements but I guess that will come somehow.

Was Capt'n's letter worth waiting for? Dad delayed sending it because he misread the address and thought it was for me.

With both compassion and realism, Orra responded to her mother's distressed wail:

I'm sorry you are feeling so weary—but you have enough to account for it all. If only the housework didn't weigh you down, and if Papa's behavior were perfect, and if Francis were on his best behavior and if there were no extras — social or financial . . . you might not be so tired when you get through a week of school. Teaching is your job, let everything else slide.[8]

During her term in Albany, Orra's interests were consistently twofold: first, her growing medical experience and, a close second, her love of the outdoors, especially the Adirondacks. In 1927, she proposed to her mother that they earn some money by publishing a folio of Adirondack flowers and scenes:

I had another inspiration about you and your summer vacation, to write a book on Adirondack Flora — not technical, but intimate, a sketchy thing, perhaps almost in the shape of notes interesting in detail, pleasing in style and I think the Adirondack Mountain Club would welcome it! My supervising physician really gave me this idea when he said he was so interested in those mountain top plants, that he didn't know what they were and didn't know anyone that did.[9]

Although the book on alpine plants was something Mrs. Phelps and Orra could have produced, money and focus were lacking. It would be more than forty years before Orra would author a chapter on alpine/arctic plants.[10]

Gardiner Littell, Orra's friend from her Silver Bay and Baltimore days, now lived only thirty miles away in Hoosick Falls, where he taught history at a private school. He often took Orra on rides in the country, out to dinner, shows, and even to Williams College for a football game. She once wrote home of their being at an overlook in the Helderbergs, enjoying a view of Albany's city lights, a romantic setting. There is no record of whether she and Gardiner were anything more than friends, but they did see each other frequently. That fall, he came to visit the Phelpses and may have proposed marriage.[11]

The Phelps home in WIlton, N.Y. for more than fifty years, from March 1918 to June 1968. (Porch now removed)

In Albany, Orra met many people who would become lifelong friends, both in her medical profession and in her Adirondack activities. During her internship, in December 1927, Orra wrote Mamma:

> I told you I had a patient who works in the Conservation Commission office. When I went to see him Sunday he introduced me to his visitor, Mr. William G. Howard, the Superintendent of State Forests — see his name on Conservation pamphlets. Mr. Howard superintends the state nursery, the repair of trails, and the opening of new trails including the Northville-Placid Trail, described in his Adirondack Mountain Club publication.[12]

Charles L. Haas and Sylvia Bessie (Phelps) Haas, the author's parents, married at the Phelps home in Wilton, N.Y. in 1928. (left to right) Kay Phelps, Harmon Servis, Charles and Bessie Haas, Orra Phelps, and Phoebe Phelps.

> We talked trails. He was interested that Lawrence
> and his scouts had climbed Santanoni from Cold River.
> Says that is one of the next trails they want to open up.[13]

Through this chance meeting and subsequent conversations, Mr. Howard and Orra became good friends. In February 1928, he sent her an autographed copy of the New York Conservation Commission's Annual Report. It was he who proposed Orra for membership in the Adirondack Mountain Club, which had been formed in 1922. On April 4, 1928, she began her more than fifty-five-year membership in the organization, fulfilling her need for hiking companions and participation in an organization devoted to preservation of the wilderness.

That spring, Orra applied for a position in public health in Saranac Lake, New York, hoping to live and work in the heart of the Adirondacks. If she lived there she could climb mountains and hunt for special plants every weekend without driving three hours each way. She went there by train to interview, but a man was hired. She also applied for the position of Medical Director of Montgomery County Schools, based in Fort Plain, New York, but had heard nothing definite.

As she had enjoyed the arts and cultural events in Baltimore, Orra also did in Albany. She was invited to join the prestigious Yaddo, a cultural center for artists and writers,[14] in Saratoga Springs and later lunched with a descendant of James Fenimore Cooper near Albany.[15]

Captain Coulter and Orra continued their friendship, and in June, Orra wrote:

> The Captain writes that he will come to West Point Friday and I would like to have him drive up to the farm on Saturday, but my coverage will be away, so I doubt if we can. Could you and Leon come down and we'd all picnic in the Helderbergs.[16]

Two weeks later Carleton came to visit again, and Orra wrote, "The Captain came Saturday at six and left for Boston at nine a.m., but I took some time off and went to Pittsfield with him and came back by bus."

On June 9, 1928, at the end of Orra's internship, she was the maid of honor at Bessie's wedding to Charles Louis Haas at the family's Lea O' Mountain Farm in Wilton. Despite the close relationship these two sisters had, their lives diverged. Bessie proceeded to life on the Haas farm in Victory Mills, New York and to raising four daughters. Orra, on the other hand, continued her medical career and her involvement with the Adirondack Mountain Club as an active club member, frequent hiker, and naturalist.

Orra may have been saddened by her inability to find a man whom she loved and whom her parents would accept as her husband. As she had written earlier, she had no say in that matter, but did in her chosen career and interests.

Orra's second sister, Kay, educated at Mount Holyoke and Smith, lived near New York City most of her life and practiced psychiatric social work. She, too, lived a rather spartan life, did not marry, and hiked and socialized with the Appalachian Mountain Club. Kay broke with her mother over dating a man whom Mamma did not like. She also felt she never had her mother's approval as Orra did. On May 31, 1928, twenty-five-year-old Kay wrote to Orra concerning her feelings about their family.

> I was glad to get your letter and hear your views on the subject of the family, etc. I don't think you got some of my points, but that was probably my fault. What I meant about adjusting to my atmosphere was not the family should when I was in theirs, but that nobody even saw me in mine, where I'm adjusted and am in a degree successful in the eyes of my group. When I go home, I feel out of my element — yes, inferior — because all of you talk about and do things you are interested in and can do well — that I can't. I don't want to participate in the things you do, except camping, but I do feel insignificant. I'm sorry I've given the impression of feeling superior — I certainly do not.
>
> For all these reasons and others I don't think I want to get a job at home and live at home. You've asserted yourself as an adult, as an independent person in the family's eyes, particularly Mamma's and you are accepted as such. More credit to you . . . . I feel all the while I'm with Mamma that she's trying to put me back in the cradle — not consciously of course . . . . My experience has been that the Phelpses love to feel that they're helping form somebody.

All spring, Orra had been making plans for another mountain trip, gathering hiking gear and provisions for a hundred-mile trek with her mother through the heart of the Adirondack wilderness. Late in June 1928, she went to New York City to get last-minute advice from Lawrence, who had hiked in that region with his scouts, as well as get some desiccated vegetables for the trip and material to make a tent according to her brother's specifications. Lawrence wrote to Orra on May 27, 1928 with his travel recommendations:

> Dear Orra,
> Your enthusiastic letter of camping plans deserved an answer before. It sounds good to me . . . On the tent I agree that the space at the very back of the usual lean-to

type is wasted. Moreover I like a tent that can be carried flat. Enclosed is a plan for a 6'x7' trapezoidal shaped tent to be made of 9½ yds of 36" stuff or 7 yds of 54" stuff. This includes flaps... Ground cloth = 4¾ yds of 36".

Tent to have a front that will close, inside mosquito curtain, standing height at front — 5', pole or rope over limb at front, two side guy ropes to form wall at front, stakes at back corners and middle ... ought to give you room to sit up in front.

Orra's brother, Lawrence Phelps, at Heart Lake lean-to.   *1930 photo*

Orra had also purchased a complete set of topographical maps of the Adirondacks from Schroon Lake to Elizabethtown on the east and from Saranac Lake to North Creek on the west and everything in between. Wherever they might hike she was as prepared as possible.

Undaunted by the warnings from the sporting goods salesmen about tent-eating porcupines, uncrossable streams, and blood-thirsty punky flies, Orra was never able to get enough of the beauty and majesty of the mountains. Fortunately for the author and readers, Mrs. Phelps recorded their remarkable 1928 study of the mountain flora and fauna and Adirondack people and places seen during their five weeks hiking in the big woods.

— 11 —

The 100-Mile Adirondack Botanical Hike
1928

Author's note: *Much of this chapter is taken from Mrs. Phelps's diary and log of their trip; the rest has been fleshed out in a manner consistent with earlier records.*

Few women braved the Adirondacks in 1928, and almost none went without a male guide; but Orra, Mrs. Phelps, and Dorothy Caldwell, a family friend and fellow Adirondack Mountain Club member, embarked on a five week botanizing trip from the small lumber town of North River, New York, headed for Heart Lake. Relaxing in camp clothes and being free from schedules, society, and housework were part of the joy of their trek. The women planned this trip as a vacation, as a tonic to quench their thirst for the outdoors as well as a chance to see how many unusual plants they could find.

The three botanists were motivated by similar desires, plus they felt pleased with themselves for being among the first women to hike a good part of the newly-cut Northville-Placid Trail.

They began their plant list as soon as they arrived along the Hudson River, spotting bluebells and butterfly weed plus three ferns: the oak, narrow-leafed spleenwort, and the narrow beech.[1] The local driver who knew the road to Thirteenth Lake could not be found, so the three women began hiking in the afternoon heat with Orra and Dorothy toting heavy duffel rolls.

Near a thirst-quenching spring at an old homestead, they noted *Penstemon digitalis*, the white foxglove beard-tongue.[2] That night they chose a camping spot by a waterfall, where Mrs. Phelps wrote in her diary on July 5, 1928:

106

Orra relaxes along the trail during a long hike in a photo dated August 1, 1928.

While Dorothy and I gathered balsam for our bed, Orra pitched the tent and then fished with no luck, so supper was brown rice fried in bacon crumbs, then cooked in water, tomato soup, bread, tea, and wild strawberries. Just as the sportsmen warned, the punky flies were fierce and, even though we tried two kinds of fly dope, neither worked.

At bedtime the heat was still unbearable, so they lifted the edges of the tent, unfortunately letting in punky flies which bit so fiercely that Orra made a smudge fire at 2:30 a.m. In the flickering shadows the three women flapped towels, directing the smoke toward the tent, then rubbed soot on the inside of the tent to discourage the tiny, tenacious critters.

The next day along Thirteenth Lake, they noticed where porcupines had ripped the tree bark to eat the cambium layer, part of their ten-pound daily diet. As long as the porkies did not gnaw their tent, man and beast would peacefully coexist. More botanical finds included *Pyrola secunda*, the dainty one-sided *Pyrola* and *Cypripedium acaule*, the moccasin-flowered orchid with its deep pink, heavily veined pouch.[3] Back at the tent, Orra built another smudge fire, then patted wet baking soda on their punky-bite welts while Dorothy checked the fly honeysuckle in Gray's *Manual of Botany*.[4]

Mrs. Phelps continued in her diary:

> As we were packing to leave, a man dressed in white shoes,
> light trousers, and a silk shirt came along the trail and
> smiled a superior smile at us in our camp clothes . . .
> Now the hotel boarders will have something to talk about!

When they climbed the steep Puffer Pond trail, they came to a
particularly turbulent stream, churning down a wide sluiceway. After
deliberating the safest way to cross, Orra chopped down a young tree,
skinned off its branches, and slid it across the brook. She then scrambled
across huge boulders above the rushing water. The others slid the baggage across the pole to Orra and crossed from boulder to boulder without packs.

Their keen eyes spotted more plants; some in huge patches such
as *Mitchella repens*, partridge-berry, and some in smaller clumps such
as the *Goodyera*, rattlesnake plantain, with whitish veins crisscrossing
the darker green leaf. As they approached the Puffer Pond shelter,
Orra whispered, "Sh-h, there's a baby woodchuck." An eight-inch ball
of brown fur sat quite tamely in the root of a large yellow birch, but
scuttled away with their arrival.

The shelter was equipped with cooking tools, three mattresses,
and a boat. Later, when only their oars broke the stillness of dusk,
they caught sight of two deer feeding. By bedtime, Orra had invented
a way to outwit the punky flies; she weighted bug screens made of
netting with pebbles and strung them over a pole just above their
heads. To keep their feet covered, she anchored their blankets with
stocking knots. Ax and bowie knife within reach, they were prepared
against intruders, large and small. Mamma wrote:

> Praises be we were soon comfortable!
> We were roused at daybreak by the wood thrush, robin,
> and winter wren to a glorious pink sky. By 4:30 a.m. we
> were out on the mist-shrouded pond and at the edge could
> faintly make out a lovely deer as well as another porky.

For the first time on the trip, Orra baked hot biscuits in her reflector
oven to add to bacon, coffee, Klim (tinned milk), and Ralston with raisins.

Later, as they hiked along the pond, the women came to a mushy place filled with dead frogs — minus their hind legs. Some unknown party had dined on frogs' legs; Orra and Dorothy buried the remains. The group passed a soggy log where insects fed on fungi and a fat toad snapped his bug lunch; a food chain in action. In another wetland, they found two bladderworts, wild calla, and mad-dog skullcap.[5]

Orra heard cowbells as they neared Carroll Brook, settled by the Carroll family in 1849. From Mr. Carroll, Orra and Dorothy learned the whereabouts of the trailhead for Chimney Mountain where Orra, the geologist, was intrigued by caves and the sixty-foot-tall chimney-like formation. In that area they found purple clematis and both the fine and bush yellow honeysuckle. Once down, they chatted with Mr. Carroll, who philosophized (and swore under his breath) as he tinkered with his car, "These are the things that keep you from heaven, also the cursed punkies."

From the conversation, Orra realized she knew Mr. Carroll's brother, a physician, whose patients Orra had seen at Albany Hospital. She was beginning to be known by Adirondack folks as the doctor who liked to hike. Finally, the curious woodsman asked, "Do you know where you are headed for?" He just shook his head when Orra calmly answered, "Yes, Indian Lake, and then a month more hiking on our way to Heart Lake."

The next morning Orra used earthworms dug the night before to catch four bullheads. Mamma wrote:

> So we had fish, pancakes, and strawberries, oatmeal, and coffee. From the boat we saw water lobelia, spatterdock, and freshwater sponges as well as two red efts.[6] A friendly white-throated sparrow and a chipmunk ate chunks of hominy Orra put out, then a pair of large dark gray mice with short tails came and finished the tidbits.

They observed three kinds of butterflies sipping nectar: a yellow one, the Adirondack white bar, and the silver wing.[7] And their bird list grew with redstart, nuthatch, rusty blackbird, gulls, and robins tending a nearby nest. Mamma wrote:

> Just before retiring Orra called us to see a saw-whet owl,
> which flew toward us and lit in a yellow birch. Then
> another came closer and a third lingered near the tree
> where we'd seen the first. All the while they kept up a
> peculiar rasping noise, like a file raking across a saw
> blade.[8]

They awoke to rain. Orra heard the brook rushing wildly and
knew it had risen overnight. She found that their butter tin, which
hung in the cold water, was safe. As they hiked out to Carroll's Inn
they spotted Deptford pinks and *Habenaria fimbriata*, the large
purple-fringed orchids along the trail. This lovely many-flowered
orchid grew in two-foot spikes; its flower clusters more than two
inches across. The lip of each one-inch flower seemed like a tiny
ballerina's tutu, fringed and flaring, with dewdrops hanging like
glass beads.[9]

Dorothy then treated them to a five-dollar taxi ride through the
rain to Indian Lake, their next destination. There, by previous arrangement, they received mail, sent out cards, and bought extra food. Heading for Snowy Mountain, they tramped along the west shore of Indian
Lake until they found a tent site. An old hand at planning and logis-
tics, Orra repacked what they needed for the next day's hike into one
knapsack and cached the rest behind a big sugar maple.

Mrs. Phelps described the summit view:

> From the fire station we gazed south, across lakes and
> mountains. The western view was most wonderful . . .
> over a steep cliff, dropping to a deep dark basin hundreds
> of feet below and across the endless expanse. On the
> mountain top were two cabins. The newer one, built by
> Mr. Fish, the fire warden, was very neat, with many
> shelves, homemade table, and chairs, where we rested
> and chatted.

Orra and Dorothy descended early so Dorothy could start home
after having been with them for their first week and a half in the
woods. With prior permission, mother and daughter tented in a cow
pasture carved by pioneer settlers from the spruce and hardwood for-

est. They flopped, exhausted, only to be awakened by a leak in the tent. Orra fixed that and they tried to sleep again, but heard cowbells clanging closer and closer. Several attempts to chase the curious cows and horses away failed. Mrs. Phelps later wrote:

> We struck the tent by the light of a birch-bark flare, saved for our breakfast fire. Piling our things onto the ground cloth, we stumbled forward, Orra carrying two corners and the flashlight and I behind, ax in hand, gripping the other corners. Fireflies attending our way, we dragged the whole thing under the fence and set up camp in the corner of a hayfield, out of reach of the herd. Gradually the thud of hooves and clanging of cowbells melted away.
>
> The next morning when we retrieved the rest of our things, we found the cows had stepped on Orra's stove, overturned our waterpail, and drained the prunes.

The two women quickly recovered and hiked out to the road. They were grateful for a twenty-five-cent bus ride from Sabael to Indian Lake, where they began walking toward Blue Mountain Lake (part of the original Northville-Placid Trail but later re-routed). When they stopped at a trout-breeding brook, Orra found a tiny flowered *Myosotis*, the sky-blue forget-me-not.[10]

Part way on their hike, a lurching bus gave them a lift to Blue Mountain Lake, where Orra's former patient, Mrs. Potter, awaited them. Word had reached her that Dr. Orra and her mother were hiking her way, so Mrs. Potter invited them to stay overnight in her simple schoolhouse home. They shared a tasty meal and all helped with the dishes, sharing their adventures as they worked. Although their bedroom was tiny, they slept soundly in sheets scented by the mountain air.

Orra repacked their knapsacks and sent the heavier things ahead by stagecoach. When the driver hefted Orra's "lighter" pack he said, "I wouldn't want to carry this far. It's heavier than any guide would tote." They still had three more weeks of hiking ahead! He did not know of Orra's perseverance nor that she had the energy, strength, and endurance of an athlete.

Mother and daughter hiked around Rock and Cascade Lakes, botanizing again. Mrs. Phelps continued to share with Orra her

Mrs. Phelps at Stephens Pond lean-to on July 18, 1928.

vast store of knowledge. They found new varieties of blackberries, two sundews, water shield, and arbutus. Mrs. Phelps's account continued:

> We crossed the lake on a beaver dam and finally reached Stephens Pond and an AMC shelter.[11] Our bed was built up from the ground on two lengthwise logs with small poles strung across, then balsam and our ground cloth, not very comfortable looking, but I rested while Orra built a fire and cooked spaghetti.
>
> We had been in the woods for two weeks and on July 18th at Stephens Pond, we counted eighteen different kinds of ferns,[12] and saw a log bedecked with a pretty sundew colony. There were deer at the water's edge and a fox running along a log, a "Peabody" bird and a wood thrush. While serenaded by bullfrogs, Orra caught sunfish for lunch.
>
> In the afternoon we hiked to a marsh where beavers must have raised the water level, for the loosestrife (not in bloom) was half way under water. A great blue heron flew low over the wilderness scene.[13] While we rested, Orra sketched some of the plants. As we were returning

to Potters for another overnight, we found two more orchids, the greenish-white, round-leafed orchis and coral
root.[14]

Like pioneers, the Phelpses rode in a high farm wagon to the foot
of the Blue Mountain Trail. The hike up was steep going but views
from the 3,759-foot top rewarded them, looking out over Blue Mountain Lake and the narrows, Raquette Lake, Long Lake, Tirrell Pond,
and the distant mountains. Orra climbed the fire tower, adding to the
growing list of Adirondack fire towers she had climbed.

The Guide to Adirondack Trails: Northville-Placid Trail[15] notes
how Blue Mountain was instrumental to Verplanck Colvin's
Adirondack high peak survey. Dynamite was exploded on the
peak each night at nine o'clock, with the resulting flash serving as
a sighting location for the crews on other peaks.

That evening, Orra and her mother were joined by Beth Hyde,
the daughter of Mrs. Phelps's Mount Holyoke College friend, Mary
Hyde. The next day Mamma found a clump of exquisite pale pink
twin flower, *Linnaea borealis,* as they reclimbed Blue Mountain with
Beth. The *Linnaea's* tiny fragrant twin bells became one of Orra's
favorite flowers.

On Sunday, the women chuckled when the Potters's housekeeper
told of "a local knicker-hating rector, who admonished women for wearing knickers and insisted that they swim after dark so as not to be seen
attired in bathing suits." The rector's wife offered home remedies to their
parishioners: the oil of angleworms for removal of scars, daisy tea for
babies who had difficulty urinating, and chewed raspberry leaves to relieve bee stings — recipes handed down by her herb-doctor grandmother.

Mrs. Phelps wrote:

> We finally tented beside the Raquette River,
> cooked dinner, fixed our punky screens, and flopped.
> Before we knew it, a winter wren sang our breakfast
> call. That day we planned to hike three miles to Long
> Lake for the $1.50 steamer ride around the lake as
> Beth's guests. Along the way we saw *Polygala* and
> floating-heart, its small white flowers resting on
> water-lily-like leaves.[16]

The boat ride was charming, our small steamer darting from one side of the lake to the other, delivering gro-
ceries and mail. At Plumley's fishing camp a man proudly
displayed his freshly-caught, seven-pound pike.

According to the Northville-Placid Trail guidebook, the original
Plumley's was at the southern end of Long Lake, settled in 1830 by
Joel Plumley. His son, "Honest John" Plumley, gained fame as an early
guide for "Adirondack Murray," the first to extol the Adirondacks as a
vacation area.

The next day, Wednesday, July 25, the Phelpses hiked one and
one-half miles south along the Raquette River to Buttermilk Falls.
Later, Mrs. Phelps stopped at a farm for fresh eggs. The farmer's wife
asked, "An did yer be after waitin' for the hen herself to lay it?"

Mrs. Phelps wrote, "I slipped my hand under and got a warm one,
then soberly bought fifteen potatoes for twenty-five cents." As she returned to their tentsite, she passed several canoeists either fishing on the
lake or making carries around the rocky sections. It made her think of
George Washington Sears, pen-named Nessmuk, and his diminutive
ten-and-a-half-pound canoe, the *Sairy Gamp*, light enough for this one
hundred-and-five-pound man to portage in the Adirondack woods.

Made in 1883 by the master boat builder, J. Henry Rushton of
Canton, New York, it was one of five canoes made specifically for
Nessmuk. The *Sairy Gamp*, now at the Adirondack Museum, on permanent loan from the Smithsonian Institution, was named after a
character in Dickens's Martin Chuzzlewit, "a tippling nurse who never
took water."[17]

They lingered along the Raquette for two days, enjoying the raspberries, resting, and scoring cribbage games on a wooden box Orra
had marked. Mamma squeezed into Orra's bathing suit and, much to
Orra's amusement, laid newspaper across the muddy shore to get in
and out of the water without squishing mud between her toes. Then
Orra took her turn in the refreshingly cold water.

On Friday, they hiked to Deerland and took the bus to Long
Lake, where they received word that Leon would be married to
Gusta Will on Monday. For months, Leon had been courting Gusta,
whom Mrs. Phelps did not approve of because she was not

well-educated. Prior to leaving on their trip, Mrs. Phelps had no word of Leon's impending marriage and, had she known, might have tried to discourage Leon. Mrs. Phelps's possessiveness of her adult children was well known. So, with Mamma away and out of reach, the lovers arranged a quick marriage. Orra and Mrs. Phelps had been in the woods for three weeks and could only telegram congratulations.

Learning that Leon, one of her two favorite brothers, was to be married, Orra trusted that he was happy with Gusta despite Mamma's concerns. It was sad for Orra and her siblings that their mother could not always accept her adult children's choices.[18] Orra's own friendship with Captain Coulter had also been clouded by Mrs. Phelps's prejudice. Because Orra wanted to nurture her mother's mental and physical health during their five-week vacation, probably little was said of their differing views. Orra's faith allowed her to pray for her brother's or her own happiness, then leave it in God's hands. Her mother did not have that sort of religious faith.

They bought more supplies in Long Lake and Orra repacked their duffel, sending things they did not need ahead to Heart Lake. They rode the steamer north amid freight for various camps, arriving at Plumley's Camp in a torrent of rain. Frank and Annie Plumley, descendants of the original Plumleys, provided room and meals and cooked the catch of the day, most often, huge pike or bass.

Mrs. Phelps jotted in her diary:

> Mrs. P. runs the camp. She advertises in Field and Stream. Very friendly person. Doesn't see a petticoat save her own from Christmas to Spring... After Orra hunted in vain for the trail and returned soaking wet, Mrs. Plumbley remembered an open shelter on the next point and sent a man to show us where. Orra contrived a hood for the fire, cooking a gorgeous supper over a sheet of metal. Orra wrote Captain Coulter and later we enjoyed camp talk. Only mice nibbling on our bananas marred our sleep.

They now began the last but potentially most difficult part of their journey, leaving Long Lake for the primitive Cold River country, and heading for Heart Lake along another part of the Northville-Placid Trail. They would be hiking more than twenty miles without a store or house in sight. In 1928, the trail was broad and open, with few mucky places up to the Big Horn cabin where the ranger lived. Mrs. Phelps wrote:

> As we passed through Shattuck Clearing we found turtlehead and three more orchids: adder's mouth, quite a few stout *Spiranthes*, and one slender *Spiranthes*.
>
> After we crossed Pine Creek on a log, we came to the ranger's cabin. Orra heated soup and we ate our sandwiches on the roofless back porch. Warden Cole took quite a friendly interest in Orra and gave her some worms and a sinker. He said he'd come up about six with a rod to show HER how to fish. Shortly after four we forded Cold River, near the junction of Moose Creek, using poles for balance. Its frigid water sluiced between slimy rocks challenging our crossing.
>
> At the first shelter we found slender fragrant goldenrod with its flat top, another very downy goldenrod growing on the ledges, double bunchberry and *Houstonias*. The ranger came at six as promised, but told Orra the fish wouldn't bite because the water had risen six inches. With so few people hiking through, the ranger seemed lonely and chatted more about the trails and sights ahead.
>
> We awoke early, packed, and Orra took a photo up the river. The view up the river is lovely but this AMC camp lacks good water, latrine facilities, and nails for hanging gear. The trail followed the river, broad and open through white cedar, balsam, and spruce woods, edged by acres of arbutus and twin flower. Just beyond our campsite we found a nine-pole teepee frame with a stone fireplace in the center, a balsam bed for one and a cache of food nearby."

It may have occurred to the women that a hermit could have a private estate here, with Santanoni and the Cold River for contemplation.

Big Eddy, a large pool with an interesting waterfall two miles farther northeast on the Cold River, was their next destination. Water swirled down between huge boulders, eddied around, then rushed on. Nearby they found a peculiar low shadbush, with a long leaf and long fruit. In a wetland that lured them a bit off the trail, they got what seemed to be the yellow-flowered honeysuckle and the narrow-leaf gentian with its rounded sky-blue flower lobes.

Where the view opened along the river, Mamma sat and rested and wrote notes of the trip while Orra read. Here in the heart of the wilderness, both Orra and her mother were content. These two naturalists were having the time of their lives, exploring the new trail and all the fascinating plants, birds, and reptiles while soaking in the fresh mountain air and sunshine.[19]

They passed a newly built lean-to whose logs had not yet been chinked, then pressed on to the Big Dam at the now abandoned logging center, where in times past logs piled up until spring floods floated them down river. First they decided to camp just below a big bank, to get the best mountain view, but saw two snakes lazing there. So they pitched Orra's tent by the brook. After dinner, Orra read from St. Matthew, then teased their minds with word puzzles.

Views of the Milky Way and Cygnus above promised a cloud-less night, but before they slept, it rained. The next morning, while getting stones for the fireplace, Orra found two more snakes, so Mamma said the joke was on her. Mamma's account continued:

> At each turn of the trail we never knew what to expect. We heard the black-throated blue warbler singing, "I am so lazy," and shortly after Orra found a small meteorite, heavy and pitted. Once we thought we'd lost the trail, but Orra went ahead a quarter mile until she found a marker. When we stopped to rest, Orra caught two nice trout. Even as the trail turned into a mud wallow, Orra had great fun placing rocks advantageously, which she then tried to walk across but sank to her boot tops. We then came to a trail junction and a shelter where someone's food was stashed. We settled in and ate our Johnny cake, trout, and pea soup. Just as I was washing the dishes, a dark hairy man appeared carrying a heavy pack. Evidently he expected to use the shelter.
>
> We didn't invite him to share the lean-to so he put up an odd looking tent about five to six rods away. When he started to get firewood, I went and offered the use of

the fireplace. He refused and built his fire right in the trail. I confess to being worried about him. While we played cribbage, he kept strolling up and down, a queer duck, bald with a narrow fringe of hair. He wore a low sleeveless jersey and, where his arms and neck were exposed, he was very hairy. He said he was carrying a thirty-pound pack containing food for three weeks, but expected to be two months on the trail. Speaking with a strong accent, he seemed unwilling to have a conversation. He had an unattractive face, rather retreating chin, and close shave except for a small mustache.

We hung our tent as a screen and went to bed early, but left an observation hole under the table so we could keep an eye on him. Orra hooted at my fears. My bed would have been softer had I gotten the balsam Orra suggested, but I feared going out in the dark. Mercifully there were no punkies so we slept without netting. Today, Monday July 30, 1928 was Leon's wedding day and I thought often of him.

Tuesday. The man didn't kill us. Once in the night I was roused by prolonged cat-like yowls and awakened Orra who said it was an owl. Must be a new kind. I slept extra well considering.

While we were deciding to get up, Orra suddenly saw the initials LHP, LL, JA, and JZ 1927 carved on the roof board by Lawrence and his three boy scouts last year.

Then a chipmunk came through a chink in the wall and, after three attempts, reached our provision shelf. Watching to see what he would do, I started to investigate, when whiz-bang, the tin of flour crashed off the shelf and a white cloud settled on the poncho I'd set out to dry.

Orra reclaimed most of it, making the best pancakes from wheat, graham, and corn meal flour. As we packed, a winter wren came and lit on the sheet iron stove not eighteen inches from me. Beautiful tiny creature, how can he hold so much pure music?

The trail was well cut and wide, with many nice views as well as tumble-down corduroy bridges. We quickly came to Duck Hole, where the signs read . . . "Bradley Pond, Lake Sanford. Had AMC marker and blue Conservation Commission marker. East sign bore red marker: Preston Pond, Indian Pass, Marcy (our intended route) and the West sign: a red marker and AMC marker: open camp 1¼ mile, Coreys, Tupper Lake." Duck Hole was a very lovely opening in the big woods, with a balsam bough lean-to reinforced by old cotton blankets. Although beaver work made it wet and many trees were down, there were plenty of good campsites. We were refreshed by the cool stream and occasional nibbles.

Preston Pond glistened dimly though the trees and *Cornus stolonifera*, the American dogwood, appeared along the trail. Passing more old buildings, we came to some posted property and Hunter Pond. After four weeks' hiking, we found the familiar Indian Pass trail and at last the Henderson lean-to.

The next day along the trail we enjoyed more *Habenaria* orchids and deep green holly fern, *Polystichum*, as well as a row of pure white Indian pipes standing as though in a pipe rack, then in contrast, the brilliant red cardinal flower. We had a hearty dinner of tongue, spaghetti, cake, and fruit, then played cribbage, winning one game each.

Mamma struggled uphill to Summit Rock, where hikers have a spectacular view of the 1,000-foot cliff known as Wallface. She later recorded:

We enjoyed the view even more than last summer. The magnitude of Indian Pass is overwhelming, its huge cliffs, gigantic boulders, sweeping view to the south. . . . The worst part was going down the northeast side. Orra took off the packs and we slipped and slid down, but no harm was done. We finally came out to Scott's Clearing and found the lean-to empty but dirty. Orra's two nice trout added to our supper of rice, hot biscuits, and apricot-raisin shortcake.

The mountain sandwort which was abundant in the gravel last year was all gone, but we found huge animal tracks. I worried about bears, but Orra calmed my fears, saying it was a large dog, chasing deer.

We packed candy and other nibbles in a small pail and expected to get raspberries for lunch. After crossing the Indian Pass Brook below the dam on a high corduroy bridge, the trail we followed was very obscure in places, so we broke branches as we went to mark it. We passed wonderful views of MacIntryre, then a more open

tote road and finally came to Scott Pond. Beavers had
worked there recently raising the water level so I thought
the *Spiraea* might be flooded.

We took a census of the flora there. The blue gentians
were magnificent. Orra counted forty-six flowering stalks
on one plant. Low *Hypericum* also abundant. We sat on a
well preserved dam, mesmerized by the rocky gorge below.
Orra took a photo. On our return Orra found a little marshy
place with hundreds of pitcher plants and much northern
bog growth. On up that trail I found what I suspect was an
unusual willow by a streamlet where we drank, but we found
no arnica. Orra hunted for a good place for a picture, finally
finding one by bending back a pin cherry.

Then she said, "Now we'll eat." I opened the pail
and alas — I'd picked up the wrong pail and had toted a
can of milk and a bit of bacon all the way up (not crackers and cheese, chocolates and lemon drops packed in
other can). Great joke! I remembered three lemon drops
wrapped in a bit of wax paper in my pocket and they
had to do until we got back to camp.

Immersed in nature for almost five weeks, Orra and Mrs. Phelps
had covered more than one hundred miles, with many side trips
and backtracks. Many of their plant finds were recorded as the most
northerly New York locations ever found for those species, according to Dr. Homer House. Years later, Orra would again hike along
the Northville-Placid Trail, exploring even more remote areas, such
as Oluska Pass, and bushwhacking up trailless peaks.

While the Phelpses were doing their final day's packing, two
young men approached on their way into Indian Pass. They asked,
"By any chance are you Mrs. Phelps and Dr. Orra? Jed Rossman is
looking for you." The Loj's caretaker had received a shipment of
mail and the items Orra had shipped ahead by stage from Blue
Mountain.

The women had returned from the wilderness to friends and to
another chapter in Orra's multifaceted life, her medical career. The
position in Saranac Lake had eluded her, but the one in Montgomery
County and Fort Plain, New York was open and school officials there
were waiting for her acceptance.

— 12 —

Medical Practice Begins
Montgomery County, New York
1928 to 1930

On September 4, 1928, Dr. Orra Phelps began her professional career as Medical Inspector of Schools of Montgomery County, New York. Orra soon became an integral part of her community, bonding with people of all ages. She threw her heart into her work as well as her play.

Because she needed her own car to serve the district's fifty-six far-flung schools, Orra bought a new Chevy and her roommate, Asta Olson, a young art teacher, taught her to drive.

Orra received her first driver's license on October 10, 1928 and by November was logging over two hundred miles a week, doing the rounds, often returning to help families with personal needs. Orra described their first landlady, Mrs. Getman, as:

> . . . a robust German widow, a Lutheran and a Republican, who owned a square red brick, flat-topped house in Nelliston, New York. Our rooms open into one another and Asta has to pass through mine to the living room, which doesn't sound very good but as we are expected to live in the whole house and just sleep in the bedrooms, it isn't so bad. Room and board, which seems good, are ten dollars a week.

This was the first of three places where Orra lived between 1928 and 1945 in Montgomery County in the Mohawk Valley.

On October 3, 1928, after only a month at Mrs. Getman's, Orra and Asta moved again to live with Rev. and Mrs. Kreuenza and their two children. The family must have been a better match, for a few days later thirty-three-year-old Orra wrote of taking the Kreuenza youngsters hiking.

Even as a young doctor, Orra related easily to people of diverse ages and backgrounds. When they found a sizable grape vine they all swung on it, oblivious to age and professional differences. In her words:

> We went cross lots for about two miles, then struck onto a wooded hill and then up and down we roved. We found a wonderful grape vine swing and each had a turn till our hands were tired from holding our own weight. We had a fire and hotdogs and bacon. Found hickory nuts, too poor for squirrels!

Orra took her New York Medical Boards in Albany in September 1928 and her license to practice medicine, number 23382, finally arrived on March 4, 1929. That is the day she said she was finally fit to practice in the state.

The travel that her school duties demanded went on despite wintry weather. On February 20, 1929, Orra wrote home:

> Dear Mamma,
> Monday and Tuesday I tested 480 pairs of ears and finished Fort Plain, now getting ready to do other towns, . . . We have had another all day snowstorm and snow is drifting, all this on top of roads already ridged with deep icy ruts and ridges. The driving isn't exactly dangerous, little danger of getting stuck but it's rough on the car and rough on the driver. I wish it would hurry up and thaw at least to clear the main highways. Below zero here this a.m., but it can't last much longer.

Orra enjoyed driving from school to school, in spite of some occasionally difficult weather, experiencing nature from her car. "My route took me into a wooded gully, beautiful with light snow." Farther along, she spotted many birds including horned larks, while chasing measles, whooping cough, mumps, chickenpox, and possible scarlet fever, meningitis or infantile paralysis cases.

Orra delighted in sharing her interest in natural history with her patients and neighborhood children. She took them to the Erie Canal to see the highest lift locks in the country at Little Falls, New York and taught them about birds, plants, and other natural subjects encountered en route. Such trips often doubled as after school medical check-ups with area students. In the spring of 1929, she wrote Mamma:

> Saw acres of large white trilliums similar to the sights we saw in northern New York. To show you how much water we have on the roads . . . a sandpiper flew and flirted, lit and flew again several times in the road ahead of me . . . a regular teeter tail.

As a practicing physician, Orra had reached the goal her friend Captain Coulter had urged her to achieve. He had believed in her, loaned her money, and nurtured her through the difficult years of medical school and her internship. Because they had continued to correspond, sharing his military career and her medical one, she was especially pleased to receive his invitation to West Point for the April 6-7, 1929 weekend.

She took the Friday afternoon train in a blinding snowstorm to Poughkeepsie, first visiting her hiking friend, Mary McGehee, at Vassar. After overnight and breakfast at the Alumnae House, Orra took the train to Garrison, New York, then ferried across the Hudson to West Point in a small gasoline launch. As she hoped:

> Captain Coulter was waiting on the dock at West Point and there ended my responsibilities. I do not know when I have spent a weekend with someone else looking out for my every need and planning my entertainment. He took me to the home of Lieut. and Mrs. Bradley where I was shown my room, and though the Bradleys urged us to take meals with them, Carleton insisted in taking me to the mess, [eating in] a small private dining room.
> After lunch we "inspected" the Mess Hall and Cullum Hall, where the hop was to be, its walls covered with tablets and trophy cannon. There is a balcony on the side toward the river — which looks right down to

the river—a glorious view. At the riding hall we watched a polo game for a while, then went to the library where there were many more trophies, old historical documents and portraits. Mounted outside the library doors [are] the cannons that fired the first and last shots in the Civil War. At the museum we saw Hessian flags among other historic flags, models of fortifications, collections of pistols, guns, sabers, Indian relics, *etc.* After seeing the old chapel, now a museum, we went for a drive down through Bear Mt. Park. It was lovely, but would have been lovelier on foot.

After supper at six we watched the cadets march in, then Carleton took me back to Bradley's to dress for the hop. Officers should be in tuxes but some were in uniform. Carleton thinks a formal dance should be formal. The girls' dresses were very pretty and mine was quite all right in every respect [Orra wore a deep raspberry chiffon, with multiple handkerchief points around the skirt, a dropped waist, and cap sleeves.]

We danced till twelve. As the last dance began Carleton pointed out a cadet officer in the balcony, waiting to stop the dance. At the stroke of twelve he signaled, the orchestra stopped short, there was a roll of drums, and every cadet turned and led off for the door with his girl and by 12:30 I was in bed.

Sunday morning Orra joined the Captain for early Mass. She wrote, "None of the service fazed me . . . but meeting the Reverend Father on the steps and being introduced . . . nearly did!" They attended the Cadet Service, and though the cadets had marched in, the Captain's silver bars assured them of preferential seating. Then, when they visited the Officers' Quarters, Orra wondered about propriety but trusted Captain completely. Orra's recollections continued:

After a grand steak dinner, we went for a drive . . . and saw hosts of daffodils, bloodroot, magnolias in bloom, dogwood almost out, forsythia, cherries, plums and peaches out. We drove through Bear Mt. Park and saw a beaver pond. Got back in time to see a glorious parade, then sped to Newburg

. . . for the 6:40 ferry . . . Time to say good-by, too . . . I slept
some on train . . . got here 11:55 p.m.

An August 27, 1929 letter showed that Captain Coulter was still
very much on Orra's mind.

> Dear Mamma,
>   Last night Kay and I went to see "Journey's End," a
> very strenuous war play . . . scene laid in a British officer's
> dugout seventy yards from German lines. Acting was
> excellent, wit rare, and characterization splendid. The
> hero was built and acted like the Captain but didn't look
> like him.

Orra plunged into her work with gusto, examining hundreds of
students' eyes and ears, throats and teeth, hearts and lungs. In so doing, she dealt with some truly poignant cases. One was Marie,[1] a
seven-year-old diabetic, whose rural immigrant family knew nothing
about diabetes, couldn't afford insulin, and spoke almost no English.
After she had collected Marie's blood and urine samples, Orra and Marie's
twelve-year-old sister, Anna, who spoke English, drove one hundred ten
miles round trip to consult at the Albany Hospital Diabetes Center.
    Enlisting the aid of an older sibling was commonplace in the
Phelps family, and in Marie's case, it served both her and Anna well.
On April 9, 1929, Orra wrote:

> The trip went nicely. The older sister learned the
> diabetic's lesson quickly and also how to make the sugar
> test. I went home with her so I could see her prepare one
> meal for my patient and give one dose of insulin. She has
> to give her sister two hypodermics a day.

That evening, as Orra explained diabetes, Anna translated for her
family. Through June, Orra regularly drove Marie to Albany for follow-up
evaluations, trusting the family would faithfully continue the treatment
and that Marie would be fine over the summer vacation.
    Orra decided to take a course that summer at Columbia in New
York City. She took the course, "Diseases of the Eye," probably be-

cause Mrs. Phelps's chronic eye problems as well as those of some of her students begged for the latest medical information.

Orra applied her special skills and knowledge when she assisted in a gratis eye surgery in Little Falls, writing, "Today Dr. Burdin, a surgeon, and I did a free operation . . . I, giving anesthesia and he doing surgery to straighten a squint on a nine-year-old girl. Family will only have to pay the hospital." Knowing how crucial eye care was, Orra often drove children to optometrists and even purchased glasses when families could not.

September came and, like the school children, Orra returned to her September-through-June duties. She was shocked to find her special patient, Marie, hospitalized and almost comatose from neglect. Orra confided:

> I found Marie at the hospital, barely conscious. I learned one thing from the mother and the nurse: she had not had any insulin for a month . . .Of course she was sick. I haven't found out yet why, but it seems they just stopped giving it to her and didn't tell anyone. Well, she's getting better.

Lamenting that there "isn't time for all I want to do," Orra worked to improve Marie's diet, made several trips to her rural home and to her Albany physician, plus did special research on the subject. Finally, Orra decided Marie would be better off boarding in Fort Plain with a family better able to meet her needs and attending school with children her own age, rather than in her one-room school. Once this bright child's health was restored, she caught up on all she had missed due to illness.

Through Orra's efforts, state aid of five and a half dollars a week provided Marie with special nutrition and insulin, while her family agreed to pay seven dollars a week for board.[2]

Intermingling her medical practice with her mountaineering, she shared her remarkable summer 1928 one-hundred-mile hike at the fifth annual meeting of the ADK Albany Chapter. Their December 1929 newsletter gave advance notice:

DR. ORRA PHELPS, one of our own members, has promised to give us a talk on her trip over the club's Northville-Placid Trail. Dr. Phelps is the only member to have attempted this, and we look forward with keen interest to hearing her account of this hike. Dr. Phelps will also bring her photographs illustrating the trip.[3] [Nearly seventy years later, the same photograph album was found intact in Orra's dusty archives.]

Within days of this exciting talk and in response to her 1929 Christmas greeting, Orra received the unexpected and tragic news that her friend, Gardiner Littell, had died following an operation. His family wrote, "We feel no thought . . . at this time as keenly as your Christmas card to him. Yours, Sincerely, John S. Littell." A yellowed news clipping enclosed read:

Gardiner Littell, 27, a graduate of Kent School in 1920; Harvard, 1924. Returned to Harvard to study for his M.A., at the Sorbonne and traveling a year. Two years teaching History and English at Hoosac School. Returned to Harvard for the second post graduate year to complete study for his Ph.D.

His life was full of many interests — church, friends, music, architecture, art, literature, civics, economics, history. He had accepted an appointment to be acting Asst. Prof. of History at U. Maine. Prof. A.M. Schlesinger of the Dept. of History at Harvard said, 'He was one of the finest young men who passed under my charge."[4]

Orra had suddenly lost her very special friend, known since their Silver Bay days. Although Orra's letter to him has been lost to history, surely they had mutual affection. Years later, Orra remarked that she had had three marriage proposals but whether Gardiner was one of the three men who proposed, one can only speculate.

From April to December 1929, Orra's old letters contained no word from Captain Coulter, hinting another possible loss. Finally, in December 1929 Orra's friend, Ann Sawyer, wrote telling Orra what she may have sensed, that Captain Coulter was engaged to be married to another long-time friend, Sally George, of Baltimore. In a November 6, 1931 letter to her mother, Orra wrote of feeling blue, one of her rare admissions of inner frustration and sadness.

> I'm sorry if I was somewhat cool and indifferent over the weekend. I felt rather blue myself over things in general, hating myself in particular. I thought I was coming down with the grippe, but I am fine.
>
> I can't get caught up with my obligations. I owe twenty letters, books, bulletins, and medical journals are piled around me, not even skimmed . . . dresses and stockings need to be mended. I have time after work or dinner when I can do things but I don't feel like it.

The cause may have been Carleton's forthcoming December marriage. Orra saved her December 1931 wedding invitation but did not attend. In April 1933, Orra heard that the Coulters had a son, Carleton III, and were happily stationed in Hawaii.

There are no letters detailing the final separation between Orra and Carleton. Had they decided during their West Point weekend not to marry—to go their separate ways—even though they cared deeply about each other? Orra's reasons may have been family responsibilities, religious differences, and perhaps her desire for independence. Poignantly, Orra carried thoughts of him into her old age, when she still recalled him with fondness.

Orra had experienced so many challenges that would have sent a less grounded woman reeling. Losing two fine young men tested her mettle, but she survived. The inner peace and stability that gave Orra the strength to bear these losses, while carrying her daily load and living with her own inner difficult choices, was reinforced by her deep religious convictions.

In her formative years, Orra had frequent opportunities to grow her faith; with her family, at college, at Silver Bay, through inspirational sermons in Baltimore and Washington, and through her life-long connections with friends in the ministry. In prayer, she placed her worries and sorrows with God. After a weekend religious retreat at Briarcliff Lodge in January 1930, Orra tried to share her feelings with her mother, hoping it might help. She wrote:

This is one of those forwards that is written last. I want to assure you of my love—you know it's there all the time—but somehow it's nice to get an extra assurance. You are very brave, too, to give me up so courageously. I hope your lonesomeness may change into a real fellowship in the Spirit.

The power of the Holy Spirit is certainly working in this place! That may be a rather startling thing to say, but it is said reverently and with deep conviction . . . and why not tell the whole truth . . . the reality of God, and Christ and the Holy Spirit, are talked of freely here as facts of experience not as mysteries of religion.

The constant talk—the meetings and the same people would soon pall and the stimulative effect would soon wear away if there were not so much truth—and so much fresh power daily revealed from so many sources.

You will want to know what has happened to me—nothing strange—just this—I know that the way of Christ is the only way for me, that with Him my life is serene, steady—harmonious and outgoing. Without Him my life is one constant turmoil, a conflict of purposes and desires, and war of wills—"That I would, I do not and that I would not, I do." In other words, Christ is a Savior, and someday I'll tell you in particular what I had to be saved from—in brief it was self, sin, and the world.

Next, Christ is the solution for all the problems of human relationships, in the home, at all stages from children to grandmothers, for the problems of divorce, the eternal triangles, the brother and sister relations—jealousy—impropriety and discipline.

And Christ is the solution for all problems of human relationships in society, for drink, crime, industrial wrongs, politics, and in the professions—including medicine, finance, and education.

The power of Christ is the only power that can reach down through every strata of society, reach through class distinctions and through racial differences and national barriers and lift humanity up—and that is just the work of this group. But first, last, and always the problem begins with individuals and therefore changing things begins there too. So these people get the name of "life changers."

Orra in her 1928 Chevy, packed for the Gaspé Peninsula trip in 1930.

> I have always felt that Christians ought to be the
> happiest people in the world. And I've always wondered
> why they are not and that is where so much popular
> criticism of the church arises. Certainly the church does
> not make very many people happy . . . I leave here Sun.
> at 3 to get back to Fort Plain.

In a conscientious move, despite the financial crunch of the Great
Depression, Orra managed to repay, in February 1930, the entire five
hundred dollar loan taken while at Johns Hopkins, leaving herself
with little until her next payday. With the same deep sense of responsibility, Orra cared for her rural school children. Even as a new physician, she had the maturity and devotion to think primarily of her
patients. One part of the job she mentioned disliking, however,
was dealing with parents of mentally ill, abused, or neglected children. She explained, "I have had jobs this week I don't relish . . . an
interview with a mother, [followed by taking] a child to a mental
clinic. Tomorrow another meeting with the County Child Welfare
Agent."

Between July 25 and August 15, 1930 Orra, her mother, and Mary
Hyde, her mother's college friend and one of Orra's many mentors, drove

3,575 miles on a Nova Scotia trip. Mrs. Phelps's diary transports the reader to Montreal, Quebec, Percé, and the Gaspé Peninsula.

Grill-work enclosed gardens and houses in Montreal seemed to cling to the cliffs like swallow's nests; the crusty habitant bread in Quebec, lifted out of courtyard ovens that baked twenty loaves at a time, tasted delicious and proved to be fresh-keeping until the last crumb; and locally grown flax was homespun into household linens in villages along the coast. The sea-carved rock formations, the tidal bore, the cliff-grasping plant life, and the maritime birds awed the trio of women.

On their return, Mary Hyde wrote on August 10, 1930:

> I am brought to question, perhaps needlessly . . . but have wondered — is your job big enough to give you the zest and satisfaction you crave. You have such splendid capabilities: perhaps this is all you need now, as it keeps you within easy reach of home and all. But sometime, you will do something bigger, unless I underestimate, as it is quite possible, all that you now have to do.
>
> It may be that just your work is the one thing that New York State most needs — in taking care of its children and you are helping build up the men of tomorrow — to be sound, physically and spiritually. What bigger work need we wish. And you are such a great comfort and pride and joy to your mother. We're very thankful for you just as you are. Be comforted and made strong and your heart have great faith and joy in God.
>
> With love, Mary Elizabeth Hyde

Unfortunately, we are not privy to Orra's reaction to Mary Hyde's questions because there are no further letters on that subject. Orra may have known she could have been doing something more important, but during the time she was in Fort Plain, she gave of her energy and talents freely to patients and colleagues, students, neighbors, and family.

While Orra Phelps was busy as a school physician, civic leader, and, as we shall see, guidebook editor, she also wove a rich fabric of interpersonal relationships. She found friends among her colleagues, but also mentored many others. When an abusive marriage left her friend, Yolanda, feeling worthless and tormented, even contemplating murder, then suicide, Orra wrote encouraging letters, which Yolanda answered in December 1930:

> Dear Orra,
>   Your letter . . . was beautiful . . . and the prayer was wonderful . . . I've read it over and over. I'm going to keep it always. He did not strike me. . . which. . . surprised [me]. He has such a temper and is such a dangerous person. It was nice of you to invite me to Ft. Plain. I can't come now in [my] weakened condition . . . If I get back on my feet, I shall certainly come up and spend a weekend with you. Meanwhile won't you write again?
>   Sincerely, Y

It is not clear from Yolanda's letters how Orra and Yolanda knew each other, whether from college or Silver Bay perhaps, but with Orra's encouragement and prayers, Yolanda finally freed herself from her abusive marriage. Orra continued to mentor her friends and care for her patients, and was now, beginning in 1930, busy gathering data for the new Adirondack trail guide.

— 13 —

Doctor and Civic Leader

Professional career development gave Orra the freedom and the means to fund the other passions in her life. Her commitment to the betterment of her world included active participation in the Adirondack conservation issues of her day as well as help in forming the lives and minds of youth through Girl Scouting.

None of these activities diminished her professional role; they in fact complemented and balanced it. Orra's supervisors recognized the quality of her medical work by offering her the position of Assistant Medical Director for New York State in February 1931. They hoped she could guide others across the state to improve their medical service to schoolchildren. On February 16, 1931, Orra reflected on her medical career:

> Dear Mamma,
> Dr. Howe, from New York State Department of Medical Service offered [me] the job of Asst. Medical Supervisor for NY State, in charge of rural schools. I am not thrilled, but flattered. I will not accept it. I know the salary isn't much over what I earn now and I wouldn't take a state job for three times what I earn now. I know my interest in the present job lies not in administration but in the contacts I make with individuals.

Those same state officials witnessed Orra's expert medical attention as this October 1931 letter relates:

> Came in for a bit of glory through an unfortunate accident yesterday. I was at St. Johnsville while a state supervisor of nurses was visiting. We were watching an eighth grade girls' gym class running a relay backward across the gym. A girl stumbled and fell backward. Without a sound she got up and clung to one wrist. I went over to take a look and said,

133

> "Broken wrist? Colle's Fracture." We splinted it and took her to Dr. Feldstein. I told him what I thought and . . . he didn't think it was broken, but x-rayed it. I went out while the film was being developed and when I returned he said, "There's a break there — Colle's fracture." That with a state supervisor of nurses looking on.

In September 1931, Dr. Phelps spoke in Montreal about her work as the only rural school medical inspector in New York State at the American Public Health Association Conference. Of particular interest to her were papers on children's hearts, hygiene, and improvement of posture. At a party on Mount Royal, she shared mutual concerns with fellow physicians, enjoyed the band concert and good food, and was especially taken by the view of the Adirondack Mountains across the St. Lawrence River.

During these years, Orra also made substantial civic contributions to the community. The most significant was leading a large Senior Girl Scout troop from 1929 to 1943 in the Fort Plain area, continuing the Girl Scout leadership she had previously sandwiched into her overloaded Johns Hopkins schedule in Baltimore.

Orra was greatly concerned about the women and men of tomorrow. They were closer than just scouts; they were like family to her. Dou-

Orra poses with her Girl Scout troop on their Indian Hill trip in 1934.

glas Ayres and other colleagues admired the way she taught young women civic responsibility and leadership as well as about rocks and minerals, birds and plants, mountain climbing, outdoor cooking, camping and woodcraft, and good sportsmanship.

Even after several of these young women left for college or careers, she continued to mentor them as they matured. Orra began her work with the area Girl Scouts in 1929, a few months after coming to Fort Plain. She wrote, "Dear Mamma, Wed. afternoon I went to a scout meeting and have undertaken instruction in stars, rocks and trees etc. Read through the Scout manual to see what is required."

For Girl Scout week Orra described their exhibit in the local hardware store window. All it really needed was Orra chopping wood or rustling some stew as she explained in her November 6, 1930 letter:

> It has my tent pitched, ground cloth spread, a pack basket (borrowed) near at hand, mess kit, small knapsack, ax, flashlight, map, compass, bird books, first aid kit, all spread out to view. It looks fairly well.
> Tomorrow I am taking the girls to Sprakers Gorge. We wanted to climb Tomany Mt. but too many mothers thought it wasn't safe for their dears to roam in deer hunting territory.

The 1930s depression forced Orra to put off thoughts of a better job as prompted, in part, by her mother's high expectations. Orra's Baltimore friend, Mary McGehee, counseled in August 1932:

> I think you very wise to hold onto your job in Fort Plain for the business situation is certainly tight . . . The men and their families (in tent cities here) were certainly a ragged and pathetic looking crowd but decent and making the best of a bad situation. I saw hundreds of them on the road between here and Washington after Hoover brought out the tear bombs. Some were walking, some had the most ramshackly looking old cows and others were riding on trucks. I am all for the khaki shirts.

In December 1932, Mamma also empathized, "I'm sorry to know that your salary is cut but a heavy cut is better than losing a job. Hang onto that one till you see a better one even if it takes you to Texas."

Then in March 1933, Orra confided:

> There are many rumors and some facts out regarding schools next year. I expect to get some money this week. Some of the state money is in and I ought to be paid up to date. Believe me, I'll hang on to some too. One part about running behind is that just running expenses look so much bigger when you come to pay room, board, garage, insurance.

On one of the few trips she took in 1933, she introduced the scouts to part of the Northville-Placid Trail. Orra then hiked from Wakely Dam to Cedar Lakes on her own, adding to the portion of the trail done with her mother in 1928. A.T. Shorey's glowing recommendation on the area read:

> May 28, 1933
>
> Dear Dr. Phelps,
>   Have just had another glorious trip to West Canada Lake. Spent night at Wakeley Hdq . . . fine place. Early the next morning went down the Cedar River Flow by boat, up Cedar River to the carry. Then hiked with about 80 lbs on my back to the dam at Cedar Lake. Then by boat to head of lakes; then "shank's mare" to West Canada. In the pool in front of Mud Lake lean-to caught a $1\frac{1}{2}$ lb. brook trout. Then next afternoon late went to Brook Trout Lake and caught nine brook trout in half an hour, the smallest weighed $\frac{3}{4}$ lb. Came out via Perkins Clearing by Whitey and Pillsbury Lake. What a trip.
>
> AT Shorey

After school and on weekends, Orra often drove carloads of students on trips, even though she was not their official teacher. On April 4, 1933, she wrote Mrs. Phelps:

> I took students to Albany on Sat. to the State Museum and to the weather bureau. Most got a good deal out of it. Sun-

Orra uses her "light axe" to chop firewood at the Cedar River lean-to.

day four of us took a hike near "Big Nose," a 560-foot-high fault scarp near Randall, NY and found a dogwood grove. I have some branches in water . . . Crocuses here are out, the river is filled with boat traffic, but buoys are not yet planted . . . purple grackles are here and the osprey.

Orra accompanied the Fort Plain High School orchestra to Syracuse in May 1933 for a district competition, fully enjoying the musical events. As if they were her own children, Orra was proud they won second place and that a thirteen-year-old cellist won first place in another division. Doc Phelps took her scouts and friends mountain climbing countless times. On October 13, 1933 she wrote:

Dear Mamma,
The trip last Sun. came off in fine style, in spite of mists and clouds that shrouded us until we were just at the foot of Snowy Mountain. Three car loads started. The B's continued on for a drive rather than climb so ten came back in two cars, six men and four girls. The mountain was just as steep as it was the first time, but it wasn't quite as slippery. The foliage was past its "red" stage up there, but we did see lots of red on the way up.

> It seems to me that this is the most glorious fall I have ever seen.
>
> After the clouds rolled away the big mountains — Mac, Caribou, Colden, Gray's Peak, Marcy, Haystack and Giant were all clearly visible and easily identifiable. Richard Franyman and J. C. Fox caught a half grown porcupine that was eating in a small ash tree. They shook him down and captured him in a leather jacket. He was photographed and then shortly dispensed with by the ranger.

In an October 6, 1933 letter, she told of being cultured — attending a Study Class banquet — and the next day being natural and leading hikers up Snowy Mountain. Orra was comfortable in both milieus, enjoying each with grace and enthusiasm. As her life unfolded, however, she chose the company of naturalists, botanists, and other outdoor-loving people more and more. The naturalist and mountaineer in her grew with each new adventure.

As the depression dragged on, Orra's funds ran perilously low. Milk prices were depressed, so rural families had less money to support their schools. Orra was paid by each sub-district, piecing together her total salary. For private cases, she sometimes received a basket of vegetables or a meal with a family, houseplants, or homegrown herbs. In September 1933, Orra was shocked to learn that the school board treasurer had committed suicide when an audit found school funds short. Her paychecks and those of others could not be cashed during the investigation.

Trail Guide to Adirondack High Peaks, Northeast Section
1930 to 1934

During the years from 1930 to 1934, many knew Orra Phelps as "Doc" — the Girl Scout leader, educator, good neighbor, and mentor. She shared her knowledge and love of nature with her troop and mentored those who needed her strength and wisdom. This was also the time when she began work on what would become the first book of the Adirondack Mountain Club's *Guide To Adirondack Trails* series.

By early 1930, when the ADK's membership totaled 834,[1] the club needed a qualified person to spearhead the proposed, more comprehensive Adirondack trail guide work. Orra Phelps, serving on the club's Board of Governors, the Committee for Johns Brook Lodge

Johns Brook Lodge view of Armstrong and Gothics, 1930. Note the young trees.

(JBL), and the Trail Guide and Outings Committee offered to be editor of the new guidebook. Realizing its historic significance, she saved the June 3, 1930 telegram by which the ADK confirmed her appointment as Guide Book Committee Chairman. Thus began another of her major contributions, one which would culminate in a new trail guide for ADK and the hiking public.

The amazing part of these years was how Orra managed to undertake several challenges simultaneously, doing each with gusto and panache. She became a member of the Adirondack Mountain Club in April 1928 and immediately joined hiking parties, gave programs, and shouldered responsibilities. When she and other club members went hiking in the Adirondacks they were frequently frustrated by the lack of up-to-date and comprehensive trail information.

In 1928, trail information available to adventurers like Orra Phelps was either outdated, strictly local, or incomplete. The New York State legislative reports of Verplanck Colvin's Adirondack Mountain surveys covered the years from 1872 to 1900. Seneca Ray Stoddard, the official photographer of the Adirondack Survey from Glens Falls, published a guidebook in 1874 and a tourist map in 1880. In 1922, the Adirondack Mountain Club had published Robert Marshall's thirty-eight page account of the forty-two High Peaks of the Adirondacks. It lacked relative trail length or difficulty, intermediate distances, hiking times, locations of many safe water supplies, open shelters, trail markers, or natural history information.

In the same year, T. Morris Longstreth had published *The Lake Placid Country, Tramper's Guide*, another slim volume with distances, hiking time, and shelter locations, but only for Lake Placid area trails. The second ADK trail publication, *The Northville-Placid Trail* by William G. Howard in 1923, detailed only that trail's conditions, route, and markers.

Two of Orra's best sources were the New York State Conservation Department recreation circulars, such as No.8, the 1925 twenty-page *Trails to Marcy*, loaded with trail mileage and information on open camps and markers, and the United States Geological Survey (USGS) quadrangle topographical maps. Orra deftly used the latter, but how many other hikers could? Other guides and maps available at that time were an *Adirondack Trail Improvement Society (ATIS)* map and information recorded by its member, Mrs. Wood.[2] Finally, there was Walter O. Kane's 1928 guidebook, *Trails and Summits of the Adirondacks.* Each of these sources was helpful, but none were comprehensive.

At the ADK annual meeting in 1928, Harry W. Hicks, vice-president of the Lake Placid Club, had suggested that the Adirondack Mountain Club undertake writing a new guidebook, ". . . with special regard to the use of these maps by campers and trampers in all four seasons, locating trails and shelters."[3]

At the January 12, 1929 annual meeting, the report of the Special Guide Book committee was presented by Chairman Russell Miles Long (M.L.) Carson and members Arthur S. Hopkins, Walter O'Kane, and Harry W. Hicks. In July 1929, that committee published a sixteen-page pamphlet containing a map of the Johns Brook region, information about Johns Brook Lodge, and access and trail notes for twenty-three walks and climbs.

Orra had frequently camped in that region during the late twenties, when Reeta and Roy Hanmer were caretakers, when wool sheets and rough cots were in short supply, and when some single women, but not Orra, made sure there would be other women guests before agreeing to come.

Orra was right in the thick of these developments, ready with current, first hand hiking information and the zeal and vision to do the job. She made medical rounds by day, but gathered information and wrote the text for the new ADK guidebook by night and on weekends. Because both Mrs. Phelps and Orra had the foresight to preserve their correspondence, we are privy to the weekly and monthly development of that early guidebook. As early as September 20, 1930, Mr. Carson reported that Dr. Phelps had outlined the first steps taken in the guide's development. Orra and the committee had many sources of information to research, evaluate, and potentially use, in whole or in part, or to use as models.

Initially, Orra sought material on the entire Adirondack region, but later she would focus only on the northeastern High Peaks section for the 1934 guidebook. Rather than rely strictly on published information, she wanted current raw data on trail conditions and difficulty, the wording and location of signposts, and updated lean-to information. As a naturalist, she hoped to include some natural history.

Orra consulted other mountaineers, woodsmen, foresters, and naturalists by letter and phone, on the trails, and at club meetings, despite her 1931-dollar crunch. One major source was the New York State Conservation Department. As she wrote her mother on June 2, 1931, "This Sat. I am planning to have a session with Mr. Mulholland, Chairman on Maps and Mapping."

Paul Schaefer, with whom Orra had hiked and swapped trail notes, was another valuable source of trail information. Schaefer was a leading activist in Adirondack conservation, a vice-president of the Association for the Protection of the Adirondacks, author, and ardent hiker. They collaborated in many political "fights" during their half-century's work defending the Adirondack wilderness. Both believed strongly in the "Forever Wild" clause of the New York Constitution, which states in part: "the lands of the State constituting the Forest Preserve shall be forever kept as wild forest land, and that the timber thereon shall not be sold, removed or destroyed." In a September 1931 letter, Schaefer described his enjoyment of their joint camping and hiking:

> Dear Dr. Phelps,
>   Indian Pass country was a rare treat! Wallface Camp — Oh boy what a spot. You bet. I wanna go back! . . . I regret we didn't have more time than we did, . . . but [it was] a hundred times worth the effort. . . . It certainly did me good to know you would "pull through" regardless of the obstacles. My admiration for your woodsmanship increased tenfold when I saw your pack and its contents. (And that stride)!
>   Sincerely, Paul A. Schaefer

Although the above correspondence from a male hiking companion did not reference Orra's female chaperones, *de rigueur* at that time, many other letters pointedly did. On one occasion Orra's parents felt free to chide her about a projected solo trip with a male teenager despite the fact Orra was then in her late thirties. Mamma wrote:

One item in your letter distresses me quite a good deal. Have you considered the matter of you and Edgar going camping [alone] from all possible angles? To me it seems a most unwise thing for several reasons. First, the gossip that it would undoubtedly cause, (and more than you think your job depends on public opinion) and to me a stronger objection is it wise for an adolescent youth to be the 24-hour sole companion of a woman even if he is the right type of boy and she — your own discrete self. I know I would protest if any woman had proposed to take any of my sons off on such a trip. I don't doubt you could make it a grand trip from a camping point of view, but wouldn't it be wiser to take another one or two? Or if he must have camping experience send him with some reliable chap like Paul or Vincent Schaefer or ask Lawrence to get him into a camp. . . I just do not approve of the scheme at all unless you each have a chaperone. I talked the matter over with Dad before I decided to write and he feels as strongly as I do that it is unwise.[4]

During these years, Orra's work on the guidebook was intertwined with action on the compelling conservation issues of the day. The Hewitt Amendment to Article 7, Section VII (now Article XIV Sections 1 and 2), proposed reforestation of burned areas and would allow lumber interests who had planted trees in the thirties to have the right to harvest them when they matured. When it was being debated in October 1931, Orra shared in Paul Schaefer's effort to stop it. He wrote:

Dear Dr. Phelps,
It was mighty good to hear from you. It always is . . . because with your letter is an intangible something — a breath of the forest, the spirit of the hills; something I don't quite understand yet know is there.
These days I am fighting the Hewitt Amendment . . . this misleading, unnecessary amendment to that great barrier of commercialism, Article 7, Section VII . . . Pass the amendment and watch the ADK Park neglected. . .
On the Adirondack trails,
Paul Schaefer
P.S. I know your perspective will be unbiased.

Another contributor, Arthur T. (A.T.) Shorey, was also a staunch defender of the Adirondack wilderness, crew leader for the cutting of the "Shorey Short Cut" trail, and later a guidebook editor. In June 1932 he philosophized:

> Dear Dr. Phelps,
>   From what I have seen, I feel that the preservation of the "wild" nature of the Adirondacks depends on a ceaseless fight by those who love it. The region is in danger every moment. The north country people need educating . . . They are the ones who abuse the region, prey on game, steal wood — do as they please . . . The boarding houses and hotels resent the use of the preserve by any who prefer to camp. They desire everyone from outside to use a boarding house.
>   The Guides want all hunters to be compelled by law to use a guide if they go into the woods to hunt or fish . . . Already fishermen are going to West Canada Lake by plane. This winter a plane will take ski parties to Lake Sanford, so they can ski back through Indian Pass.
>   Scientific forestry is out of place in the Forest Preserve . . . There should be reforestation but not in solid stands of one type. Why not spread them out so they

The Mt. Marcy shelter built by Pirie MacDonald.

can grow into things of beauty . . . Lean-tos are needed at West Canada, So. Canada and Cedar Lakes — also at Spruce.

Sincerely, A.T. Shorey

Like Shorey, Orra wanted to experience the entire amazing Adirondack region, from west to east and in all seasons. Her plan in 1933 to ascend Marcy in winter caused her mother to agonize over the dangerous climb. Rationally, Mrs. Phelps knew Orra was well prepared for the rigors of the climb and was safety-conscious, taking only well-calculated risks. Still, she fretted:

Dear Orra,

Your letter just received . . . Must say I am more than a little frightened to think you even consider Marcy in the winter. Ralph England ought to have his neck wrung for even suggesting such a dangerous climb. I've heard the experiences of several men and they are too terrible to think about. Never could see why folks want to climb snow clad peaks anyway. I can go into raptures over snowy paths in the woods and icy water falls and frozen brooks but the ice clad summit of a mountain probably with a zero temperature and wind blowing at an eighty mile gale doesn't seem to me attractive. However your life and your legs are your own and if it delights you to put them in peril, well all right.

With much love, Mamma[5]

The 1933 Phelps party of Mt. Marcy winter climbers shown leaving from winter camp near Johns Brook Lodge. At left are the Johns Brook Lodge caretakers, the Hanmers and their son, Alphonse.

In spite of her mother's fears, Orra did climb Marcy from Winter Camp near Johns Brook Lodge on January 1, 1933. She led George,

Fred, and Grace Wagner, Ed Park, and D. Abbott. James Goodwin, at the time a guide at the Underbrook Lodge and a High Peaks climber for seventy years, was in another group attempting to reach the Marcy peak first that year. He shared his memories of Orra:

Orra and Fred Wagner pause at the top of Mt. Marcy, January 1, 1933.

My first meeting with Orra was at the Winter Camp of the Adirondack Mountain Club, next to JBL, one winter when we were all racing to make a first ascent of Marcy . . . I believe for the year 1933 . . . and because it had been storming, the caretakers of the camp thought the Albany people would never arrive . . . and we were actually all asleep when the Albany crowd arrived about midnight . . . They threw us out of the camp . . . Rightfully and there was another camp for us to sleep in. The Albany group was led by Orra Phelps . . . and we were glad to get to know them at the time . . . but they were not very pleased with us because we got up earlier and beat them to the top of Marcy. They had planned a newspaper article . . . printed about their first ascent of Marcy for 1933 . . . and unfortunately we had taken the steam out of their plan. We have seen so much of Orra Phelps, thereafter, even though I was not an intimate friend.

The last time I met her, when she was in her eighties, I believe, was on a trailless peak, Seymour. She had already been up and was coming down when I was leading my group up there. It was a great experience just to have seen her and to be able to talk with her again. Her knowledge of all of the Adirondacks as far as nature study was concerned . . . with particularly being an authority on the vegetation above the timberline area . . . was outstanding . . . I wish I had known her a lot better than I did.[6]

Loaded with medical samples and literature, Girl Scout handbooks and badges, and Adirondack maps and notes, Orra moved for the last time in Fort Plain in September 1933. In her new storefront apartment on the Wagner Block facing the park, she hung out her sign, "The Doctor is IN/OUT." It was here that the new *Guide to the Adirondack High Peaks, Northeast Section* began to take shape. In November 1933 Orra wrote to her mother, "Devoted all day Saturday to ADK work . . . map and estimating page material for Guide Book. Did more work Sunday. Orra."

The scope of the book must have concerned Orra. Limiting the first edition to the northeastern High Peaks enabled the committee to focus in depth on that area. In the 1933 ADK Annual Report, she proposed six sections to be covered in a series of future ADK guides. When Orra Phelps attended the ADK annual meeting in New York City she gave the following Report of the Guide Book Committee, January 1933 to December 1933:

> Since the last Annual Meeting of the Club the Guide Book progress has taken several lines other than the Trail Data, which has been the main work in other years.
>
> The committee is grateful to those members who have taken time to collect and to report trail conditions.
>
> As an aid in simplifying the work of trail description and mapping, a scheme has been adopted of dividing the entire Adirondack Park Area into six sections: A Northeastern Section including the Marcy and Lake Placid territory, a Northwestern Section including Saranac and west to Cranberry Lake Region, a Central Section including Indian Lake and the West Canada territory, a Western Section including Old Forge and Big Moose country, an Eastern Section including Lake George-Schroon Lake territory and a Southern Section including the Lake Pleasant, Piseco Lake region.
>
> A Key Map is planned that will show the area covered in each Section Map. Each section, it is hoped, will

eventually be reproduced on maps of like scale, sufficiently large to be readily interpreted and small enough to be convenient.

At the Governor's Meeting in December it was recommended that the Guide Book Committee concentrate its efforts on the Northeastern Section, and prepare for its publication.

Signed, Orra A. Phelps[7]

The 1934 Guide Book committee included only Orra A. Phelps, M.D., Chairman; William G. Howard, William Mulholland, A.T. Shorey, and Howard Carlson. She thanked Mr. Hicks and ATIS for contributions . . . but she carried the bulk of the job. As Bill Toporcer, a member of the earlier committee wrote, "The fact probably is that the [1934] guidebook project was practically a solo job done by her."[8]

Howard Carlson handled most of the business details for the new guidebook to the Adirondack High Peaks. Orra wrote to thank him for "rounding up information."

> I do feel that this publication is going to be the biggest step ahead we can take . . .The suggestions about the signs directing and indicating distance to Johns Brook Lodge strike me as fine.
>
> The work of checking the elevations and correcting them is going on all the time. Even the U.S. Geologic Top. Survey sheets are sometimes quite inaccurate. This doesn't help when the hiking populace demands accuracy.
>
> Sincerely yours, Orra A. Phelps[9]

During January 1934, Orra reviewed the trail data with her committee. Orra and A.T. Shorey pored over maps to prepare a composite for the guidebook. In March 1934, Orra found suitable maps through John McCombs Ross of the Utica Engraving Company. The club's total cost for their two maps, one an 18½" x 19½" Northeastern Section and the other a Key Map of the U.S.G.S. quadrangles, was $105.49, thanks to Orra's thrift. The larger map had trail information superimposed in red.

Orra's skillful attention to detail, gained from her medical practice and botanizing, was invaluable to the multi-faceted aspects of publishing the trail guide. Her April 5, 1934 letter to Howard Carlson addressed issues regarding ease of use—an important concern for target markets, marketability, and competition.

> I wonder if you think it would be advisable, looking a long way ahead, to change the size to conform to that of the new Appalachian Trail Guide . . .The size of their book is 4^1/$_2$" x 6^1/$_2$". . . . This size would reduce the number of pages and make a flatter book. Maps would not have to be folded quite so much . . . My thought is that someday when the Appalachian Trail Conference has completed their series of Guides to the Appalachian Trail . . . , our Adirondack area will more readily receive the recognition it deserves if its Guide Book [is] comparable to those of other areas.[10]

Orra prepared a sample copy of the guide, allowing the printers to make a dummy and set a typographical sample. With a facsimile of the map, detailing size and placement of folds, they would submit a price for folding and insertion. Then the final decision could be made on placing the entire order. The 1934 guide had a dark green, waterproof, flexible cover, was pocket-sized, and did not attempt to be encyclopedic.

During this time she wrote a table of contents which she sent to the committee members, with the admonitions that,

> . . . anything we want to add must be thought of now . . . feel free to criticize—it might better come from you now . . . than . . . from others when it is too late. Show this to as many interested persons as you wish and get their reactions.[11]

Orra's work on the book did not seem to diminish participation in her other passions. In early April, she wrote home:

> What between the Guide Book and special Girl Scout affairs—Camp Committee—I have been dashing around. I expect to get another slam of work done tomorrow on the Guide Book. I sent off four page reports to four members of the Committee yesterday.[12]

However, her many activities seemed to leave little time for much personal correspondence. By May 31, 1934, Orra wrote:

> Dear Mamma,
> How busy is hard to describe . . . There's been so much to do I can't half think of all of it. Last Sun. I worked on Guide book almost all day and Mon. and Tues. school work. [Wednesday Orra escaped for some fishing but on her return] found Shorey here, had a bite to eat, and studied maps till nearly eleven. I was so sleepy.

On June 21, 1934 she wrote,

> Dear Mamma,
> I ought to write you a long letter but I fear I'd get all mixed up with the Guide Book. Last weekend... I went to L. Placid and Heart Lake trail finding. Then Sunday I interviewed Mr. Hicks and climbed Cascade Mt. Monday I ran up Colden alone, a great trip round-trip in five hours. I got back a little before two and left for home. Saw two deer, three porkies, including a baby, snowshoe rabbits, ducks, and a scarlet tanager. Also found the enclosed twayblade at about 4200 ft. on Colden.

Orra and friends on a canoeing and fishing trip out of Fort Plain, N.Y.

The Adirondack Mountain Reserve – Ausable Club owned part of the High Peaks region of the Adirondack Mountains. Another group, the Adirondack Trail Improvement Society (ATIS), provided Orra with current, accurate trail information.

On June 26, 1934, Orra received a letter from Henry Goddard Leach, President of the Ausable Club, stating which trails they maintained and which the State handled within the Adirondack Mountain Reserve. A member of the ATIS Executive Committee had used an odometer to measure most trails converging on Johns Brook Lodge, making their map one of the most accurate.

Orra delivered the manuscript titled: *Guide to Adirondack Trails, Northeast Section* to Mr. Carlson in New York, traveling down by night boat from Albany on June 30. They reviewed the copy together and met with Mr. Leach concerning the ATIS region.

Orra received a letter dated July 16, 1934 from Russell Carson about the length of his bibliography. He also congratulated her, saying:

> You have done a great job for the Adirondack Mountain Club and Adirondackers generally, and are justly entitled to a huge amount of satisfaction and pride. Best regards and a huge congratulation.
>
> Cordially, R.M.L.C.

On the same date, Mr. Carlson wrote that he had:

> . . . read the first batch of galley proofs and think the contents of the book are fine. Am especially well pleased with the amount of information in the book not already in the Conservation Dept. publications as in the case of the Ausable Lakes region.
>
> H.C.

Orra wrote Miss Roseanne Mullarkey, Secretary of the ADK Mountain Club, on August 22.

> I had to work right with the typist in many cases. I had notes and often had to dictate corrections. I have advanced some money for typing. Enclosed are bills for the typing, drafting, stationery, and postage.
>
> I have certainly had a busy summer—working in a hospital and trying to finish this on the side. Here's hoping the Guide Book proves worth the effort.[13]

Finally, on September 17, 1934, the first copies of the guidebook were ready for shipment. Then, on September 22, 1934, Mr. Hicks wrote Orra in *Simplified Spelling*, Melvil Dewey's attempt to reform spelling.[14]

Dear Dr. Phelps,
Our 100 copies of the Guide Book came and already several have been sold. It seems to me you have done a thoroly[sic] good piece of work for the first edition . . . I do want to express my profound appreciation personally of your leadership in this new and difficult field of effort of the ADK. Without your intelligent and enthusiastic devotion to the woods, it could not have been done. You have faced the difficulties with courage and discrimination and I am sure the entire hiking fraternity will wish to speak of their appreciation of what you have done...
Sincerely, H.W.Hicks[15]

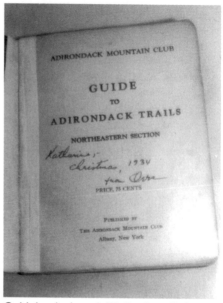

Guidebook signed, "Katharine, Christmas 1934, from Orra"

Orra received numerous congratulations. On September 25, 1934, Russell Carson wrote Orra:

Dear Dr. Phelps,
Heartiest congratulations. The Guide Book is great, and is a great step forward for the Adirondack Mountain Club. You have done a great piece of work for which forever you will have great satisfaction, and for which the Adirondack Mountain Club will be forever your debtor.
Cordially, Russell Carson[16]

By September 26, Orra had received her first copies and sent one to her mother. Mamma replied, October 3, 1934, "Dear O., Guide Book received and I'm proud of you. It is a real bit of work and deserves heaps of praise. Many thanks. Hastily, M."

Another congratulatory letter, dated October 4, 1934, came from a fellow hiker:

> Dear Dr. Phelps,
>   I have just finished reading your guidebook and I can't resist writing to tell you what a splendid job I think it was, and I know that my opinion is shared with a great many Adirondack lovers.
>   I have read several guides to the Adirondacks and not one is half as useful as yours will be. Now that such a book is available, the demand for closed huts and more civilization in the mountains should be largely eliminated.
>   Cordially yours, Kim Hart

President Leach of the ATIS thanked Orra for his complimentary copy and acknowledged her mention of the "quiet work of the ATIS and family names recorded for several trails—the Hayes Trail, the W.A.White Trail and Maghee Clearing. . . ."[17]

The total cost to publish the first guidebook came to nearly $800, including $498 for printing. Treasurer Bell had to take a three-month loan of $500 to cover club expenses, but felt that sales in the spring of 1935 would offset costs. These first editions then sold for seventy-five cents.[18]

— 15 —

Personal Relationships
1935 to 1940

As Charles and Orra Parker Phelps aged and their professional incomes decreased, roles reversed dramatically, with daughter Orra and son Lawrence shouldering more parental duties. They paid their parents' bills, with occasional help from the other working siblings. Orra was their personal confidant, counselor, and physician. For the most part, she was uncomplaining and readily drove sixty miles from Fort Plain to Wilton to help them.

Charles Phelps by the fireplace, in 1940.

Mamma was strongminded, ambitious, and independent for a woman of her times, but Papa still felt he should have the last word. The two argued a great deal about women's emerging rights and independence, changing marital roles, their children and finances, and whether Mamma should learn to drive or be allowed to attend college reunions, botanical outings, or other meetings.

After Mr. Phelps lost his Farm Bureau Agent's position in February 1919, they subsisted on Mrs. Phelps's teaching salary, until her retirement in 1933, and on Mr. Phelps's Justice of the Peace income, plus money from serving chicken dinners and selling jam, canned goods, and farm

154

produce. It wasn't exactly the gentleman farmer's life the Phelpses had hoped to live.

Sometimes Mamma complained so bitterly about Papa's depression or raging that Orra would take one or the other of her parents to Fort Plain for a week to relieve the pressure at home. This seemed to help. Orra wrote the following advice to her mother in May 1935:

> Papa [with Orra for a few days] has seemed quite well. I would suggest . . . that meals be based on several items rather than on a casserole. Cut down on the quantities and spread out the varieties. Unless it is out of reach serve spinach once a week and carrots, yes carrots, once a week and if poss. serve a vegetable and a small salad individual service at noon and at night. Cut out most of the "creamed" substances or make the creaming very thin.
>
> Your last couple of letters told or implied how mad you got at him. That is not quite right, maybe, but you do get mad when his behavior "cramps your style." He is going to need "handling" and I don't see how I can do it all the time from here. I know it is a distasteful job but I don't see but what his health and Francis's peace of mind are in your hands — and your happiness and freedom to go depends upon their mental stability — so you've got to work for balance — a compromise between going and catering to them. If this seems like "strong medicine," there are times when I feel like making it a lot stronger. Doubtless I haven't told you anything you didn't know. What I should be able to do is to fill you with courage and renew your spirit for the fray. At least I have taken a share in the responsibilities.

Dr. Orra—or, as many called her, "Doc"—served her district zealously as a medical doctor, and also shared her enthusiasm for natural history with teachers, giving assemblies on the mountains, conservation, birds, botany, and other natural history topics. She was especially close to Douglas Ayres, the longtime Fort Plain High School science teacher whose science room was just around the corner from her medical office.

Many a morning, she would drop by his room to tell of horned larks she had seen, a fox and her kits, or a sapsucker's cavity nest. In

John Fox, Orra, and Doug Ayres in 1942.

turn, he shared tales of birds he had seen, plants needing identification, and, sometimes, Native American artifacts he had found.

The author interviewed Doug Ayres in 1989 in his artifact-loaded living room, where the bright-eyed octogenarian recalled his heydays with Orra:

> Once I had a field trip up . . . near Cherry Valley. I took an earth science class to see the falls at the headwaters of Canajoharie Creek. When . . . something like that was in the wind, Doc would say, "When are you going?" and "Care if I come along?"
>
> "Why sure." On the trip one of the girls slipped on the trail there . . . and just rolled over and over down the talus slope . . .
>
> Well, I was worried and felt very responsible . . . I said, "Hey Doc, check to see if she's all right." She was, but you always felt so secure when Doc was along, because she was so expert in her field as well as in the outdoors field. . . . A very unusual and talented person. She was so modest about her own accomplishments and knowledge that some of the people didn't

realize that they were talking with a person who was a master of the out-of-doors.[1]

At about that time, Orra shared a laugh with her mother and Ayres. She wrote, "I had venison last night and learned today that three state laws were broken to get the deer, maybe four. It was killed by a car, at night, on the 19th of November and was a doe."[2]

Her wide range of community service gave Orra a choice of many different companions with whom she could flee to the mountains or marshes when taking some time out for fun. In 1934 she wrote:

> Dear Mamma,
>   The G.S. hike on Sat. simmered down to three, which is a very nice sized group. The girls got a kick out of watching a pair of bluebirds in their chosen apple tree. The female was cleaning out the hollow limb. One of them had never seen a bluebird before! We found an Indian campsite which had been plowed last fall and had the easiest picking of pieces of pottery that I have ever seen — all on top of the ground, and some in fair sized pieces. I found one beauty of an arrowhead, a bird arrow, not an inch long and perfect. Also found one larger with a broken point. That makes two arrowheads in one week. We also found a mud turtle out sunning. I was surprised. Is it or is it not early for these?

Orra preferred to work outdoors during the summers rather than inside a local hospital. The Girl Scouts provided an outlet in which she could combine her personal passions with her professional skills. Camp Kowaunkami on Caroga Lake, New York hired Orra as a summer Girl Scout camp leader and staff medical doctor in 1935 and during subsequent summers. Years later she recalled:

> It was there that I got to know the girl that later camped with me in the Adirondacks, Elsa Jane Putnam. She was one of the senior scouts. . . . When we went on a camping trip out away from the main camp, I had to teach her how to chop wood.[3]

During the summer of 1935, Orra led her senior scout troop on another Northville-Placid Trail section, making their 9.5 mile segment her third piece of the long trail. As she reported some forty years later when she completed all sections:

> The [most southerly] section from Upper Benson [near Northville] to Canary Pond, a distance of 9.5 miles, was probably hiked in 1935. This section has a moderate upgrade, interspersed with several ponds with beaver dams and lodges . . . Some time in the early thirties, I walked to Rock Lake lean-to with my Girl Scout troop. The next day we walked as far as Canary Pond, then returned to Rock Lake lean-to to spend another night. I cannot give an exact date, but would guess 1935.[4]

While Orra was teaching others she continued to learn botany from her mother, "the real botanist" as Orra often said.

> Tell me again what I should call the fragrant poplar that does not have a heart shaped leaf? And Carolina poplar — is what is called cottonwood around here . . . not the white poplar? Spent some time looking for a tree trail for the scouts within the village limits . . . . What does wahoo look like in the month of November?[5]

Orra loved to tend plants in her own garden. Her scouts shared in this passion by growing a troop garden together with her for some years. She recounted that once the scouts met her "for a tour of three gardens. I 'spieled' on plants — perennials, annuals, bulbs, shrubs, etc. There were pools in each garden but each was a distinctive type."[6]

For winter fun, Orra shared outdoor cooking and snowshoeing with her scouts. She wrote:

> I invented a new dishless dinner. Spread bread with sausage and toast it on a stick. Very good. The fire we built settled into a two-foot hole in the snow. Everybody had a grand time in spite of cold feet part of the time.[7]

Orra also liked quoits, pinochle, and jigsaw puzzles. She organized troop dramatic sessions and presented plays, went Christmas caroling, and taught the Scouts to dance the Virginia reel, all laughing riotously in their fun. The mouth-watering taste of hot maple syrup and the smell of the crackling fire inspired Orra to organize a trip to a sugar bush in April 1936. Orra explained to her mother:

> I wound up Girl Scout doings by taking them to a sugar bush after school. We bought a gallon of sap and were given a kettle to boil it down over an open fire. We were just outside the sap hut as it's called here. There were 10 girls and only 3 had been on such a party before. Pans of snow were filled at nearby drifts and forks were handed round. A little is enough for me, but some girls seem to have no limit. For all the patches and drifts of snow [after late storm,] the woods were full of hepaticas. The rock that outcrops there is apparently lime and the hepaticas were acute [or pointed leaved], but the ones we found back of the county farm last Sunday on dolomite were the round leaved.[8]

'Gusta' and Leon Phelps.

Papa knew Mamma needed to get away to have more intellectual stimulation and professional activity. As he aged, he became increasingly dependent on her emotionally, fearing he might die without her care. There were times, however, when he showed he cared about Mamma's well-being. For example, in January 1936, he suggested that Mamma spend time with Orra in Fort Plain or take the Ski Train north for a weekend.

Mr. and Mrs. Phelps, Sr. also took separate vacations to visit Leon and his wife, Augusta, in Rochester, New York. Leon, a Cornell graduate, had farmed the family land until he moved to Rochester as a state foods inspector in about 1928. He never returned to farming. Though he and Augusta had no children, they were happy together.

The senior Phelpses used their separate vacations to visit Orra's third brother as a means of relieving the stress in their own relationship and the starkness of life on their farm.

Papa was injured in an auto accident while visiting Leon in Rochester in December 1936 at 74 years of age. Orra took leave from her job and gave up her Christmas vacation to nurse him back to health at the Nathan Littauer Hospital in Johnstown, New York. She brought him to her apartment for several more weeks of recuperation after his hospital stay. Mamma did not go to Fort Plain, writing that she trusted Orra's competence and unworried attitude would benefit him more than her nervousness. By summer, he was fully recovered and able to hike in the Adirondacks.

In 1937, Orra's thirty-nine-year-old sister Phoebe gave up her work as a Columbia University-trained social worker to live at home and care for her parents. Not only was she embroiled in the daily family struggles, but she was virtually penniless because her only income was from the sale of a few purebred collies she raised and from her small summer camp at the Phelps farm. Therefore, Phoebe asked Orra and Lawrence for money as well. Orra counseled her parents on their relationships with Phoebe:

> Phoebe is having a tough time and needs more freedom . . . I do wish Phoebe would feel she has a right to live her own life and that it is not her bounden duty to sacrifice herself and stay at home always and forever for your sakes. That is the real thing that keeps her from going out after a job.

There are few indications that trips or vacations were taken together by the senior Phelpses. Papa felt he should stay at home with Phoebe while Mamma was away. He would then take his turn when Mamma could be at home. Her mother enjoyed having Orra's company and undivided attention on their special outings when they shared mutual interests not shared by Mr. Phelps.

One trip the three of them did take in 1937 was a hike from Heart Lake to Lake Colden and then along the Opalescent River to Hanging Spear Falls and out. Leon met them at Tahawus with his car.

Papa was forever chasing schemes that were too labor-intensive for him to handle alone. The schemes, such as the care of his orchard, depended on the family or hired help for success. When the stress built up, he raged unmercifully at the others in the house. In January 1939, Mamma wrote to Orra:

> Dad went to Town Board meeting yesterday — came home tired and as I had radio on to hear the opera, [he] declared his nerves couldn't stand it, so went to bed. Just before supper he came down and raged at Phoebe for general neglect and shiftlessness! Poor Phoebe flared — don't blame her one bit. Whereupon he went into a rage. I do not believe you've ever seen one of his tantrums where he stamps and pounds and swears. He was the worst I have ever seen him — threatened to kill himself, etc. We finally got him calmed down.

Orra's medical practice would, at times, become serious, such as when eighteen-year-old Tom,[9] one of her former students, contracted tuberculosis. She found treatment for him at the state-run Ray Brook Sanitarium, as was common with TB patients at Dr. Trudeau's famous Adirondack Cottage Sanitarium. However, recovery was slow, aided by the oxygen-rich, evergreen-scented mountain air, rest, and diet as much as by any medicine or procedure. Orra sent him dried fruit and nuts and visited him whenever she was in the mountains. He shared his pain and hope:

> Dear Doctor,
>
> It's been some time since I got your letter. I have been here six weeks this Sunday. It seems like a long time. I am feeling quite well and have gained six and three quarters pounds and . . . . am taking pneumothorax . . . . I started Wednesday with 400 cc., Thursday I took 600 and tomorrow I get it again... after I have been fluoroscoped. It bothered me quite bad [sic] the first two days. I had pain in my back and chest, and still I get them now and then. It makes me cough quite a little and

> I am short winded. I hope everything goes all right and I
> get a good collapse, then maybe my trouble will clear
> up.
>
> Sincerely yours, Tom[10]

Meanwhile, Dr. Phelps worked to educate the public about tuberculosis. On April 9, 1937, Orra wrote Mrs. Phelps:

> Hectic week. The publicity meeting on Early Diagnosis of Tuberculosis is in Canajoharie tonight and I
> have to be there. This is the third public meeting and
> I have also had three assembly programs in high
> schools... not to mention one in Nelliston.

When a strange skin malady occurred, Orra diligently researched the problem. On May 25, 1937, she wrote:

> Dear Mamma,
>   Busy days . . . have been chasing a skin eruption
> that is epidemic in Canajoharie . . . with no illness to
> speak of. I had a clinic and presented eight cases this afternoon. Four of the Canajoharie doctors were there. Very
> interesting and by careful tactics, I brought them around
> to my diagnosis — *Erythema infectiosum* — a recently
> described disease new to them — and to me till recently.
> I have to write some doctor in New Haven now and see
> if we can get some more dope on the thing.

Over the years, Orra continued her close personal relationship with her Mount Holyoke mentor and friend, Dr. Talbot. When Talbot asked her to help a Mount Holyoke geology student, Orra obliged by hiking with her into the mid-New York State glacially-ground gorges, examining rocks, faults, and folds, and searching for fossils.

Through her network of friends, Orra substituted for the Sunday school teachers at the Dutch Reformed Church and helped with church suppers. She cheered at basketball games, sang while chaperoning hayrides, and dressed in costume for charity events. Once, she was the hit of the evening when she dressed as a European peasant carrying a physician's anatomically correct baby.

Orra's large network of friends continued to expand with her ADK work, as she climbed more mountains, marked maps for fellow hikers, and even gave a radio broadcast from the top of Marcy at the 1937 centennial celebration of its first ascent.

Nineteen thirty-eight also marked Orra's twentieth Mount Holyoke College class reunion and her mother's fiftieth reunion. Although the two women had hoped to attend together, Mr. Phelps had been ailing and feared his wife's absence. His letter reveals how dependent he was on his wife and daughter. It also reveals that he based the decision regarding his wife's attendance at the reunion solely on his own health and needs. He wrote:

> I am sorry to be so much trouble but if I get in shape to allow your mother to make her So. Hadley trip June 11-13, I must have the best care and no increase in worry between now and then. Please do your best to help out this weekend.
>
> With much love, Dad.
>
> PS Written in bed Tuesday am.[11]

Despite such tension, the Phelps family also had times of cheer and excitement: holiday gatherings, birthday parties, and visits from their grandchildren. On October 28, 1938, Phoebe Phelps discovered a large patch of the rare climbing fern, *Lygodium palmatum (Bernh.)* in their neighborhood. Mamma wrote an article about the find for the *American Fern Journal* [12] and invited the State Botanist, Dr. Homer House, to come to see it.

The day Dr. House came, Mrs. Phelps had to be in town unexpectedly and so missed his visit. Mr. Phelps held court and enjoyed their important visitor.

The Phelpses' large flower garden was another source of pleasure and pride for the family and friends. In long Monet-like flowerbeds, with wide grass walks in between, grew tulips, iris, peonies, lilies, roses, petunias, forget-me-not, delphinium, dahlias, asters, and chrysanthemums. Orra started annual seeds in her apartment and brought them home to transplant, ordered bulbs and perennials and helped Phoebe, Francis, Mamma, and Papa maintain the garden. Orra shared in her family's joy, from

January's seed ordering to October's last roses. In one of Mamma's letters to Orra, she wrote of her friend's compliment to its beauty. "Mrs. Holmwood came to see our garden one day last summer and said, 'It is a garden one can't forget . . . you go into it and it enters your heart.' "

Dr. Phelps's general practice continued to be as busy as ever. Among her patients were an embittered boy whose leg was amputated, a young woman with breast cancer, the flu-stricken Superintendent of Schools, and a Girl Scout who had been badly burned. Personal thanks and words of courage paid Orra more than money ever could. On May 25, 1938, a letter came from Nathan Littauer Hospital, Johnstown, New York, in a child's penciled scrawl.

> Dear Dr. Orra Phelps,
>
> How are you? I am getting along better. I have been in the hospital five weeks.
>
> My dress caught on fire and I forgot all I had been taught in Girl Scouts about fire. The doctor says I am going to be able to be out in a short time . . . I hope he will let me get up soon.
>
> The burn was worse than they thought. I get so lonesome. My mother is working and can't come and see me, only nights.
>
> How are the scouts getting along up there? Our troop seems to be getting along pretty good.
>
> Your friend, E. A.

Despite all her Adirondack activities, Orra was a central part of whatever was happening where she lived in Fort Plain. She and the other women of the town hurrahed when an illegal liquor still was raided in September of 1939.

> Dear Mamma,
>
> Big news in Ft. Plain News was discovery of a big liquor still and raid by Federal Inspectors. Three huge tanks and the apparatus were in the room next to the gym where the boys play basketball. They smelled something strange and the man who rented the room told them it was disinfectant. I'm wondering what percentage of the Ft. Plain male population knew all about it.

During her years in Fort Plain, Dr. Orra Phelps was a popular speaker on medical as well as natural history topics. She spoke to the Kiwanis Club on hearing loss and her work as medical inspector, to the Girl Scout leaders and Girls' Club mothers on sex education for teenage girls, to her friend John Fox's business class on industrial health programs, and to the Parent Teacher's Association on health and safety in the home.

Orra also wrote countless letters and articles urging action to improve health care. When Fort Plain prepared a fifty-year time capsule in 1939 to be sealed in the science room wall, she wrote about measles, a disease she hoped would be eradicated by 1989.

Orra helped behind the scenes to organize the Fort Plain science teachers for a district Round Table of Science Teachers conference, held in Saratoga Springs January 25, 1940. Orra was especially pleased when the Canajoharie School exhibited pictures of the New York Conservation Department work. Orra explained:

> In the set on forest fire prevention they have as contrast
> to some burned areas — the views of the MacIntyre Range
> from the dam at the end of Flowed Lands. I had a great
> time telling people how often I've been there!

Although Orra had no children, she enjoyed each of her sister Bessie's children as her own, as did the other childless siblings. As Bessie and Charles Haas's family grew, Orra and the other aunts and uncles helped provide baby clothes and took early photos.

Orra was always concerned about Bessie's health, fearful that her weak heart or anemia might overwhelm her. She consulted with Bessie's physicians during and after each pregnancy. Bessie had difficulty delivering each of her four daughters: Phoebe Louise in 1930; Mary Kay, the author of this book, in 1934; Dorothy Orra in 1937; and Rachel Ann in 1940. Rachel's twin, the only male child, died at birth. When Bessie was hospitalized for three months from December 1940 to March 1941 with complications following her last delivery, Orra consulted regularly with specialists and her physician.

From time to time, Orra took the girls from their home on the Victory Mills, New York farm to Fort Plain or to the

Adirondacks for vacations, helped them make balsam-stuffed pillows, and shared birding and botanizing. She knitted warm sweaters and mittens and sewed snowsuits and dresses. Orra's letters brought Bessie current advice on shingles, contraceptives, and vaccinations. She also provided comforting salves for Charlie's chronic psoriasis and calmed Bessie's fears of meningitis and scarlet fever.

Scarlet fever was a health problem that Orra took very seriously as these letters attest. On December 13, 1940, she wrote:

> Dear Mamma,
> The Nelliston school board finally closed the school Wednesday noon on account of scarlet fever . . . The health officer and I got in our licks with them, by issuing an order that all children who had been in school on Tuesday or Wednesday had to remain isolated in the home for seven days — until Wed. Dec. 18th so we do not have a flock of possible contacts wandering through Ft. Plain. So far — no serious kickbacks. Rumors run wild of this one or that one being sick with scarlet fever.

Two days later she continued with her no-nonsense opinion:

> Nelliston scarlet fever affair is quiescent and as far as we can observe here, the children are staying home pretty well. I did not expect 100% cooperation, but rather wanted to produce a psychological effect. If contagion was bad enough to close the school, it was bad enough to keep the pupils isolated. It was the parents who put pressure on the trustees — so it was right, it should be the parents who had the burden of proper supervision of the children handed back to them.
> Orra

The two sisters' lives diverged. Bessie's life was full with her husband and children and endless farm and household work. Her social life included the Quaker Springs Grange and the Schuylerville Library, Eastern Star, Dutch Reformed Church, and Garden Club. Orra's life was filled with Scouts, Adirondack Mountain Club hiking and leadership, her medical career, and caring for the elder Phelpses.

Bessie emulated the domestic side of their mother's life while Orra carried out the academic and outdoor side. For example, Bessie arranged flowers, became a flower show judge, and won Saratoga County Fair prizes for her baking. On the other hand, Orra searched for, collected, and preserved wild plant specimens for the New York State Museum.

— 16 —

Mt. Marcy Centennial
1937

Orra had accomplished much by 1936. She and her brother, Lawrence, remained key factors in the emotional and financial stability of their family. By this time, Orra was the Medical Director of the Montgomery County School System and held a Governor's position in the Adirondack Mountain Club. She had also written the first book of the ADK's *Guide to Adirondack Trails* series.

Her perpetual Adirondack mountaineering gave her many opportunities to gather information for what she recognized would be the updating necessary for subsequent editions of the "*Guide*" as well as to contribute botanical specimens with her mother for the New York State Museum. If someone had asked, Orra's goals at this time would have been to run the best medical practice she could while learning more of the Adirondacks with each trip.

Members of the Albany Forty-Sixers: (left to right) Bess Little, Helen Colyer Menz, and Ida Sawtelle, all friends of Orra's, photographed February 13, 1937 on their trip to Mt. Marcy.

As if in preparation for the 1937 Mt. Marcy Centennial, Orra often "took to the woods" for several exhilarating jaunts during 1936.

Having the capacity and the interest to participate in almost any outdoor adventure, the Adirondack Ski Train trip and winter sporting day sounded exciting to her.

In February 1936, Orra and her mother rode the Ski Train from Saratoga Springs to North Creek, New York, where trains chugged in from Schenectady, Albany, and New York filling the small town with merrymakers and tourist dollars. Many paid two bits to ride a privately owned school bus to the top of nearby Gore Mountain Ski Slope in order to ski down. Mrs. Phelps hobnobbed with young friends between the North Creek Station, the hotel, and the Union College Ski Lodge, while Orra, Alton West, and two young friends snowshoed nine miles through nearby woods.

Being outdoors in the pristine winter air with fresh snow bedecking balsam boughs and brooks, was a "slice of heaven" for Orra. Orra and Al West shared many happy times together over the years. The son of Lake Colden forest ranger Clint West and his wife, Mary, Al was a Union College graduate and a sum-

Mrs. Phelps (left) with Aimee Birkenbine and Alton West.

mer ranger at Marcy Dam. He shared Orra's love of the outdoors, the mountains, and vigorous activities such as climbing and snow-shoeing, as well as photography and music.[1] He was a gifted tenor and once sang "The Lord's Prayer" for Orra from Wright's Peak.

The next 1936 challenge was Orra's July climb up Colden's famous trap dike, across Avalanche Lake from the "Hitch-up Matilda" floating bridges. The trap dike is a steep-walled gorge cleaving Mt. Colden's western face, rising abruptly from Avalanche Lake's talus strewn shore, parallel to the great open slides, and visible from the MacIntyre Range and from airplanes. Differential erosion of the metagabbro igneous intrusion and the harder anorthosite granite of the High Peak dome formed the dike. Pioneer birches, balsam fir, ferns, and other mountain plants cling to crevices, misted in wet times by cascading waterfalls.

In the mid-thirties, very few women would consider such a rigorous climb, which required pulling oneself up over sheared rocks, creeping along slippery ledges, and gripping narrow shelves with no next step in sight, up or down, for hundreds of feet. Orra felt the struggle was worth it because she wanted to achieve another goal. She wasn't racing the others, just pushing her own limits.

She could also check the mountain-top flowers again and see her favorite summit view from Colden. Across its alpine meadow, past its large balanced boulder, she could see Avalanche Lake, Lake Colden, the Flowed Lands, and the panorama of surrounding mountains. Orra's success proved that she was ready for almost any climb.

Orra looks over Flowed Lands, one of her favorite Adirondack venues. The lake, south of Lake Colden in the High Peaks, was formed in the mid-nineteenth century as the result of the damming of the Opalescent River by the proprietors of the McIntyre Iron Works.

Why did she climb the dike? Because she was an explorer and this was a new, difficult, and geologically interesting area to climb, with possibly new flora to discover. Orra was delighted to be among "a select few," including Orra's two female friends and two male students, to climb the dike with Al West. Being in Al's company was a special pleasure for Orra.

A few weeks after the July climb came the medical emergency of September 6, 1936, when Orra hiked to Lake Colden to suture John Russ's ankle, as described in Chapter One. Also in September, Orra made the 20.8-mile loop from Heart Lake to Lake Colden with Mrs. Phelps and Al West, to the top of Marcy, down to Johns Brook Lodge, and out to the Garden. With Mrs. Phelps as chaperone, Al and Orra enjoyed their times together. Mrs. Phelps savored her part of their adventures, as shown in remarkable photos of their group. Al wrote in September 1936:

On the back of this framed print is written, "Holiday Greetings & Best Wishes, John." The picture shows Orra and John Fox at a fire observer's hut on Woodhull Mountain.

Thanks for your note and the two snapshots, one of
Colden from dock . . . The tri-C's began their work on
the new trail between the Range Trail (near Snow-birds)
and Slant Rock. That day, beginning at the R. Trail they
completed the job to the height of land including marking it. Color of markings: yellow. ATS Shorey was on
hand to see that the job was properly executed. Trail finished Thurs., authority: J.H. Hopkins; told me Sat.
morning. [Later named Shorey Short Cut.] Sept 27 —
Winter came early this year. Thurs. a.m. everything was
white. Still a good bit of snow and ice on trail and top.[2]

It was not just the mountains that lured Orra, but the northern
waters as well. In October 1936, Orra wrote of fun canoeing with
John Fox and her neighbor's boys, George and Fred Wagner, using
their canoe on Spruce Lake, north of Dolgeville:

I rode most of the time and the boys did the paddling
except about the last quarter mile. John R. Fox was the
fourth person in the party and that made the canoe full.
The reservoir is long and narrow — perhaps two miles of
lake and two more of winding stream that was sufficiently
deep to navigate. In spots the color was grand but there
were also long stretches of rusty alder. We saw evidence
of beaver work in the past but no recent cutting. The
prize event of the day was seeing an osprey dive for a fish
but apparently he did not get one. We did not see him as
he hit the water, but heard the splash.[3]

A February 1, 1937 letter to Mrs. Phelps gives a first-hand glimpse
of the ADK annual meeting, Orra's involvement in the club, and what
impressed her and what did not:

The trip to NY was brief but satisfactory — delightful
in spots. I met Bill Walker and introduced him to a few
governors before the meeting. The session was a hot one —
much resentment over certain resolutions. People felt that
their integrity was questioned and much heat and bitter-
ness flew around. Finally the peacemakers patched it up
and as a result the afternoon session was smooth as silk . . .

After PM session I went back to Brooklyn, put on my red dress and satin slippers, fixed the wave in my hair, and with [brother] Lawrence, went back to the dinner. The exhibition of old Adirondack pictures (mostly Stoddards) was great. I wish I had had hours to look at them. The dinner was very good and the speaker, Pres. of the Audubon Society, was excellent though he did not put in much about birds.

As the mountain snows began to melt, Orra could hardly wait to be in the woods again. The basis for her 1939 article in *High Spots* was a June 1937 camping trip to Slant Rock, a huge boulder with a slanted overhang deep enough for refuge, 6.8 miles from the nearest parking lot. Orra wrote her mother:

Keene Valley trip was very [satisfactory with] just my load of "kids," Olga, MaryAnna, and Lenig. We hiked in to Slant Rock on Sat. Long trip but we rested at noon at the JBL Lodge where Mrs. Hanmer was in charge for the weekend with twelve people there from Scotia, Albany, and New York.

I've always wanted to camp under Slant Rock, so we stayed there two nights. I'm thankful it did not rain for in spite of the slope and protection it looks as if in a rain the water would have dripped off most anywhere. As it was at night the moisture dripped down from the soil on the rock. We were very comfortable on balsam beds in spite of the snowdrifts all around us. We had to walk around one to get to the stream for water.

Sunday we climbed the Range Trail, intent on Haystack. We had to navigate old snow for the whole one and one-half miles and it was sloppy. We got wet but on top it was hot so we took off our boots, wrung out the water from socks, and dried them. Of plants I saw two kinds almost in bloom, the willow and *Diapensia*.

We chose another route home which proved to be much better — much less snow. The last of it was the new cut off that Shorey and Al routed. It was scenic. On Monday we did nothing but pack up and hike out taking it leisurely. Flowers in the valley were numerous and lovely: pin cherry, shad, white violets, spring beauties, red and painted trilliums, foam flower, and hobble bush.

One of the pesky things I have to do in the next few days is send out bills. I wish I had a secretary. I hate that kind of work, but must collect or starve.

While camping at Lake Arnold on June 19, 1937 with Orra and Al West, Mrs. Phelps wrote of seeing an arctic three-toed woodpecker hunting grubs on a dead spruce, grasping with two of its toes in front, one behind. She noted, "He looked regal in plain shining black upper plumage,

Two Colyer sisters, Helen Colyer Menz (left) and Mary Colyer Dittmar.

barred sides, and an yellow crown patch."[4] Mrs. Phelps also recorded witnessing the August swallow migration of tens of thousands of birds, crowding every branch and wire in every direction. The massive flock included barn, bank, rough-winged, and tree swallows, at times whirling and darting around.

Her position on the ADK Board of Governors gave Orra privileged access to the exciting preparations for the 1937 centennial celebration of Marcy's first ascent. There were to be four ascents made by groups along the four main trails to the summit. Orra chose to join a group approximating the original bushwhack.

It was writer Hal Burton's idea to broadcast the event. During an interview by the author in 1989, he recalled:

I thought that up...I couldn't go because my newspaper had an assignment for me in Mexico. I called my friend, Osborne, a newspaper owner. They thought it was a dandy idea... and they got GE to haul a huge broadcasting unit up there...It was immense. Broadcast over WGY.

Mary Dittmar also recalled the difficulty of getting the broadcast equipment to the top of Marcy, "They hauled it to a lean-to till the horses could go no more, then people had to put it on their backs . . . the rest of the way."[5]

Over August 4 and 5, 1937, Orra Phelps made the historic and daring centennial climb, alone most of the way, bushwhacking up Mt. Marcy by approximately the same route Professor Ebenezer Emmons, New York State geologist, and his party climbed in 1837. Joining some two hundred forty people on top, Orra described her ascent:

1937 ASCENT OF MT. MARCY VIA EMMONS' ROUTE IN 1837
Short Wave Broadcast From Marcy's Top by Dr. Orra A. Phelps

In making arrangements for this celebration, the Adirondack Mountain Club planned to have parties make the ascent of Mt. Marcy by each of the four main trails, one from Keene Valley, one from Elk Lake, one from Tahawus Club and one from Adirondak Loj at Heart Lake. It was also suggested that a party follow the route taken by Prof. Emmons and his companions 100 years ago. I chose to join this party. At the last minute the leader chosen was unable to be present. Though I knew of no others planning to attempt this route I resolved to undertake it.

On the afternoon of August 4th I drove to Sanford Lake and parked my car. With a light pack I took the old road that leads past the abandoned iron mine. About three miles from the start the old road brings one to the banks of the Opalescent River. The Emmons party, starting from Tahawus and traveling east through the forest had reached the bank of this stream in this same vicinity. They followed the stream to its source on the north side of the crown of Marcy. I followed the trail which leads along the west bank, then crosses and continues on the east side, and brings one to the splendid Hanging Spear Falls. On up through the gorge which is still wild and lovely, the trail at length comes out at Flowed Lands. This was not, in Prof. Emmons' day, a beautiful lake, but was probably a broad marsh.

In following the trail around the lake, I crossed its second outlet, Calamity Brook, and made my way in the twilight, to the foot of Lake Colden. Here the explorers had camped one hundred years ago, so here I camped. In accordance with previous plans a friend [Lyle L. Louden] joined me here.

In the gray mists, next morning we again took the trail that follows the Opalescent and leads past the narrow rock-walled flume where the falling waters thunder. The clouds and mists were still thick when we reached Feldspar Brook. The trail to Marcy follows this branch, but Prof. Emmons and his party had followed the main branch of the stream, so from there on there was no trail and the stream was our only guide. It was a lovely stream with many mossy boulders and frequent waterfalls. We proceeded upstream jumping from stone to stone. Now and then we had to climb up the banks through thickets of balsam and spruce to surmount waterfalls. In places we walked the trunk[s] of fallen trees. We stumbled through the tall grass and low shrubs where there had been an old beaver dam. Occasionally the mists lifted and we had a glimpse of the near mountain slopes that were on all sides, but the top of Marcy was not to be seen.

The stream grew smaller. We climbed up a rock crevice that was very steep and straight. Above this the stream seemed to disappear but we could hear it now and then under the moss and tree roots. The spruces and balsam grew more dense and scrubby. We heard in the distance what no one in that first party heard, the voices of many other climbers on the trails and on the top. At last we broke through the scrub balsam onto open rocks and saw the bare granite peak ahead of us. From then on we went up over the rocks with the rest of the climbers.

It is thrilling to be here on top of Mt. Marcy today but I don't believe we can be half so thrilled as were those early adventurers who were here one hundred years ago.[6]

The Marcy Centennial crowd on August 5, 1937. More than 240 people gathered at the summit, including Orra Phelps, M.D., who climbed along the route taken by geologist Ebenezer Emmons during the first recorded ascent of Marcy in 1837. Orra delivered a radio broadcast from the summit over Schenectady radio station WGY.

On a vertical rock wall just below Marcy's summit is a bronze plaque, commemorating the first recorded ascent by Emmons and the Centennial date. It includes the known members of the first ascending party and reads, in part:

1837 - Marcy - 1937
Also known by the Indian Name
Tahawus
Meaning "Cloud Splitter"

To express what climbing these mountains meant to her, Orra Phelps wrote the following verses in the spring of 1937 and chose the title "Tahawus" for her song. It has since become the Albany ADK Chapter's and the Adirondack Forty-Sixers' song, sung to the music of "Austria," making another lasting contribution to both groups. It was published in the same *High Spots* edition as the centennial celebration, December 1937.[7]

TAHAWUS

Great Tahawus, we salute thee,
Mighty Cleaver of the skies.
Of the summits of the forests
Thine the crown that towers most high.
Suns of summer, snows of winter
Make thy grandeur more sublime,
We come humbly seeking blessings
That thou givest all who climb.

On Tahawus' slopes we tarry
Build our evening campfires bright.
Comrades of the trail together
Here find shelter for the night.
Wind for music, stars for wonder,
Mystic dawn, then glorious day.
Great Tahawus, strength thou givest,
For life's ever upward way.

by Orra A. Phelps, M.D.

At about that time, Orra also sandwiched in two more segments of the Northville-Placid Trail. Of her fourth trail segment, she reported:

> The 12.5-mile part from Rt. 28 to Shattuck Clearing was also done in two parts. In 1936 or 1937 I hiked from Rt. 28 north to Kempshall Mt. In 1974 I hiked the other end of that trail south from Plumbleys' on Long Lake to the Kempshall Mt. trail [again because the official NP Trail was rerouted].

These extraordinary jaunts in 1937 seemed to be warm-ups to the enterprising hikes Orra would tackle in the next few years. Leading a few other hardy travelers, Orra ventured ". . . way the Hell and gone"[8] back into the wilderness more than twenty miles from civilization to see the Adirondack hermit, Noah John Rondeau, at his Cold River hermitage.

Cold River Country, the Hermit, and the 1941 Trail Guide

PART I
ORRA VISITS THE HERMIT

As described earlier, Orra and her mother enjoyed a five-week botanizing "vacation" during the summer of 1928, traveling over one hundred miles, much along the newly cut Northville-Placid Trail. While on the trail, Mrs. Phelps noted seeing ". . . a nine-pole teepee frame with a stone fireplace in the center, a balsam bed for one and a cache of food nearby."

Ten more years would pass before Orra would meet Noah John Rondeau. Rondeau, who took to the woods at thirty-three in 1916, became an Adirondack legend. In his book, *Noah John Rondeau, Adirondack Hermit*, Maitland C. DeSormo referred to Rondeau as "Hizzoner, the Mayor of Cold River, population one."[1]

Alone—except for rare encounters with hunters—Rondeau fished, trapped, and hunted and grew a few vegetables, sweet peas, and gladioli in the rocky soil above the river. Only rarely did he make the trip of twenty-two miles to Coreys, New York for staples.

Rondeau was a poet, musician, in-comparable woods-

Noah John Rondeau's home at Cold River, with a cabin and log teepees.

(Left to right) Orra Phelps, Noah John Rondeau, John Fox, and Mr. Sterno at Noah's Cold River Camp in 1938. By that time, Rondeau had lived alone in the Adirondacks with few visitors for more than 20 years.

man, and voluminous correspondent. He was also a master at caching tinned food and pans in hollow logs and caves around his "village" and along his trapping routes. Twenty-plus-foot logs, notched by Noah's ax into firewood lengths, made up his teepees. Standing well above drifted snow, the poles could readily be whacked apart to stoke his stove.

By charring the middle of larger logs in an open fire, Noah prepared firewood-sized chunks for his woodpile. Both the partly charred chunks and the ax-cut sections fit neatly into his fifty-gallon oil drum stove.

Noah shares a laugh with visitors.

Orra recalled that although Rondeau was short, he had dug down the dirt floor of his teepees about a foot so he and his guests could easily stand up inside. Around Noah's hearth, the group shared stories. Orra told the tale of how a friend, toting an eighty-pound pack, was crawling through the "hole" on the Avalanche Pass Trail, when he realized a bear was rustling along toward him from the other side. For several moments neither budged. The bear snorted and pawed nervously.

Noah in front of his shack.

The hiker backed out of the way and waited until the bear lumbered past. Only then was it safe to proceed.[2]

Orra approached Noah's outpost in 1938 from along the Averyville-Duck Hole segment of the Northville-Placid Trail, Orra's fifth piece of the trail. She and Mrs. Phelps had hiked northward to Duck Hole from Shattuck Clearing in 1928, but had turned off the trail toward Indian Pass and Heart Lake then. She recorded her first visit to Rondeau[3] as follows:

> In 1938 I agreed to lead an Adirondack Mountain Club backpacking trip. The plan was to be out a week, based at Rondeau's and climb the Sewards. Three men and two women [Bob Street, Alice Waterhouse, Merrill Winne, Oxerman and Orra] started at

Orra and Noah outside his lean-to.

Averyville and hiked down the N-P trail. We spent the

Enroute to Couchsachraga in 1938. Noah John Rondeau led their party.

first night at Moose Pond lean-to. Continuing the next day we passed a CCC encampment with a large number of (12-man) pyramidal tents near Cold River lean-to and

arrived at the Big Dam. Rondeau made us welcome; more than that, he offered to guide us on trips!

Next day Rondeau led us, with packs, up into Oluska Pass where he selected a campsite and made camp. The men had an umbrella tent. Alice and I had my homemade two women tent. We pitched it in a spot I chose. When done, Rondeau said, "If you'd gone three feet further, you'd have been on top of one of my traps!" He went back of the tent and pulled up a trap.

Orra peaks out from the two-person tent she shared with Alice Waterhouse.

We started early next morning for the top of Seward where we found Howard Nash's copper emblem. We went on to Donaldson. There we had to wait a spell for mists to clear so we could get our direction for Emmons, then we "crawled" to that summit. On the descent from Emmons, Rondeau knew how to avoid the cliffs. The mists gathered into rain. Next morning when we planned to climb Seymour, which yesterday had looked very near, we could not even see it. So we broke camp in the rain and traipsed back to

Noah and Orra on the trail.

Rondeau's home on Cold River. He made us welcome again, Alice and I in "Town Hall," the men in the other shack. We used his fireplace in the log teepee.

According to our schedule we were to start for home the next morning. The day dawned frosty but bright and clear, a perfect day for climbing. Noah John urged us to stay, bribing us with the promise of a trip up Couchsachraga. We considered. Would our food supply last another day? We were out of coffee but had enough else. "Need coffee?" asked Rondeau. "Wait five minutes and I'll get you some." And with that he disappeared into the woods. He was back in "five minutes" and handed

me a vacuum sealed pound tin of Beechnut coffee, saying, "All the better for being all winter in a cedar log!" It was agreed, we'd climb "Couchie."

First we must cross Cold River, either by jumping the gap in the old dam,

Crossing Cold River in Noah's leaky canoe.

or be ferried one at a time in the hermit's leaky canoe. One man tried to jump and his near miss quickly persuaded the rest of us to risk the leaky canoe.

I do not know whether Rondeau's route was similar to the present recommended route. He led; we followed. I remember one place where head high balsam hid old blow down and Rondeau, the shortest in the party, was practically out of sight. I remember also his steering us to one side of an insurmountable sloping ledge somewhere near the top. We were "up" by noon. The men climbed trees to get a view to the southwest, down the Cold River valley. "Couchie" is not a favorite mountain for its views.

Marcy Dam.

Since we were now a day late by schedule, as soon as we reached the dam and ferried across, we packed and started up the trail. We reached the CCC encampment about supper time, now nearly deserted as the men had gone out for the weekend. We were invited to make use of an empty tent and had the luxury of a little wood stove for cooking and very welcome warmth.

The homeward route next day was via Duck Hole, Preston Ponds, and Lake Henderson. Here Alice and 2 men walked on to the gate at Tahawus Club where their car

Alice Waterhouse pauses with Noah John Rondeau.

awaited. I, in the company of one, took the Calamity Brook Trail to Flowed Lands, thence to Lake Colden, Avalanche Pass, and Marcy Dam, arriving for a late supper at camp[4] there. The day's trip, with

L. Morgan Porter presents Orra a copy of the new guide book on June 1, 1957. Years earlier, Orra mentioned Morgan's wheel in her memoirs of Noah John Rondeau.

pack, 19.30 miles by Morgan's wheel.[5]

Forty years later, Orra said her ascent of several peaks with Rondeau had inspired her to complete all but four of the forty-six peaks over 4,000 feet by 1939. However, World War II interrupted her early completion of all forty-six.

Deep in her cartons of old letters, Orra saved three from Noah John, written in his elegant flowing script. One letter, written on January 7, 1939, recalled her visit to his "Wigwam" on August 29, 1938.

> Dear Dr. Phelps,
> This is the Mayor of The Wigwam! How Da Do? Oh! It was August 29th. I was dressed in my leather; It was nearly sun down. And Dear Miss Phelps came along to The WigWam. I heard the tread of her rubbers; The rustle of Her Blue Denim. I ran to the WigWam Door, Threw open the Shuter [sic] and tumbled over the Rocking Chair on the Floor.
> She drove Her ReinDeer and called them by name. On Table Cloth, On Supper, On Dish Water, On Bon Fire, On to Bed, On Fluffy feathers,

On Ye Packs, On! On Donaldson, On Emmons, On Ye Trails, On Little Balsam, On Couchsachraga.

Well, Dear One, I'm sure You don't know one thing; about how Sweet You was among the Cotton [grass] and Sun Dew Flowers. Your style captured both of my Eyes.

And your Brown Bread struck me in the Mouth and unresistably got me in the Stomach.

Well last Hunting Season I got a Deer and a Bear.

Dec. 21st I left the WigWam at daybrake [sic] and came to Bartlett Carry Club.

I had wonderful Christmas. Christmas Eve we had a Splendid Tree. And Christmas Day I helped my Friends, eating a twenty pound Turkey. I got a load of Good Useful Gifts from my many Good Friends.

I got the combination package that Miss Waterhouse sent from Adirondack Mountain Club members.

I'm glad to Thank You here. And I got The Special Package of Sweets that you sent from Fort Plain.

I Thank You Miss Phelps for the Gifts and for Your Benevolent Lovable Spirit.

Needless to say, You don't need any round about excuse to come to my WigWam next Season.

You've got to climb Mount Seymour and further The Mayor knows you are Lovable and He wants to see You.

I got a splendid letter from Mrs. Hudowalski and one from Merrill Winne. Again I Thank You Dear One. Most of all for your wonderful ways and accomplishments and serene Spirit, from which I enjoy so many Happy Memories of recollection of your visit in the Cold River Valley.

And here are my Best Wishes for You for the New Year; To make 1939 The Most Satisfactory time in all Your Life.

Most Sincerely, N.J.Rondeau.[6,7]

Jan. 7th. 1939.

Corey N.Y.

Dear Dr. Phelps

This is The Mayor of

The Wig Wam! How Da Do?

Oh! It was Aug. 29th.

I was dressed in my Leather;

It was nearly sun down.

And Dear Miss. Phelps

Came along to The Wig Wam.

6.

Again I thank You Dear One

Most of all for Your wonderful

ways and accomplishments

and Serene Spirit, from

which I enjoy so many

Happy Memories of recollection

of your visit in the Cold-

River Valley.

And here are my Best

Wishes for You for the New Year;

To make 1939. The most

Satisfactory time in all

Your Life

Most Sincerely

N. J. Rondeau

Copies of the first and last pages of Noah John Rondeau's January 1939 letter to Orra Phelps (see complete text on previous pages) in which he recounts meeting her a year earlier. The letter's boyish charm, graceful, flowing penmanship, and poetic language appeared in sharp contrast to its author's rugged lifestyle.

PART II
1941 GUIDE MATERIAL ACCUMULATES

As official ADK map marker, Orra received many requests for custom "marked maps." She hand-inked the hiker's best route, adding trail corrections and other bits of information. In return, these hikers furnished Orra with updated trail information.

The following letter from Herbert Kates, a New York illustrator who, together with his brother, Jerome, sketched and kept journals of their climbs in the Adirondacks, is an example of how Orra shared and gained information used for the Adirondack Trail Guides.[8]

> Dear Dr. Phelps,
>   Although it seems a bit selfish, we, too, have kept the Moss Pond trip to ourselves, for sometime we might want to repeat it and it would be a shock to find an open camp and a garbage pile at the edge of the Pond. One of our objectives this year is to climb Macomb. In the May 1938 issue of the Bulletin the map of Marcy region shows a trail leading from Elk Lake-Dix trail to the summit of Macomb. As it is not on the Marcy Quadrangle you sent us, we're wondering if it still exists. Do you know anything about it?
>   We expect to be in the mountains towards the end of August and we're hoping to meet you again.
>   Sincerely, Herbert S. Kates[9]

Orra knew the trails as well as the skyline profiles of the peaks. In one of Mrs. Phelps's letters she mentioned Orra's sketching the mountain skyline to memorize the many views and peaks. A young friend's letter also gives testimony to Orra's familiarity with the mountains:

> I will give you an A+ on the picture you said was Four Corners from Skylight. I thought it was a rather good shot from an angle that isn't too frequent and wondered how good your old memory was — and found it was very much better than mine.
>   Bill[10]

Mrs. Phelps learned of developments through her own network of friends and kept Orra updated about changes such as at the Heart Lake area where a two-and-one-half mile ski trail was opened, cut by the Conservation Department on Wright Mountain, across the side of Whale's Tail down to Adirondak Loj. Superintendent of State Forests Director William G. Howard summarized their policy:

> Ski trails of the so-called wilderness or cross-country type should have a definite place in our Forest Preserve development. On the other hand, trails developed especially for downhill racing, slalom hills, or open slopes have no place in the Forest Preserve, for such facilities are not consistent with maintaining its wilderness character.[11]

For years, Loj caretaker Orville Cobane and Hal Burton taught skiing there and Alice Waterhouse maintained the ski trails. Although Orra did not ski, she went snowshoeing and bushwhacking across these trails many times.

In the fall of 1939, Orra received information from Al West about the Marcy Dam washout.

> Dear Orra,
>   Bob Byrne and Lawrence West took a run up to Marcy Dam before winter set in and the southeast end of the dam went out, and the pool below the dam is filled with the rocks that went to make up the dam. What a mess!
>
> Al[12]

The next summer, Orra wrote her mother more about Marcy Dam, "The work on the dam is expected to take two years. At present they are blasting rocks and snaking huge hemlock logs around. The big boulder below the washing pool is no more — blown to bits. Orra"[13]

By late June 1939, Orra could again concentrate on trail-checking for the 1941 trail guide. She still ran a very close personal budget, but gave the trail guide work high priority, often spending her own money. A few people helped Orra with these tasks. One was her now-recovered TB patient, Tom, who sometimes drove while she checked trails for the guide and reconditioned the mileage wheel she used to check the trails' distances. She wrote home:

> This trip is to be more domestic and less arduous camping than usual. The tent is a small one borrowed from the St. Johnsville Boy Scouts . . . cots, with mattresses and even the coffee dripolator. Marianna is my only assistant. We have all my old maps in the car — and a new sheet of almost every one in this part of the mountains. We also have all the trail data, guidebooks, and colored inks for marking maps.
>
> We left Ft. Plain yesterday at 1:20 PM and went to St. Johnsville to collect my cyclometer wheel. Got to (Sharp's Bridge) campsite at 6:45. Right back of tent are beds of Moneses, the one-flowered pyrola, and they are lovely little white stars.[14]

Orra's quest for Adirondack information also included exploring a new slide on Wright overlooking Marcy Dam; one Al West had spotted from near Indian Falls. She gives an account in her July 16, 1939 letter to her mother:

> Morning dawned rather gray with mist swirling around the peaks. We [Al, Marianna Snell and OAP] went to Avalanche Camps and then worked our way back down stream on the far side of the brook till we reached a tributary. As expected we found an old lumber road which made going simpler. We climbed and the road led us first to one side and then to the other. We saw one big green-white orchid plant, several of the spiky white ones, and at higher levels, lots of *Linnaea* still blooming.
>
> Well, the first sign of the slide was just a huge new channel of the brook, full of debris of trees and branches. The channel itself was just a wide stony ditch. The bottom of it was mostly hard pan with all sorts of stone in it. We had lots of fun picking out the . . . "foreign" stones . . . those transported thither: Potsdam sandstone, quartz, and pink granite. Al found a large chunk of magnetite iron.
>
> There may have been 1/8 mile of this ditch before we came to the slide. The foot of this was a pile of trees swept off the clear slope above. Some were nearly bur-

ied. I stepped on a trunk of one a foot in diameter that showed only in one place — rest was entirely buried in more branches and soil.

The bare slide was about 200 feet across the base and maybe half that at the top. It was about 400 feet long. It was not as steep as it looked and the rough rock permitted our walking on it almost anywhere. We decided to climb it, which didn't take long.

At the top we had to bushwhack . . . a little awful scrub balsam and then we were on top of Wright. The views all the way up the slide had been grand. We started off Wright down the ski trail, then bushwhacked across the Whale's Tail notch ski trail and followed that to Marcy Dam.

In 1982, Orra wrote Landon Rockwell:

One of the special things I remember about the (1939) trip was the ancient geology revealed in the "cut," now probably overgrown. I have a photo of a huge boulder that was moved onto the old lumber road. The cross logs from which the road was made show in the picture. I am backed up to the boulder, [which] is about a foot higher than my head.[15]

In October 1939, she presented her accumulated trail information at the ADK Governors' meeting at Heart Lake. Of the meeting she wrote:

Meeting — 14 governors present. Business was straight forward — no fights, no controversial issues. Sunday, I was intent on a new trail, if not a new peak so I chose Porter from Keene Valley-Baxter House route up and a different way down. Mr. and Mrs. Knauth and Bob St. Louis (Conserv. Dept. man) joined me. Views were entrancing — blue sky, clouds, a little autumn color in the valley, and snow on the tops of the high mountains.[16]

Orra also shared trail information with the Utica Tramp and Trail Club. A. J. Renssing wrote of their mutual interests:

Dear Dr. Phelps,

Your letter of Oct. 30, 1939 gives me a chance to get in touch with you . . .The last time any of our local club saw you was on top of Mt. Marcy at the Centennial climb and then they were in such awe of you that they did not make themselves known. However, I hope I have the pleasure of meeting you at the round table discussion of maps covering the Northville-Placid trail as you suggested in your letter.

Very truly yours, A. J. Renssing[17]

In her January 15, 1940 letter, Orra described the Utica meeting: "The people were a jolly congenial crowd — 'real' people — not affected. I was introduced to the crowd and made a short speech about the new guidebook in the making. After dinner there were cards and dancing — but for me there was a series of interviews — and map studies. I learned a good deal about new regions."

PART III
1941 ADK GUIDE BOOK TAKES SHAPE

After the January 1940 ADK Annual Meeting in New York City, Orra's guidebook work increased. She hoped for a June publication, but on March 7, 1940 she wrote to her mother:

The Guide book work creeps ahead. I am now receiving word from all the Governors with regard to changes in the format. Fortunately, all agree with most suggestions that have come in. I have a man working on the map for the Northville-Placid Trail and I'm studying how to divide the Marcy sheet up into small sections for maps to accompany the text. Have had one photographic enlargement made — on which I expect to put trails, then have the whole thing rephotographed.

Either because of continuous close map work or simply having reached the age of 44, Orra needed eyeglasses. In early April 1940, she wrote her mother:

"Have just been fitted to glasses! Yes, the kind one has to use for reading. I can read without them of course, but if I don't have them [now], I'll have to wear them all the time later."

There never seems to be enough time for busy people to do all that seems important. In addition to her school physician's job, she worked summers as a physician/leader at a scout camp, and raced to the mountains to check trails every chance she had. Her June 1940 trip to Marcy with the scouts served the dual purposes of trail checking and scouting. When planning this trip, Orra wrote home that everyone was eager to go, but that she was concerned that some scouts might have severe reactions to bug bites. They planned to take mosquito netting and every kind of skin medicine Dr. Phelps could find.

Viewing the rare plants atop Marcy again prompted Orra to think long range about educating people about their rarity. In 1940, taking a step toward protecting New York State's rare plants, she wrote her mother:

This photo of Orra at her desk appeared in "Trail Expert," an article in *Upstate Monthly*. She maintained a staggering number of personal and professional correspondences along with her duties as a doctor and her work writing and editing trail guides.

I would like a list of what you consider the one hundred rarest plants in New York State. Of course there are some things that are rare when considering the state as a whole, but plentiful in their own location, like the lotus. And of course no such list can be exact and accurate; it doesn't have to be for my plan.[18]

In order to document, photograph, and educate people about rare plants, Orra needed such a list. Her mother returned a list of one hundred sixty plants that she considered rare in New York. Mrs. Phelps lamented that many were too far away or too inconspicuous to photograph, but over the years Orra pursued them, usually traveling with a "photos to get" list.[19] As she developed slide shows of rare plants, she gained first-hand information of habitat and growth.

Over the years, Orra became one of the state's best field botanists on rare plants. She continued working to educate people about rare plants in New York State and was an advocate for their protection the rest of her life.

On July 5, 1940, Orra lamented to Mrs. Phelps:

> If ever I wished I could be in two places at once, it is now. . . . The revision of the old guide book is just about done — it's only the new section that is unfinished. Perhaps we'll let it go to print without all of the Eastern Section completed.

On September 22, 1940, she wrote: "The index is about half typed. This is no small job because there are seven pages, double spaced for half of it." By November 28, 1940, final corrections were still being added. Orra voiced her strain:

> Mr. Shorey sent me about twenty corrections—after I thought it was okay. Some of his items are worthwhile—things I had not been informed of; others were (mere semantics).

In addition to her medical practice, scouts, and civic work, Orra kept up with guidebook correspondence, checked proofs, and sorted maps and other material stacked on every chair and on the floor of her apartment. She had such a store of Adirondack trail and woods information that the writer of an article in the Upstate Monthly titled "Trail Expert," advised any general defending the Adirondacks against foreign invasion to commandeer her whole apartment.[20] Finally, the new guide book went to print. Before the January 1941 annual ADK meeting in New York City, Orra wrote:

I'm still worried about a costume for the NY Dinner.
Wish I could wear overalls and Bean boots. I do expect to
go, because I believe the Guide Book will be out. Go and
get my "brief glory"![21]

Although Orra gave an extraordinary amount of time to research-
ing and writing the 1941 trail guide, she never forgot her needy parents. She recognized Mamma's need to have respite from her husband's
outbursts, but still to take a responsible course of action. In letters,
Orra advised her mother to calm herself by "taking some part of every day up in your own room, doing things you like to do — reading,
cards, or crossword puzzles."

Fate struck while the Phelpses were preparing for their fiftieth
wedding anniversary celebration in the spring of 1941; Charles Phelps
died fighting a grass and brush fire on their farm. At age seventy-nine
he was finally at peace. The ghosts that haunted him in tortured dreams,
the fears of his disabled son's rage, the misunderstandings with his
wife, and all the unfulfilled goals now lay at rest.

The Phelps family gathers at Christmas in 1939. (Adults in back, left ro right)
Lawrence, Orra, Francis, Phoebe, Mr. Phelps, Mrs. Phelps, Charles, Bessie,
Leon, Gusta (children in front) Phoebe, Dorrie, Mary Kay.

Charles S. Phelps

Saratoga Springs, Apr. 12, 1941 - Charles S. Phelps, 79, a Justice of the Peace in the Town of Wilton for the last 12 years and former professor of Agriculture at Conn. State College, died yesterday fighting a blaze which threatened his farm.

Phelps's death was due to a heart attack, induced by suffocation. The body was found by a crew of the State Conservation Dept. forest fire fighters who were rushed to the scene. George McDonnell, forest ranger, recovered the body, driving his fire truck through the blaze to reach it.

Phelps had obtained a permit to burn brush on the farm. The fire apparently got out of control and, shortly after 1 PM forest rangers stationed on a nearby mountain sighted the blaze and rushed a crew of men to the scene. The blaze burned over 8 acres.

Phelps was a graduate of Mass. State College. He taught agriculture at CT. State College from 1888 to 1903 and later served as farm bureau agent in St. Lawrence and Saratoga counties. At the time of his death he was writing a book on the history of agriculture. He is survived by his wife and seven children.[22] [Courtesy of *The Saratogian.*]

Many people such as the scouts, ADK friends, teachers, students, and neighbors wrote to console Orra to ease the pain of her loss. Aunt Bessie Gammons wrote:

> Purposely waited until you should be back in Ft. Plain before writing so to express myself more freely.
>
> Am sure you can have no regrets, for you have appreciated your father and have been most kind to him. I wonder whether his going will make your load less or greater. I cannot see how either your mother or Phoebe can go and leave the other alone on the farm. It seems to me that poor Phoebe [then unmarried and living at home] has quite a responsibility.
>
> You have a big load, with Francis and the home, and I appreciate how many sacrifices you have to make. You are a wonderful woman and I know your father appreciated you.

For Orra, it was a big loss and yet a relief. She could not change her father's world; only temporarily relieve its stress. After his death, she went to the mountains for solace and to regain a feeling of oneness with herself.

Although there are no letters or records of Mrs. Phelps's reaction to her husband's death, it must have been a sad end to a long shared life but at the same time a release from her concerns for him. It marked the beginning of Mrs. Phelps's nine years as an independent woman, marriage in 1942 for sister Phoebe, and a significant career change for Orra.

Lt. Commander Orra A. Phelps, M.D., United States Naval Reserves

The onset of World War II brought a new focus to Orra's life. She joined the local Defense Council in February 1941, taught Red Cross First Aid classes, packed Bundles for Britain, and helped organize and direct First Aid posts, practice drills, and black-out strategies. She even drove in the dark with no headlights during blackouts.[1]

War restrictions meant the rationing of gas, tires, and sugar. The rationing of milled cotton also resulted in a shortage of Girl Scout uniforms. Orra curtailed her visits to Francis, to Wilton, and to the mountains because, as she wrote on May 31, 1942, "Beside the rationing and one's conscience or patriotism — the gas stations are all out of gas, [now at the] end of the month." Many of Orra's young hiking friends such as John Fox, Jim Louden, and Al West had enlisted, so the ascent of the four High Peaks she hadn't yet climbed would have to wait until after the war.

Robert Owens, Orra's friend, summed up the ADK membership sentiment:

> Guess we're all up to our necks in the emergency and it is becoming increasingly difficult to maintain the activities and program of . . . the ADK. I am sure it will survive and have a glorious future, but these are tough times . . . Many thanks for your untiring and unselfish service for the club,
>
> Yrs, Bob O.[2]

As World War II escalated, straining the nation's medical resources, Dr. Phelps offered her services. Years later she candidly confided to a friend that she felt lucky to be able to leave a job without wider horizons at a time when doing so was considered patriotic. In May 1943, Orra submitted her application to the Navy. Some of the Navy's requirements included appropriate medical training, learning to construct model airplanes, having no dependents under eighteen, and passing a physical exam. Because she was over thirty-six and was not a medical specialist, she accepted the appointment of Lt. W-V (S) (MC) US Naval Reserves in Arlington, Virginia. She braved the largely male world

Lt. Orra A. Phelps USN MC, MD

of military physicians, feeling a duty to serve her country in time of war as well as seeking increased financial security, new challenges, and further achievement through another form of service.

There was no preparation for war like the military death of a hometown friend. Days before she left, young Marine William Fox, the grandson of her fellow Fort Plain physician, Dr. Walter Fox, died of pneumonia after having been wounded in action. Orra was personally stunned and saddened. She sent flowers but, more importantly, she shouldered some of the grieving grandfather's medical load.

Orra Phelps left the modestly paid life of a country school doctor and her many personal friends to report for duty on January 17, 1944. She joined a medical staff caring for a two-thousand-person torpedo factory near Washington, D.C. Clinical work, meetings about emergency procedures, and blood bank work replaced medical exams for school children's measles and mumps. She missed the close interpersonal relationships she had in Fort Plain but soon began to visit area hospitals to see hometown boys who had been injured.

Lt. Phelps as a member of the U.S. Navy Blood Donors Staff in Washington, D.C.

En route to her service, Orra visited briefly in New York City with brother Lawrence, who wrote his impressions of their new officer to Mamma:

> Think Orra was quite self conscious in the uniform. Lots of people both in and out of uniform looked her over...out of the corners of their eyes. She was busy telling the rest of us the ranks of the various insignia that we saw.
> A red-cap stopped her stripes uniform and sneaked us down a back way to the train. He was obviously disappointed at the quarter tip. I judge that Orra will have to jack up her snobbishness to fit with her rank. I sense that the Army and Navy have very definite social strata. Orra inclines to cut through such strata.[3]

From Alexandria, Virginia, Orra described her headquarters and personal housing:

> The Torpedo Station is a huge great block of a brick building and several other lesser but still large buildings

right on the banks of the Potomac River. There is a high wire fence all around and Marine guards. After I had saluted the guards, I was admitted and went to 2nd floor Personnel Office. . . . I met Warrant Officer (clerk of records) Ericson and Captain Simmons. . . . There are two other doctors, 50 WAVES and nearly 2,000 employed civilian women. I turned over the proper papers and was driven to . . . where I have a room at 506 North View Terrace, with a Mr. and Mrs. Arthur King.

The house is in a very nice suburban location, fairly new and the accommodations, bath and laundry privileges, seem unusual in this crowded place. My window is west and looks out on a slope that has some trees and a hedge and birds have been hopping around all afternoon. Mrs. McKay says the mockingbirds are thick here.

Late this afternoon, I walked back downtown and found a place to eat dinner — no meals here, but there is a cafeteria at the station and so probably I'll get most of my meals there. As I was walking a few blocks from here I was thrilled to hear the characteristic call of the white-throat! Hope I see one next time.

Planes have been zooming around all the time. I have seen as many as eight at once. I am going to live all day at the Station, reporting at 0800 and staying till 1730 but this should permit a half hour off because its supposed to be only a nine hour day.[4]

Within a few days, Orra had adjusted and wrote of feeling relaxed, even at work. The senior physician, Dr. McSweeney, who was at times loud, stern, and given to swearing, had been grand to her, saying, "You'll go far in the Navy" and "You have very interesting hands."

Orra's close friend, Alton West, served in the South Pacific.   *1942 photo*

Orra liked that he wanted to go trout fishing with her in upstate New York after the war.[5]

During her personal time, Orra visited the sick and the wounded service men. On February 29, 1944 she wrote to Mrs. Phelps:

> I saw a Marine from Guadalcanal with a malarial chill yesterday. His teeth chattered till he could hardly hold the thermometer. But a dose of Quinine staved off the worst effects — more chill than high fever.

Then came a letter in March 1944 from her mother, who was "knocked in a heap" by getting Al West's new address — South Pacific - APO #31-B Care of PM San Francisco.

> Of all places in the world, the South Seas are the most terrible seems to me. Of course he may not have to be in the front line — surely hope not. Some have gone and come out all right but it is a fearsome place.

People at Orra's new home were also anxious. There was a constant fear that Washington would be bombed, but the first explosion was of a different sort.

> A little before midnight there was a big explosion — not in the plant, but in a building about a block away. The Marine guards dashed out with the steel helmets on — thinking they were being bombed. When we arrived this morning we learned that a boiler blew up in a four story brick warehouse (next door), used by the Army to store microfilm records. It blew the end out of the building exposing three floors and the outer metal sheath of the boiler sailed right up and came down on our roof. I went up and saw it. It must have gone 1,000'. No one was hurt. All quiet now but the gaping wall and pile of rubble, just like the result of bombing.[6]

Orra took advantage of the many professional opportunities for women in the service. She was invited to the Women's Medical Association meeting and wrote:

The U.S. Navy Staff in Washington, D.C.

It was pleasant to meet the others. There were three other
Navy Women MDs there [for] a total of seven in the
Washington area. The subject of the meeting was typhus
fever and the . . .discussion was good because there were
some doctors who had some experience with typhus.[7]

Her May 18, 1944 letter home shows how Navy life introduced
Orra to different types of social gatherings:

Well, believe it or not I have seen and heard Mrs. Eleanor
Roosevelt! at the anniversary celebration of the Salva-
tion Army USO. The First Lady was the principal speaker
. . . I was rather glad I've had a first hand look at her. A
Navy band furnished the music — there were some so-
los, tenor and contralto. . . . It was a powerful hot night
and I wore the white uniform for the first.

Orra wrote of having dinner with six other Navy women doctors:

> Table conversation was mostly shop . . . but I think it should be. We have so few chances to exchange notes; men doctors get much more opportunity that way. One of the women said she hadn't heard so much medicine discussed since she finished internship. After dinner, I went to the Navy concert and was educated on the kind of music composed by Dmitri Shostakovich.[8]

Two days after the Allied invasion of Normandy on June 6, 1944, Orra wrote her mother:

> The big invasion is on. I was wakened at 5:00 a.m. by news boys, then Mrs. McKay's radio — but I could lie in bed and listen. One or two fellows who were here may be in it. Also the doctor I relieved. Betty King's husband is on the Tuscaloosa, one of the battleships reported to be in the engagements. Glad Al is in N.G. [New Guinea].[9]

Then came another wave of wounded men. Orra reported:

> Just as I left the hospital . . . a group of wounded sailors from the Normandy front were arriving. The walking cases came in station wagons, but there were about 10 ambulances . . . making rapid round trips from the hospital to the train. Bet they were glad to get here! Wish I could have made the acquaintance of one or two.[10]

Orra often visited the wounded at Walter Reed Hospital, feeling she could be of help in this way. She took those in wheelchairs outdoors; those who were bedridden she visited, counseled, and cheered, helping them to bear the horrors of war. On her evening visits she sometimes saw "ranks and ranks of men in wheelchairs" at the movies. Orra tried to find as many home-town boys as she could and bought them treats, helped visiting relatives get around Washington, and did errands. She wrote:

Went to Walter Reed and Matt may be home in a week or ten days on a thirty-day furlough. This will be before he gets his leg but he can go on crutches. Morgan has both his legs fitted but can't practice walking yet because he still has infection in one stump. But I saw him stand on them. He is 6 ft. 1 inch tall.

In September 1944, Orra visited the U.S. Naval Torpedo Testing Range at Piney Point, Md. and the dispensary there. She explained to Mrs. Phelps:

On Sunday I was invited to go to Piney Point with Captain Simons and his family. Piney Point, where our torpedoes are tested, is about 80 miles down the Potomac River from here, near where the Potomac enters the ocean (or Bay). Every torpedo has to be tested, but without the explosive head. The motor mechanism that drives it and the intricate machinery that steers and balances it is what has to be tested.

Went through dispensary — saw there two of the boys . . . some burn cases from an accidental explosion on the firing range. Then dinner . . . at Bachelors — Officers Quarters. . . . There was very nice service, white table cloth with Navy emblems woven in damask, heavy silver, white china with a plain blue band and an anchor. All the plates were set so the anchor was at the top. . . We had roast beef..

Just outside was a persimmon tree, loaded with fruit. You have doubtless heard how puckery wild persimmons are, but Mrs. Simons looked around on the ground where many had fallen till she found one just right. She sampled it very cautiously, then proceeded to eat the whole thing and said it was delicious. I was surprised. But I soon learned how to pick out a ripe fruit and sampled a couple. They were very sweet and tasty.

After dinner we drove to the dock where a 40-foot "crash boat" awaited us. It proved to be a specially built speed boat for rescuing crews of crashed planes. . . . We rode out to the barges where the torpedoes are fired, then went around the small wire net target which not only registers a hit but also times it . . . . We did not see any torpedoes fired — to my regret. I hope I may yet.

Besides the Testing Range buildings, there is little else at Piney Point — just salt marsh, shore plants, and scrub pines. No village, but a few scattered saloons, a dance hall or two, a tiny store, and a Coast Guard Station. There is no industry but fishing which includes fishing for the "tin fish." Weather perfect.

Orra was never far from the sadness of war. On July 22, 1945, she wrote home that a Navy chaplain had made a personal call to her home, notifying her landlords, the Kings, that Mr. King's brother was lost when a Japanese prison ship was torpedoed. The grave news kept coming:

Also Mrs. McKay has had a letter from the co-pilot of the plane in which her "missing" nephew was the pilot. He told her that he was either killed or unconscious from shock before the plane crashed. It was a grand letter to have though, as it told how well liked he had been by all of the crew of 10. Some of the crew known to have made safe jumps, have been imprisoned and have not been found. Others were rescued from a prison camp.

To keep her own spirit up, she invited three colleagues and, using gas ration stamps she had hoarded, took a drive along the Blue Ridge Parkway. It reminded her of New England's Mohawk Trail but with views across the Shenandoah Valley, then the coastal plain. She saw the Appalachian Trail crisscrossing the highway, but none of its lean-tos.

As usual, she gathered a few plants, which she thought to be the fragile bladder fern, a *Houstonia*, and an *Epilobium*, to send to Mamma for identification. Birds she reported seeing were a partridge, scarlet tanager, indigo bunting, and hawks. She heard thrushes and "a surprise, a junco singing his real summer song."[11]

In 1945, Orra was delighted when, by chance, she visited a National Parks Campfire Program when Roger Tory Peterson showed his Kodachromes of birds. She wrote:

Pictures were two reels of fairly common birds, close-ups of nests and feeding young, and a third reel of birds on some of the National Sanctuaries. These included pelicans, roseate spoonbills, swallow-tailed kites, little

The Phelps family in 1944, when Orra was home on leave: (left to right, adults) Francis, Orra, Augusta, Will Lohnes, Phoebe Lohnes, Phoebe Haas, Lawrence, Bessie Haas, Mrs. Phelps; (left to right, children) Rachel, Dorothy, and Mary K. Haas, the author.

egrets, and reddish egrets — including their dance!

One thing I learned was that the black and white warbler nests on the ground. Could it be what your boy found at camp? Sunday because of remarks Mr. Peterson made, we went to Kenilworth Water Gardens. It was not nearly as hot as at home . . . good breeze. . . . Lotus not yet in full bloom, lilies were fine. Birds . . . long- billed marsh wren, Maryland yellow throat, redstart, titmouse, Carolina chickadee, pewee, cardinal, and many commoner birds.[12]

During this time, Orra continued to share her interests with children. She took a colleague's six-year-old daughter to the Department of Commerce building where Navaho Indian articles were for sale. Orra wrote:

She loved the moccasins and the Indian dolls. She knew
what the drums were and even called them tom-toms. I
went there especially to price the pottery, thinking of a
birthday present for Bessie. Prices are not too bad and
some shapes and colors are lovely. I like the pure black.
It has a lovely lustre.[13]

Orra worshiped at the Washington church of her old friend,
Dr. Leo Glenn from Silver Bay, and visited the National Gallery of
Art to enjoy the Mellon collection of Old Masters. She described the
interior of the building as "beautiful, a rotunda with columns of black
breccia and marble — a fountain in the center. There are two lesser
courts with palms and potted flowers."

Orra and her mother continued to share a constant flow of letters. Mamma found out through a third party in July 1945 that Orra
had her hair bobbed and was stepping out with lipstick and all. Fear
must have struck the possessive
Mamma, who wrote:

She said you were changing,
using make up and stepping
out. Don't object — only
please don't step as far as [sis-
ter] Kay has. You are my
main stay and I won't be a
bittersweet vine that clings
till it kills — maybe just a
woodbine. I do miss you —
yet I know it is for your good
that we go our separate
ways.[14]

Orra replied:

First I couldn't think . . .
who said I was stepping out.
Finally came to me, [the girl]
who was working in the Pen-

The author, age ten, at the Haas
farm.

tagon . . . with whom I used to go to dinner now and
then. . . . The stepping out is very innocent — the

lipstick — yes, on occasions — if I don't forget it. No
cause for worry.

The author who, at ten, went to Girl Scout camp for the first
time also missed Orra and wrote:

> Dear Aunt Orra,
>   I'm at the Boy Scouts' Camp Saratoga. We (the Girl
> Scouts) are using it now. The girls can go in swimming
> twice a day. We have delicious food. Since it's Sunday we
> have extra food. For dinner we had corn on the cob, po-
> tatoes, chicken and gravy, dumplings, bread and butter
> and milk. For desert we had ice cream. We all gather at
> night around the campfire and have plays, games, sing
> songs, and talk. We can take hot showers anytime. We go
> to bed at 9 PM and get up at 7 AM. There are 60 girls
> who are divided in three units: 15 in the tent unit, 30 in
> the cabin unit and 15 in the pioneer unit. I'm staying
> until Saturday. Will you please write.
>   Love, Mary K.[15]

Although Orra had left the area, her presence was still felt as
she continued to maintain mentoring relationships with people in
Fort Plain. She wrote to the father of one teenager that her departure must have been hard for their son and she was glad to hear
from him. Her advice to the parents was straightforward and compassionate:

> One thing I should have had the nerve to tell you
> before, that has made a barrier between you two . . . is
> the — do as I say — not — do as I do — method. You
> know I don't drink, but neither am I a temperance fiend.
> I think that it's a problem every individual has to meet
> and settle for himself. But in Junior's case, his tempera-
> ment is such that drink can ruin him very quickly. His
> feelings are very sensitive and the only hope I can see for
> him is to keep him from hurt as much as possible until
> he is big enough to understand his own difficulty.
>   There is another rule for training youth that is usu-
> ally most effective. When punishment in any form has

been necessary during the day — even just a scolding — that before or at bedtime the parent who dealt out the punishment, shall re-establish a loving relationship with the child. Punishment shackles the child's faith in a parent's love, and when it continues week in and week out — it can undermine the child's faith completely until they actually hate their parents. And this is the sort of situation where gifts and good eats do not make up for love. . . .

Then too, share with him some of your own youthful mistakes, and remember what you are expecting in the way of wisdom, understanding, and obedience from a boy not yet sixteen, . . . and before you judge him, judge yourself by the same standard.

I also hope you feel the sincerity behind it and will pardon my boldness. Nothing I have said is to be interpreted as criticism of any of your family.[16]

Orra could write forthrightly to this Fort Plain family, but when it came to the triangular relationship between herself, her Adirondack hiking friend Al West, and her mother, it wasn't as easy. Her mother craved letters from both Orra and Al and thought nothing of writing and sending him packages. She fully expected Al to write to her as often as to Orra. Orra felt that Mamma did not respect the boundaries of Orra's special relationship with Al West, which prompted Orra to criticize Mamma for interfering with her male friendships.

Both worried about his welfare when he served in New Guinea, but Orra enjoyed hearing in June 1944 via her mother of his

. . .wading out to the coral reefs to pick up shells and coral. Also of swimming in fresh water and nearly drowning when he tried to keep himself on top. Didn't dream salt water swimming was so much easier. . . .They went through Panama Canal. . . . Said now it could be told . . . and was wonderful.[17]

But in the fall of 1944, the Phelpses learned that Al West, like so many service men, was hospitalized, although the letters did not explain why. Rather than share Al's complete letters, Mamma related only brief parts to Orra.

With her family and friends hundreds—even thousands—of miles away and on different continents, Orra wrote home in December 1944 that the stars gave her a feeling of unity in a fractured world. She mused, "The stars are brilliant this morning, just before I go to work — same stars here — there, in Europe — and in the Pacific and the same stars for thousands of years!"

Her mother replied, however, enclosing a poem Al had sent her. "The stars are the same for us but not for Al." The poet mused that in the southern skies the familiar Orion, Big Dipper, and Seven Maidens (Pleiades) are gone and how strange it seems to soldiers far from home.

Stoically bearing her fears, frustrations, sadness, and losses, Orra continued her medical work and mentoring. In early 1945, she described an accident at her plant:

> We just had a "lulu" of an accident — forefinger with compound fracture, and lacerations of the arm — grinding wheel pulled finger into moving parts — but consensus is he was trying to do something not in the usual routine . . . [after emergency care] I shipped him to the hospital that takes care of civil service cases.
>
> Yesterday on my half day off I had my hair done and went to the hospital to see the boys. This time I met the mother of the fellow who lives on the north side of Oneida Lake. . . . Her son is a pathetic but very famous case, one where both legs were removed at the hip joint. He has an appliance with two artificial legs and his whole body fits in it. I do not know whether he walks or whether the support rolls — but he is not a bit depressed.
>
> Almost forgot the big day we had Friday — eight visitors, subcommittee on Industrial Medicine from the National Research Council. One or two were interested in our industrial medical problems, but most were more curious about the mechanics of the torpedo.

Orra kept in touch with several young men in the service; one in particular was Carleton Keisler, her former patient. Just before he was shipped to India, he visited Orra. She took him through the torpedo plant, then he and another friend took her to a baseball game. She wrote,

"We all enjoyed it, but Washington lost to St. Louis. During the game, the two boys recalled dozens of games they had played together in Fort Plain."

Carleton was an airplane mechanic specializing in B-25 carburetors who worked with a ground crew to keep the Pacific Fleet flying safely. Orra wrote asking him to describe the things he saw. From India, he wrote long letters of his work, the different customs, and the strangeness of the land. On May 7, 1945, he wrote:

> Dear "Doc,"
> Waited a long time for that last letter. It was elegant but I would enjoy them more often.
> Where was I when I received the news that the President had died? I hadn't thought of it before . . . but think I was in our hanger [sic] changing engines on one of our planes. When we heard the news we thought the fellow was kidding but later it was confirmed on our bulletin board. Only a few had much to say . . . they hoped that Truman would do as good a job. I guess I thought it wouldn't make the war any longer or shorter. . . . I guess we are all just hardened to that sort of thing.
> Perhaps now that the war news is looking brighter we can have that dinner date in 1946, I hope. Thanks again for writing.
> Always, Carleton

In August 1945, he wrote again.

> VJ Day. Just heard the official news that Japan has finally surrendered. We are all very happy here and already are worrying how long it will be before we get back to the states.
> The P. A. system is repeating President Truman's speech. So I guess I jumped VJ Day. Won't be until the surrender papers are signed. I didn't like the news that it would take 12 to 18 months to discharge five million men. Guess I'll miss Christmas in '45 after all.
> Isn't it a funny feeling to know it's over. Still seems like a rumor. Guess I'll just have to wait until I get into civilian clothes again before it will be real. . . .
> Write soon, Carleton K.

Orra wrote of having been moved by the Church sermon on June 24, 1945, which "talked about ordinary men in service who have those qualities that can make a better world . . . courage, sacrifice, and humility."

She went on to advise her mother, who was working as a nature counselor at a church camp:

> . . . to take time to yourself . . . and relax, read what you like, find a quiet corner where you can write your letters. So besides giving something — which you always do well . . . get something for yourself. Professor Chadwick's story about looking for a hole when we see a wall ahead is a good idea, but it might also be well, when up against a wall, to lie down near it and take a nap and wake up with more strength for climbing.
>
> As for being alone — you will doubtless find some interesting new people . . . and some old friends. Do the ADK members know you are there? There's lots to look forward to, and even on your own, you'll be more content than in most other places.

There were still others who missed Orra's mentoring, such as her former Girl Scouts. Among the many who corresponded with her, Elsa Jane Putnam wrote in May 1945 that she would be working as a camp counselor and administrative aide during the summer, using the skills Orra had taught her. She wrote:

> And now because you have always been a sort of guiding light to me, and because of your sound advice and the interest you've shown, I want to tell you of three recent happenings.
>
> On April 20, I was initiated into the national Kappa Delta Pi, an honorary society in education. Then I was elected President of Cortland Chapter of KDP.
>
> Fri. May 18, I was sworn in as President of the College Governing Bd. Here at Cortland State Teachers College we have a student government and needless to say, Presidency is the highest honor one can give. I'm not saying that to boast but more because

I feel so humble to everyone at CSTC for electing me, Elsa Putnam. The thing that hit me the hardest was right after I took my oath of office. The assembly clapped, but Doc I think when I turned to face them from the rostrum, the sound was deafening. I shook like a leaf and had a wild desire to run off the stage. My senior year at Cortland is pledged to serving every student and faculty member of our assembly.

I've told you my reasons for the grand slam — you are to me a symbol of ideals and truths. When I was going to Cortland you wrote me a letter which I will treasure forever (in fact every letter of yours). Everyone should have you as a friend. Please don't think me a braggart — I wanted to tell you these things to show you I had not forgotten you or your philosophy; that I am trying to be a better person — to be a little like you, if I may be so bold.

Doc, I am not trying to be sweet and sentimental nor am I trying to throw the bull, rather I am trying to express something for which I feel very inadequate. . . . In time of happiness or sorrow one wants to turn to her best friends, the people she has the most confidence in, and express her feelings. That is what I've tried to do.

Am still looking forward to that trip to the Adirondacks after the war. Wouldn't it be nice if it could be the summer of 1946 after my graduation? Hope to hear from you.

Love, Put

Another surprise letter came for Orra, one from the other Carleton! She wrote home:

I had a three-page letter from Colonel Coulter, 130th Infantry, somewhere in New Guinea! written June 18, 1945. He went into detail to tell me what a fine regiment he commanded. Said his wife and two children were in Los Angeles with her aunt.

Orra had often wondered where Coulter was in the military and even noted in her diary that she prayed for his safety.

Coulter had lost her address for a time, and wrote that he hoped not to lose her a second time. Records provided by West Point show that Carleton Coulter was injured in action at Finschhafen, New Guinea, by a ricochet as he was showing a young soldier how to place a charge in a bunker. The bullet shattered a nerve in his right shoulder, causing his arm to atrophy, but the real hurt was leaving the regiment he had trained so well on the eve of going into combat.

Orra's final correspondence from Coulter was in January 1950. In shaky handwriting, he explained that he had been on duty in Japan after the victory, as chief administrator of a region the size of Pennsylvania with twelve million people. His wife and children had joined him. After that Orra lost contact with him. His health must have failed, for West Point records show that he died in January 1953 in the Valley Forge Army Hospital at the age of fifty-seven and was buried at Arlington National Cemetery.

Not knowing of his death, when in her eighties, Orra wondered aloud to the author if he were alive, how he might be, and where. She still admired him.

The Veterans Administration staff at Watervliet, N.Y., where Orra served after the war. *1947 photo*

Orra left the U.S. Naval Reserves on August 26, 1946, and "loafed for a month," as she called it. In October 1946, she began work as a senior medical officer for the Veterans Administration in Albany, New York. Because she did not have specialty training, she was assigned to administrative supervision of physicians performing compensation, pension, and insurance examinations. She also performed liaison work between examining physicians and the adjudicative division of the Veterans' Administration as well as outpatient administrative duties.

In 1962, she retired from the Naval Reserves with the rank of Lieutenant Commander and a military pension which she said, "saved my life." She was free to then devote almost full time to her much loved natural history teaching and service.

From 1946 until 1962, she lived at the Phelps farm during the spring, summer, and fall, but took an apartment in Albany each winter. She again made frequent visits to her sisters and nieces and restored her large flower and vegetable gardens. She became active again in Adirondack Mountain Club activities, especially with the Albany chapter, resumed her mountain explorations, and began botany classes with Stanley Smith, Assistant New York State Botanist, at the Albany, New York museum. Smith was one of Orra's most brilliant teachers, an impassioned botanist from Albany who gave over 50,000 plant specimens to the museum. For years Orra studied fungi with him and helped identify and label his collections. Dr. John Haines, New York State Mycologist, recalled:

> Orra left a large collection of fungi to the museum, but several hundred of these were of particular interest because she had begun to specialize in a group of wood-rotting fungi, the *stereums*. These fungi are overlooked by many workers, not only because they are inconspicuous, but they are quite difficult to identify. She had a good start on the group, however, and had made numerous drawings of their microscopic details. . . . It looked like she was actually working on a book.[18]

Typical of hundreds of Orra Phelps's accessions is the following record in the mycology archives at the museum:

Box 6 -Cinn-
    Hymenochaete cinnamomeus
    On bark of old balsam Christmas tree — my barnyard.
    Wilton, NY. October 15, 1961 OAP 780

Dr. Haines enjoyed working with Orra as she did research on fungi and shared her finds. He admired her personal strength, energy level, and devotion to science despite advancing years. With feeling he recalled that to him she seemed to be invulnerable, a rare quality. With a smile, Dr. Haines said:

> Orra's fungi donations arrived in all sorts of containers: old medicine bottles and boxes, envelopes, shoe boxes, cheese boxes, even in a pair of old rubber gloves. Once there was a larger box containing several specimens of fungi plus a family of live mice.

— 19 —

Adirondack Forty-Sixer

Many of Orra's hiking partners were people with whom she shared several interests. Some of Orra's friends in scouting were introduced by her to the joys of hiking the Adirondacks and became Forty-Sixers. Elsa Jane Putnam Turmelle, fondly known as "Put" by Orra, enjoyed Orra's mentorship from her formative scouting years through college and into the beginning of her own professional career.

Elsa Jane Putnam Turmelle, Orra's companion in Girl Scouting and hiking.

Just as Elsa Jane had suggested in her May 1945 letter to Orra, they spent a week hiking in the Adirondacks during 1946. These first few of Elsa Jane's forty-six High Peak climbs marked their celebration of her college graduation and Orra's departure from the military. Elsa Jane described the trip:

> We went to Johns Brook Lodge, then climbed Upper Wolf Jaws, Armstrong, and Gothics; those were my first three. Then we climbed Macomb and East Dix. Hough is the one I missed. Doc and I stopped probably within 100 yards of the top, but it was pouring rain and getting dark. That's why I later finished on Hough.[1]

Orra considered finishing her first forty-six in 1939 when she had only four left to do. However, due to World War II restrictions on gas and tires and then her years in the Navy, Orra did not make her final ascents until 1947. Elsa Jane recalled Orra's last peak:

> Jim Nye, Doc, and I . . . left Grandma Phelps at Marcy Dam and climbed Allen. We . . . picked blueberries on the way back, and then made blueberry muffins at camp.[2]

Allen Mountain, the massive 4,340-foot trailless dome with its twin peaks rising alone southwest of Marcy, Redfield, Cliff, and Skylight is a challenge to any hiker. In her Forty-Sixer record Orra described her ascent.

> Allen in 1947, my last one . . . We went the long way from Panther Gorge to Ausable inlet to Sand Brook and got on the south peak first, facing into the north peak summit. We were cut off in the clouds. From the summit, we bushwhacked back to Marcy Brook, one and one-half hours and then followed up the brook to camp through the mile of blowdown that had swept the side of Skylight.

Orra, Jim Nye, and Gerry Hunt in 1952.

Orra wanted to be a part of every exciting event, especially those that involved the observation of wildlife up close. Such photo opportunities were a high priority with her. Elsa laughed at seeing a bear on the trail when Orra was not with her.

> She was very mad . . . because Jim and I saw a bear and she wasn't with us . . . My mother worried about my

being in the mountains. "What will you do if you see a bear" she'd ask . . . I said, "If I see a bear, I'll just ask him to join me in a game of poker." So when Doc would travel, she'd find a postcard with a bear on it and write, "How about a game of poker?"

Jim and I were climbing Whiteface. The trail we were on was all smashed, trees down, because they were putting in the ski slopes. You can imagine the noise. We came around a bend and here was this bear right in front of us. Jim and I just stopped and looked at him. Then the bear quickly turned off into the woods. I said to Jim, "I forgot to ask if he wanted to play poker!" [3]

Orra became a Forty-Sixer in 1947, qualifying for that unique hiking group whose first members were George and Robert Marshall and their guide, Herb Clark. The Marshalls' record of climbs started in 1918 and ended on June 10, 1925, at about the same time Orra began her first ascents. Revealing how much she valued her own early climbing years, preserved in her copy, #47, of *The Adirondack High Peaks and the Forty-Sixers*, is Orra's hand-written record of the only fifteen Forty-Sixers who made and recorded the first Adirondack High Peak ascents before hers.

The Adirondack Forty-Sixers evolved from The Forty-Sixers of Troy, New York. Their charter meeting was held on May 30, 1948 at the Adirondack Loj. At this meeting, they elected Orra A. Phelps and Edward A. Harmes as directors, Grace Hudowalski as president, Katherine Flickinger as secretary, and Adolph G. Dittmar as treasurer.

This group had climbed all forty-six Adirondack peaks over 4,000 feet, which included twenty trailless peaks, done either with a guide or by skill with a compass and bushwhacking. When Orra started climbing in July 1924, it was considered quite adventurous for women to hike the High Peaks, especially without guides.

Orra Phelps climbed the Adirondack High Peaks for far more than just checking them off to qualify for the elite Forty-Sixers. Orra climbed, preferably on a clear day, venturing into the wilderness to see far-flung views and to find rare plants and birds; in short, to have "peak experiences" of a different sort. Rare alpine flowers of *Diapensia lapponica* and *Arenaria groenlandica*, mountain sandwort, three-toed

William Endicott and Dr. Adolph and Mary Dittmar.   *July 25, 1988 photo*

woodpeckers, boreal chickadees, and stands of old-growth pine and spruce all lured her. The naturalist in her also investigated and recorded the scope of earlier fire destruction, as on Giant and Rocky Peak Ridge, and listed peaks with treed summits: among which were Phelps, Tabletop, Street, and Nye, and those that were bare — Marcy and Haystack. En route to some mountains she found truly special places: remote and pristine Moss Pond, isolated and wild Oluska Pass, and the thundering waterfalls at Hanging Spear Falls.

When "Put" Turmelle remembered being at the top of Haystack with Orra, she spoke with reverence in her voice.

> That was one of the most marvelous times I ever had on a mountain top. With Doc when you got on the top of a mountain, you didn't just sit and look at the view, you walked around to see what kinds of plants were growing there. . . . In one spot we spent three hours, just [walking on rock]around the top of the mountain . . . each side of it, so we could get the different [micro]climates. Oh, it was wonderful.[4]

Dr. George Marshall, one of the original Forty-Sixers, shared Orra's love of mountain flora. In a letter from Marshall to the Dittmars, he thanked "Ditt" for copies of Orra's article, "Mountaintop Flora," reprinted from *The Adirondack High Peaks and the Forty-Sixers* (see Addendum). Marshall referred to various flowers he had seen in bloom:

> Thank you for sending me the copies which I ordered of Orra Phelps's "Mountaintop Flora." It is a pleasure to read this excellent piece again. One thing strikes me about it is that several plants she has listed from forested slopes and trailsides growing near "timberline" are among the earliest woods wildflowers to bloom at lower elevations at about from 1,500 to 1,600-foot elevations. From my memory of dates of blooming around Lower Saranac Lake where for several years Bob [Marshall] and I recorded the earliest dates we saw various plants in bloom, the following on Orra's list bloomed at these lower elevations by mid-June or earlier: Goldthread (*Coptis groenlandica*), Clinton's Lily (*Clintonia borealis*), Starflower (*Trientalis borealis*), and Canada Mayflower (*Maianthemum canadense*).[5]

After the Dittmars forwarded the letter to Orra, she wrote in the margin of the letter, "I met George at an ADK annual meeting in the mid-thirties — before his brother, Robert Marshall, founded the Wilderness Society." She habitually documented events that were significant to her. Finding special plants was always a thrill for Orra. At eighty-seven, she told interviewer Mary Brennan:

> One of the nice things about camping in Panther Gorge was discovering a nice clump of arnica. Arnica has such a strong smell; you can smell it anywhere the leaves are crushed. Elsa Jane Putnam and I found a patch of arnica just downstream from Panther Gorge at the foot of the stream that came in from Mt. Skylight. It was all in blossom when we discovered it. The blossoms are yellow, resembling daisies, but their odor gives it away. You can't smell anything else around it except the arnica. It smells like the ointment used for sore muscles. Arnica is not

A Forty-Sixers' New Years celebration at the Phelps farm. (Front row, left to right) Helen Colyer (Menz); Pauly Menz (Brown); Mary Colyer (Dittmar); Ethel Thompson (McDuff); (Back row, left to right) Howard Brown; Delores Fussell; Ruth Prince (KIng); Ed Hudo; Louis Knap; Nell Plum.   *Pre-WW II photo*

rare in the west, but it is rare in the Adirondacks.[6]

Elsa Jane smiled as she recalled their return trip from Panther Gorge and their free-spirited bit of irreverence:

> On the way out to JBL via the Gothics, we stopped at Gothics lean-to. We had all our equipment on top of Gothics after hiking in the rain almost a week. We emptied the knapsacks . . . and spread clothes out on the rocks to dry . . . Then we got so with it . . . that we put . . . a blouse and a pair of pants and a pair of socks and a pair of boots . . . and a bra and a pair of panties. We had these "people" out on the rocks and we took pictures . . . of them. . . . Later a young boy saw the pictures and said, "That's dirty." So Doc and I always laughed about the "dirty pictures."[7]

Forty-Sixers also tell tales of bathing behind the bushes. Elsa Jane laughingly recalled one of Orra's quick dips, again an experience of freedom from conventions that hiking in the deep woods afforded.

Orson and Lorinda Phelps at home in 1882. Phelps Mountain was named for Orson, whom Orra described as "no near relative." *Photo courtesy of the Adirondack Museum, Blue Mountain Lake, N.Y.*

> Doc and I were coming off of Algonquin, down to Colden, on the red trail. I saw this brook splashing down the mountain. [I said], "I'll stand guard," and Orra went down . . . and yelled, "Watch out." The trail went around the side . . . where you could get right back against the crook and nobody could see you. Orra often wondered what those people who came through might think . . . (had they been able to see her). There she stood . . . taking a little dip. I was wanting those people to hurry up and get by. Orra was getting cold in there.[8]

When in her eighties, Orra said she believed she was the first woman to bushwhack up Phelps Mountain, named for Orson Schofield Phelps, who, as Orra put it, was "No near relative." These two branches of the Phelps family diverged nine generations before in the 1630s.[9]

Al West wrote of their Phelps Mountain hike of July 1934:

> My dear Doctor,
> I got the prints today of the pictures we took from

Phelps Sunday. Some of them are rather good. I'm enclosing them. I think you'll be able to identify these peaks.[10]

Another letter from Orra to her mother also spoke of the event.

Had a letter from Al West with some snapshots that he took on Phelps Mt. The pictures are clear. One shows Heart Lake. One shows me holding up the flag we erected. Did any-one . . . see it with field glasses from Heart Lake?[11]

Al West atop Phelps Mountain, after he and Orra climbed it in 1934.

With hopes of earning money and spending the summer in the mountains, Orra proposed a summer climbers' camp in 1933. Paul and Vincent Schaefer and A.T. Shorey offered their assistance. Probably because of the hardships of the Great Depression, Orra's idea did not materialize. Orra's expert camping skills were legendary. When asked if she learned camping from her parents, she replied:

No, I learned to camp just by doing it. Our camping really went through a sort of evolution. When we started camping, the time my brother and I climbed Marcy in 1924, we took things in bed rolls, with the tent on the outside and slung across our shoulders. Tin cans had to be very well protected, so that it wouldn't make a hard place that would rub on your shoulder or back.[12]

In *Forest and Crag*, by Laura and Guy Waterman, Orra Phelps shared some camping tips. She

. . . rolled up potatoes, carrots, and even a can of soup in her bedroll. She transported fresh eggs in a cooking pail padded with loose shredded wheat, carried carefully by hand. Breakfast included oatmeal, dried fruits (stewed and heated), or bacon. Dinners often included meat, soup, and vegetables, most of it canned and heavy.[13]

"Put" recalled another time, when Orra pointed out a lovely clump of edible Hydnum mushrooms as they hiked past. When they got to camp and were preparing dinner, Orra said she wished she had some. "Put" hiked back five miles round trip to collect their fungi feast.[14]

Orra's friendships also included Elsa Jane's brother, Dick, who recalled hiking with Orra when she was in her early eighties:

> She asked me once, "Do you know why I stop to look at all the mushrooms and lichens? Because we're going up hill." It was always amazing to me. . . . I always walked in back of her. I'd see a plant I didn't recognize . . . and say, "Doc, what was that?" and Doc just kept on going.
>
> Then she'd say, "That was such and such" and give me the common name, the Latin name, and the family tree. She kept mentally active by looking at everything and reciting the history of the plant.[15]

Lillian Hunt shared her recollections of Orra's second Allen climb in 1953, marking the completion of her second forty-six:

> My husband, Al Hunt, Doc, Lorraine, and Jim Nye went in to climb Allen. I had made her a special Forty-Sixer patch with gold braid around it . . . and "92 R." Al handed it to her on Allen. Later he painted her . . . from a photo taken on the summit. Apparently on the way up they stopped and had Triscuits and water, then hung the pail over the stream on a limb and bushwhacked on up. On the way back they wanted some tea and Triscuits. Orra watched closely as they descended along the stream. She'd say . . . "No, not yet." Finally she sat down and found it . . . And Alan told everybody about that.[16]

Mrs. Phelps's 80th birthday party on August 11, 1947, at Marcy Dam.

Orra, her Forty-Sixer friends, and her family celebrated Mrs. Phelps's 80th birthday at Marcy Dam, just before the 1947 Allen climb. Brothers Lawrence and Francis were there, the Haas family, Elsa Jane Putnam, and Al and Lorraine Hunt. Lillian Hunt described the event:

> Everyone was there including you [the author]. You decorated the tables. That's when Grandma Phelps crossed the stream on the rocks instead of following the trail and came up the road. She did this to take a short cut to Marcy Dam.[17]

Mrs. Phelps's lean-to, on the right on the approach to Marcy Dam from Heart Lake, opened to a view toward Colden and Marcy that included two pine trees Orra planted. In her eighties, Orra told the author how she carried those trees in from Heart Lake in two five-gallon pails. Orra felt that by establishing two healthy pines she might get seedling pines to grow there. When? Elsa Jane figured, "I remember that we would visit them. The first year I went with Doc was 1946 . . . so the pines were planted before that."

Fifty years later the two white pines still flourish on the southeast side of Marcy Dam's pond.

Orra hiked with a wide variety of people. She was as comfortable hiking in all-male company (again, breaking convention) as she was hiking with family or groups mixed in gender or age. As a Forty-Sixer, one regular group of hiking partners included Jim Nye, an undertaker from Buffalo; Al Hunt, a contractor from Schenectady; and Dr. Adolph Dittmar, a dentist from the Plattsburg area, who all met with Orra annually to hike for one week. They would go to a chosen spot, establish their main camp, and hike from there.

Nye had a name familiar in Adirondack history; William B. Nye, the North Elba guide for whom Nye Mountain was named, lived from 1816-1893. Orra's friend, James Hamilton Nye, who lived from 1905 to 1977, was a direct descendant of old Bill.[18] When Jim died in 1977, Orra was asked to deposit his ashes on Mt. Jo. Bill Endicott recalled the day:

> The last time I went hiking with Orra was when she and I went up Mt. Jo with the ashes of a 46er, Jim Nye, who wanted to be buried in the mountains. We went down to the inlet of Heart Lake to the Property Line Trail. You climb a rock face, get up to a plateau, and walk out for a nice view up Indian Pass way. She deposited the remains there.

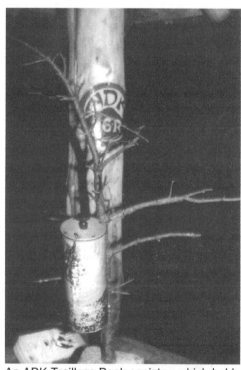

An ADK Trailless Peak canister, which holds a logbook record of each person who climbed that peak.

When Forty-Sixers speak of Street and Nye, the twin trailless peaks on the skyline across Heart Lake, they often tell of hikers getting lost and coming out either at Last Chance Ranch or at Wanika Falls, miles to the west. Orra knew the terrain and successfully climbed both peaks at least twice, according to canister logs. However, when nearly eighty, she agreed to accompany ADK Executive Secretary Fay Loope on a climb of both peaks, where they spent an unplanned night near the summit.

Whether they started late, lost time in finding their way across the vlei, or needed to rest, darkness fell before they could safely return. Being the good woodswoman she was, Orra advised waiting for daylight to bushwhack down. Her fierce pride most likely kept the matter from coming to light. She never divulged the mishap to the author, and only those at the Loj that day knew and recalled the event.[19]

Grace Hudowalski, the Forty-Sixers' historian, shared parts of Orra's Record Form, which all Forty-Sixers must complete.

In answer to the question, "What got you interested in mountain climbing?" Orra had written, "Always interested in the out-of-doors. Mountains seemed naturally interesting because of rare plants and birds."

"What got you interested in climbing the forty-six?"

"The explorer's urge — Marcy, first on trail mountain, Phelps — first trailless peak."

"Describe briefly unusual incidents in natural surroundings."

Orra's two were a trip through Avalanche Pass, alone on a moonlit night between 11:00 P.M. and 1:00 A.M., and finding Lost Pond. Hudowalski added:

"I know Lost Pond. It's not easy to find because the Marshalls had a hard time finding it. It's between McNaughton and Street Mountain. There's a mountain there that's 3,900 something . . . that has no name . . . but that's where Lost Pond is."

Under remarks for "How many 4,000-feet and over ascents have I made?" Orra wrote, "To double the 48 would be 96. A . . . careful estimate on memory but without stretching gives me 126 times up peaks over 4,000 ft. [as of 1947]."

"How many nights sleeping out in lean-to, tent, or no shelter?"

Orra answered, "That would take time to arrive at . . . but could be approximated: 200 at least [as of 1947]."

Another of Orra Phelps's accomplishments was climbing the one hundred fire towers, which afforded her both an opportunity for unparalleled views and often anecdotes and local history from the wardens.

Orra and her mother climbed many High Peaks together, but Mrs. Phelps never did have Orra's drive to complete her forty-six. Those that Mrs. Phelps did not climb, Orra shared with her by letter, phone, or in person.

In 1950, one of life's most difficult times came for both Orra and her mother. Mrs. Phelps became ill and was bedridden. The author went to live

Orra is shown with John Fox at the base of Dairy Hill Fire Tower, one of one hundred fire towers she climbed.

with them during that summer, while Orra worked. Mrs. Phelps died on July 16, 1950 at Saratoga Springs Hospital. Her death was a great loss to all the family. (See Epilogue for further reflections.) Orra salved her sadness and found peace and strength again by hiking in the deep woods.

After her mother's death, Orra did more traveling, particularly to botanical conferences or to locales where special flora grew. In August 1951 Orra and Dr. Elliot Stauffer of Rochester, New York flew to Labrador and Newfoundland, where they botanized and photographed rare Labradorean plants, including curly grass. They also learned more about the Grenfell Medical Mission and its medical care of the native people there. Twenty-five years earlier Orra had been impressed by the Johns Hopkins slide lecture presented by its founder, Sir Wilfred Thomason Grenfell, and hoped to see the mission one day. After returning from this trip she shared her slides with botanical and medical friends and gave the mission financial support until her death.

In 1958, Orra accompanied Mrs. Stauffer and her senior Rochester Girl Scout troop to Europe. The only medical problem encountered was a nasty boil in one scout's armpit and a brief hospitalization. Of special interest were Kew Gardens, the flower mart in Holland, a miniature garden in Amsterdam, and being serenaded by Venetian gondoliers.

In the spring of 1959, she drove alone from Wilton, New York to Birmingham, Alabama where the author was teaching, visited briefly, and then flew to Mexico to visit medical school friends. Among her souvenirs were chunks of obsidian and slides of local flora and fauna. Perhaps her longest trip was to New Zealand with Dr. Mildred Faust in 1978. She saw long-dreamed-of rarities: giant tree ferns, Kauri pines, 12,000-foot Mt. Cook, and glow-worm caves.

First Adirondack Mountain Club Ranger-Naturalist

1962 to 1972

One of the high points of Orra Phelps's Adirondack travels was climbing Algonquin with U.S. Supreme Court Justice William O. Douglas and a select party on June 16, 1962. The day was sparkling-clear, the sunshine warm on the alpine flowers, and the breeze just brisk enough to keep bugs down. Douglas, a world-wide climber and ardent conservationist, was taking his first Adirondack hike. As he later wrote:

For years I had seen the Adirondacks from the air and roads. Only the other day did I have a chance to hike part of their 700 miles of trails. I now know why so many people love this sanctuary and call it one of America's treasures . . . the forty-six peaks that are 4,000 feet or higher, the 200 lakes, the hardwoods and conifers that fill the valleys, the pure cold streams, the alpine flora of the barrens— these are among the great wonders of the world. . . .

Dr. Orra Phelps and U.S. Supreme Court Justice William O. Douglas atop Algonquin in June 1962. (Left to right) Dr. Phelps, Chief Justice Douglas, Dr. Marian Biesemeyer, and Herb Allen.   *Photo by Landon Rockwell*

Conservationists the country over should visit the
Adirondacks to learn from the men and women who
guard this wonderland how they can bring their own
wilderness areas under the constitutional protection.[1]

Early that morning, as the group crossed the outlet of Heart Lake,
they detoured to admire a new lean-to recently built by one of their
group, Hoverman. Douglas exclaimed, "Look, there's a deer!" It stood
in front of the lean-to, not thirty feet away. This must have been a
moving experience for Hoverman "to have seen it graced this way," as
Landon Rockwell, former chairman of the Department of History at
Hamilton College, wrote in the July 1962 *Adirondac*.[2]

With a wave of her hand, Orra cited Latin and English names of
plants along the lower trail: *Cornus, oxalis*, gold thread, Clinton's lily,
wild sarsaparilla, and twisted stalk. No one spoke of the trail clean-up
done the day before by Orra and a few others, ensuring that Douglas
would see this part of the Adirondacks at its best. Familiar birds de-
fended their territories; the black-throated green warbler sang, "See,
see Suzy, see" and the red-eyed vireo endlessly called, "Here I am,
where are you?" After another stretch of trail they rested by a cascading waterfall.

By high noon the hikers were atop Algonquin, with the panorama
of the High Peaks region surrounding them. In every direction, wave
upon wave of mountains faded to the blue horizon. Orra Phelps, Justice Douglas, Dr. Marian Biesemeyer, and the others feasted their eyes
on the alpine flora they cherished: mounds of *Diapensia* and the beautiful Lapland rosebay in bloom, and Labrador tea, blueberry, bilberry,
cranberry, goldenrod, sweet grass and cotton grass, willow just six inches
high, sandwort, and the three-toothed cinquefoil in various stages of
growth. As Rockwell wrote:

> Orra Phelps was spotting flowers, mosses, almost
> everything that grew — and confirming the Justice's own
> quick identification of his old friends. And then we were
> showing him new friends — Marcy, Colden, Skylight,
> Gothics and the rest — Eleanor Friend pointing out the
> Ranger's cabin on Lake Colden and taking pictures, Jus-
> tice Douglas taking pictures and making notes, Herb

Allen telling the Justice about the 1950 hurricane . . .
Brad Whiting making out Lake Champlain.

Watson Pomeroy was telling of the "Forever Wild"
provision. "It all goes back to the Constitution," Watson
explained. "Almost everything goes back to the Constitution," the Justice replied. David Newhouse joined them
and they discussed conservation and the constant alert
that all conservationists must maintain these days."[3]

Back at the Loj, over Nellie Cobane's sumptuous roast beef dinner, talk of conservation issues and the hike enlivened the evening.
After Sunday breakfast they easily climbed Mt. Jo, the 2,876-foot peak
behind the lodge. From its summit they viewed the blue-green
MacIntyre range they had climbed the day before.

With this exhilarating trip, Orra's ten years as the Club's first
Ranger-Naturalist began. The position had its roots in a 1930 ADK
meeting, when its membership totaled 834. Orra, on the Board of
Governors, proposed "... a week's school at the lodge, with groups
going on trips. Russell Carson stated that, although conducted outings had not been attempted in the past, he felt it was worth trying
out . . . [if] Orra [would] work out the matter."[4] Subsequently, A.T.
Shorey praised the educational work of campsite counselors and Conservation Department workers. In 1957, Dr. Arthur E. Newkirk,
former ADK president, wrote a preamble to the motion for a
ranger-naturalist for the ADK Conservation Committee. He wrote:

> Over a million people now use the campsites each year.
> But comparatively few can identify any plants or ani-
> mals or appreciate their interrelationships, yet the camp-
> ers can hardly help but be curious about the strange life
> they find in the forests and waters about them . . . The
> ranger-naturalist's job is to answer the campers' questions,
> arrange nature hikes, and to give campfire talks.

According to Dr. Edwin H. Ketchledge, professor emeritus of the
College of Forestry, Syracuse University and former Natural History
Committee Chairman, it was "April of 1962 when Art Newkirk,
Herb Allen, and Orra formed the Flora Committee." For the first

three years, the focus was on the work of the Ranger-Naturalist and on Orra's establishment of the Kelsey Nature Trail. The Ranger-Naturalist job was hardly work for Orra; it was second nature. She loved to live summers at Heart Lake and to share her passion for the Adir-

Dr. Edwin H. Ketchledge, professor emeritus of the College of Forestry, Syracuse University.

ondacks, and get paid for it. Her enthusiasm was contagious, her friendly manner when teaching beginners was inviting, and her outlook, forever young.

For three years Dr. Newkirk's nine-by-twelve-foot green tent served as the nature museum and Orra's car housed her reference books and other materials. In her field guides, she penciled where and when she found plants, birds, and mammals. However, Orra always referred to the out-of-doors as "the real museum."

Orra had previously assisted her colleague and friend, Dr. Mildred Faust, with a plant census of Franklin County. In the sixties, Orra and Dr. Faust completed a plant census of the ADK Heart Lake tract in Essex County, a valuable record to botanists such as Ruth Schottman and Dr. Nancy Slack, who give seminars there now.

As if to entice passers-by, Orra set up a trail-side display on a weather-beaten table featuring rocks, feathers and nests, and evergreen twigs and cones, beckoning people to learn more about their surroundings. Back in the shade another table offered labeled plant specimens. Orra led almost daily nature walks and helped hikers identify their finds, despite heat, rain, and annoying insects.

Orra developed the Kelsey Nature Trail south of the Loj in memory of Mr. and Mrs. Frederick T. Kelsey. The Kelsey Nature Trail pamphlet explains:

Naturalist Orra Phelps and the ADK museum tent, used for three years before the museum building was erected in 1966.

> Frederick T. Kelsey was a Charter Member of the Adirondack Mountain Club and served as its President for five years from 1936-1940 . . . During the depression years of the 1930's, when the Lake Placid Club was considering the liquidation of the Heart Lake holdings, he obtained a long term lease on the property and initiated the Adirondak Loj Chapter at Heart Lake. When [he] died the Club bought his interest in the furnishings and equipment and the property from the Lake Placid Club in 1958 for $35,000.[5]

Orra did not move plants into the Kelsey Trail, as someone asked her, but rather, made a comfortable and interesting loop trail and tagged various points of interest. In 1963, she wrote the brief Kelsey Trail Guide for visitors to learn about the trail's diverse habitats and natural history.

To illustrate Orra's naturalistic approach, in a March 1967 letter to Dr. Ketchledge, she explained why she used typed baggage tag labels back in the early sixties:

The first year I "set up" the Nature Trail with my . . . labels, tied to a limb, a bush, or a broken stick planted beside a plant, I had as a visitor an eminent botanist from the New York Botanic Gardens, Dr. Eugene Jablonski, . . . who was . . . very interested in natural history education. . . . When he had been through the trail, he said, "I like your tags. Manufactured tags and labels don't belong in a place like this!" So I put out baggage tags in the spring and take them down in the fall. Also, throughout the season I can add tags or remove tags.

That same weekend in 1963, Dr. Edmund H. Fulling, honorary curator of the New York Botanical Garden and editor of *The Botanical Review*, was also a guest at the Loj. He met his colleague at dinner, the same Dr. Jablonski, honorary curator of Tropical Botany at the New York Botanical Garden. Dr. Jablonski introduced Dr. Fulling as the person who had first described a new species of fir, *Abies intermedia*, with exserted bracts between the cone scales.

During the introduction, Orra suddenly disappeared, but reappeared in a moment with a fir cone in her hand. Coincidentally, Dr. Ketchledge had commented upon this unusual cone, *A. balsamea var. phanerolepis*, during the previous day's bryological foray. The three had an interesting time comparing this find with Dr. Fulling's southern species.[6]

Orra was so interested in learning more about arctic and alpine plants that in 1963 she traveled to Alaska. She reveled in the artic plants growing there, especially the ones she had seen atop the Adirondack High Peaks. With camera ever ready, she photographed the rare species, discussed them with Alaskan naturalists, and made notes. She also panned for gold and swooped down in a small plane over the coastal glaciers.

A year later, she and Dr. Faust marveled at Iceland's unusual petaled buttercup, rare saxifrage, geysers, and thermally heated greenhouses. Orra integrated information about these rare species with her understanding of global glaciation and plant habitats. Continuing that trip to Edinburgh, they heard Dr. Herbert Wagner, an expert on ferns, at the International Botanical Congress. While there they saw a tiny Botrychium fern, only one inch high.

In 1965, to Orra's delight, Dr. and Mrs. Newkirk funded the building of a permanent nature museum as a memorial to his parents, Arthur P. and May Young Newkirk, at Heart Lake. Built by Ken Fos-

ter and opened July 16, 1966, the museum had a roofed porch, front and side windows and, as Orra had specifically requested, a large slanted window toward the woods for viewing birds and other wildlife undisturbed. The building provided lighting, space, security, and screened windows.

Dr. Phelps brought in her 1920 vintage microscope and gave the pesky no-see-um punky fly a glass slide exposure, magnified forty times so hikers could see the tiny devil that bit so ferociously and raised such itchy welts. She added an aquarium representing the shore habitat of Heart Lake, with a collection of its

"Fingering the feathers" at the nature museum.

various inhabitants: caddis worms, tadpoles, salamanders, minnows, green freshwater sponges, pipewort, and water lobelia.

Other displays created by Orra featured different characteristics of local plants, animals, and minerals. Chunks of sparkling garnet, anorthosite, and gneiss were shown as mineral examples that could be found in the area. One display provided a rare view of the inside of a white-faced hornet's nest artfully made from pulpwood chewings. Visitors could also see pressed leaves, ferns and cones, some of which were identified while others were left unlabelled to challenge visitors to name them correctly. Under a seven-inch-diameter lens, lichen and reindeer moss from Mt. Jo's ledges looked like crumpled leather and miniature trees. Snake skins, animal pelts, and bird's nests could be fingered, hefted, and identified. It was totally user-friendly.

One June day in the late sixties, Lili and Sherene Aram, the author's two small daughters and Orra's grand-nieces, came chattering up the museum trail

The Aram family: (from left) Sherene, Dr. Ali Aram, Orra, the author, Lili, and Heidi atop Mt. Jo, overlooking Heart Lake.

carrying tadpoles in a man's shoes that just happened to be on the dock. Other hikers and club members brought in treasures they found — from large mineral specimens to egg shell fragments, antlers to snakeskins, and beaver-gnawed logs to owl pellets.

Orra explained the Natural History Committee's philosophy of the nature museum in an Ocotober 1967 *Adirondac* article, "The Nature Loj at Heart Lake":

> From the beginning it has been our policy to keep exhibits illustrative of Adirondack natural history. We want to show people things that they may see along our trails. Some of the rock specimens come from a distance, but all may be found in a day's journey from Heart Lake . . . We show diopsite from Cascade Lake and it is a beautiful light jade green. There are numerous samples of anorthosite, the rock that makes most of our mountains. The principle mineral in this rock is labradorite which often shows a blue-green iridescence and more rarely, a red-silver iridescence.

Stanley Smith, assistant New York State botanist, and Orra had continued to correspond since their botany class and research times in the early sixties. In July 1966, she offered additions to his plant collection of species from Heart Lake. As it happened, he had previously collected some from there.

Do you want a specimen of *Habenaria obtusata* (Pursh) Richards from Heart Lake? Plant has one leaf — blunt, light green with silvery sheen, scape is slender, no bract, 8-12 cm. high. One plant has 8 blooms. The spur is very slender and the lip is narrow and sharply tapered to a point. I'll press one if you say so.

OAP

Stanley Smith, assistant New York State botanist.

That summer Orra took two weeks leave from her ADK Ranger-Naturalist position. By surprise, she joined her sisters Phoebe and Kay, Tom Dunn, and Dot Plum on their trip to England, Germany, Norway, Scotland, Holland, Luxembourg, and Belgium. Another year, she tripped to Lake Louise, Jasper National Park, and Banff for the Canadian Botanical Society meeting. Everywhere Orra traveled, she fed her passionate interest in plants, birds, and other natural history topics, further broadening her knowledge and experience as a naturalist.

One of Orra's favorite groups, the Thursday Naturalists, provided another avenue for learning and sharing botanical information. The organization began in 1965 as the Schenectady adult education Advanced Natural History class with Dr. Nancy Slack, now Professor of Biology at Russell Sage College. During Dr. Slack's 1966-67 sabbatical at Oxford, Ruth Schottman, adjunct for the summer course at Pine Bush, assumed leadership.

For many years, one of their annual trips was to Dr. Phelps's gentian-filled sandpit in Wilton. Orra typically led the group, hiking in from Parkhurst Road along a sandy road cut. The sand pit, exposed when Orra sold many tons of gravel for the building of the Wilton Developmental School, had a layer of gravel containing tiny shells

A meeting of the Thursday Naturalists after their annual visit to Dr. Phelps's Wilton, N.Y. home.

from ancient Lake Albany's bed overlying clay, making the pH and moisture a favorable habitat for variegated and dwarf horsetails, fringed gentians, and other plants unusual to the area.

The author believes that Orra introduced many of the unusual plants that grew on her property though Orra noted in her diary that she found Grass of Parnassus there having come on its own. Whether Orra introduced the others or the seeds and spores arrived naturally, it still provides an interesting area for botanists to explore. Orra further shared her botanical knowledge at the National Wildlife Summit at Silver Bay and the national meeting of the Garden Club Federation at Lake Placid.

During this period, Orra realized that the old fourteen-room Phelps farmhouse was too large and rambling for a single person. Balancing reason with her strong attachment to the place, in 1967, Orra designed and built a modest new house across Parkhurst Road and a bit north of the original home. She would now back up to the eighteen-acre nature preserve she and her mother had been nurturing, view the same fields and mountain range, and have the best of both.

Her new house was built to be practical, a reflection of her nature. Its sand-floored root cellar soon stored carrots, beets, potatoes, onions, and brussel sprouts from her vegetable garden. The hub of the place, her kitchen, had room for a large table where mail of every description vied for attention with fresh flowers, bird feathers, and rock samples.

Dr. Nancy Slack (left), currently professor of biology at Russell Sage College. Her adult education class in Advanced Natural History during the 1960s led to the founding of the Thursday Naturalists. She is shown with the author atop Wright Mountain in 1996.

The Wilton Heritage Society was formed in 1967 with Orra Phelps as a charter member, showing her dedication to the place she had called home for fifty years. Although she had been active in churches in metropolitan centers, she was not a church member in the Wilton area. She occasionally attended services with one of her sisters or nieces, but during this period her religious needs seemed to have been met through her love of nature.

Most of her personal involvement during this time continued to be with botanical, environmental, and mountain climbing groups. She was a longtime member of both the Wilderness Society and the Audubon Society. Although she was a life-long Republican, she was not active in political campaigns.

In response to the wide-ranging interests of visitors to Heart Lake, the Flora Committee expanded in 1967 to become a full natural history committee with programs encompassing mammals, reptiles, birds, and more. Presenting slide talks on birds of the Adirondacks and leading bird watching tours on weekends also came naturally to Orra. These trips provided a rich source of material for the Adirondack Mountain Club's nature museum. As Doris Herwig wrote in "A Bird's Eye View" in the June 1974 *Adirondac*:

One day in 1968, Dr. Orra was taking a hike up to Marcy Dam. At the beginning of the trail, she heard "the noisiest of birds." After some study she discovered that all the commotion was being created by sapsucker parents attempting to feed their young in a poplar tree. [The following spring] Dr. Phelps found the birds had returned to their nest.

In 1970, when Dr. Orra again returned, she found the wind had felled the tree and it was lying some four feet off the ground. Ricky Cobane got a chain saw and removed that portion of the trunk that contained the nest. "First we took a wire and put it deep into the hole," said Orra. "Had to find the exact location of the nest so we could remove it in its entirety." Later they split the log open so that the inside of the nest could be viewed by museum visitors.

Although she also wrote several articles for ADK publications on flowers, mushrooms, birds, ferns, and botanical trips, she preferred to be out in the field exploring or collecting rather than sitting and writing. Perhaps that makes the rest of her legacy more important.

Orra told the author, "People say I should write, write, write" to record and preserve some of her accumulated natural history lore. Her 1970 chapter, "Mountaintop Flora" in *The Adirondack High Peaks and the Forty-Sixers*, has been a valuable reference for botanists (see Addendum.) In it, she distilled decades of observations of these rare plants in a clear, yet technical manner so that both professionals and students could benefit.

Dr. Phelps with a nature study group.   *1971 photo*

She shared with other Forty-Sixers in the planning and writing of the book, is listed in their roster as #47, the forty-seventh person to scale the High Peaks, and claimed book number 47 of the 1,200 first editions as her own. Her poem "Tahawus" is included as well as a brief biography as a contributor.

Former ADK Executive Director Grant Cole and his wife, Heidi, recalled how "at home" Orra was in the woods. One early spring, as they neared the nature museum, a chipmunk ran right up to Orra. She remarked that the little creature must have been waiting all winter for her return and its share of the birdseed she supplied.

Orra Phelps at Lost Pond, Cranberry Lake, in 1969. *Photo by Dr. Edwin H. Ketchledge*

Another time, crawling on all fours, she found cherry pit chewings under an exhibit table. She marveled at how industrious the chipmunks were to gather fruit from the nearest black cherry, twenty yards away. As Claudia Swain, a naturalist, said in the 1986 *Adirondac*, "Orra was tuned in to the natural world . . . and taught me a way of appreciating that pesky chipmunk and the subtleties of nature."

Each weekend and often midweek Orra gave slide lectures, at first in the Loj or on the lawn and, by 1967, in the Buhlman Amphitheater, named for Barbara Buhlman, the Ranger-Naturalist and Algonquin Chapter Chairman until her untimely death in 1966. According to Doris Herwig, Dr. Orra Phelps and Dr. Adolph Dittmar conceived the idea of the memorial and Orra chose the site. The Algonquin Chapter created the amphitheater.

There was a hush in the attending crowd whenever Orra presented her slides with seemingly effortless commentary, giving her visitors a vicarious tour of the woods. Her topics ranged from alpine flora, her favorite, to Adirondack birds, fungi, ferns, the Forest Preserve, Adirondack geology, and forest ecology. Her underlying mission was always to teach people to be better stewards of the vast natural gift that was the Adirondack Park.

In her twenty-five-year-old slide boxes, the author found the following poem in Orra's handwriting, which was used with her Forest Preserve slide show:

> Under the sandwort clinging close
> To the almost barren stony slope
> Filling a crevice and scarcely seen
> With broken crystals of once hard rock,
>
> Under the trees whose trunks rise straight
> To lift their crowns to sunlight and rain,
> Whose branches mesh and myriad leaves make
> A latticed canopy to cool the earth,
>
>> Under them all is SOIL
>> Soil, a priceless gift, yet free
>> Held in trust for posterity.
>
> Born as snow in a winter storm,
> Or pelting rain when thunder rolls
> As drifting mists, as morning dew,
> Or springing cool from out the earth.
>
> In dripping moss, in marsh or bog,
> Limpid, pure, in shadowed pool,
> In bubbling brook, singing or silent streams,
> And where the hidden lake reflects the wooded shore.
>
>> Where green things grow there's WATER.
>> Water, a priceless gift, yet free
>> Held in trust for posterity.
>
> The hills are clad in vibrant green
> Of poplar, birch and maple groves.
> The moss is damp and ferns abound
> Beneath the dark green bows of conifers.

The hills are home to hare and grouse;
Beneath the brake the fawn is hid,
The white-throat sings, the wood thrush broods
And man seeks solace from a world of care.

Sheltering all — the FOREST
Forest, a priceless gift yet free
Held in trust for posterity.

During these ten years, Orra and the Natural History Committee tapped their wide-ranging network of contacts and included programs given by other natural history professionals. Howard W. and Elizabeth B. Jaffee lectured on Adirondack geology; Dr. Mildred Faust on ferns, grasses, and sedges; and Dr. Edwin H. Ketchledge on Adirondack trees. There were Alpine Flora Weekends, Birders' Weekends, and Fungi Weekends.

In 1968, in addition to camp groups, the natural history program attracted over 700 individuals to the nature museum. Over 1,000 people came to the programs and walks presented at the nature museum and on the Kelsey Trail. Evening slide talks reached hundreds, if not thousands, more.

Orra was a primary source for trail and nature information for hikers and visitors. She instantly knew which trail to take and its natural features. With a few pointed questions she could answer most queries, but led people to helpful books or guides so they too could be independent. Sometimes her nature groups took day trips to other locations: Cranberry Lake, Wilmington Bog, Silver Lake, or Whiteface Mountain. She scouted the area beforehand, checking for special plants or birds or whatever was the group's focus.

When individuals or groups wanted to find a special plant, Orra guided them, once bushwhacking miles into the woods to the exact location of a clump of orchids. Another time she led a curious party to an active den of porcupines on the backside of Mt. Jo.

Several times during her Ranger-Naturalist years, Orra shared her medical knowledge as well. Dr. Ketchledge recalled one such time when he, Dick Andrus, and Orra were climbing Algonquin's northwest knob. Both men developed terrible headaches. Orra theorized that they were taking too short and too shallow breaths, not ridding their lungs of carbon dioxide. Her recommendation was to stop occasionally to take more deep breaths, and to take aspirin when they returned to the Loj. Soon they felt better and joked over whether the unnamed peak should be called Dick's Peak, Orra's Knob, or Ketch's Point.[7]

Dr. Ketchledge, who has himself given the ADK and the Forty-Sixers decades of service as a teacher, leader, scientist, and role model, to mention a few of his talents, reflected on Orra's role in the development of many people's appreciation of nature:

> Many of us end up where we are in our careers because of some catalytic event in our youth, when somebody opened our eyes . . . so we had a broader perspective on the world around us. . . . That is the thing that I honor Orra most for — the way she had done that with youngsters. . . . I am sure there are dozens and dozens of people to whom Orra was the catalyst and gave them an enjoyable experience that years from now they will look back on and see how she opened the door for them.
>
> There is a tendency in this day and age of specializing to think that achievement is measured in some new discovery, some different understanding of some complex problem. [But] if your objective is to lead new people to start at the beginning level . . . that means that you start at the level of youngsters. . . . That was Orra's skill to open their eyes to . . . what was interesting about some simple thing like the goldthread leaf versus the wood sorrel. . . . There is a subtle message in the work that Orra did and is continued by our Ranger-Naturalist program . . . in that the key person . . . makes a casual observation [and] shows the new person things she did not see. . . As soon as you start pointing out the diversity among ferns or spring wildflowers versus club moss versus tree seedlings . . . that is where the new world is . . . That's what Orra did. She just really relived the whole experience and shared her enthusiasm for it.

Orra finally retired as the Club's Ranger-Naturalist at the age of seventy-seven. She worked with succeeding naturalists, showing them locations of special park features and sharing with them her reference books and materials, and her large collection of Adirondack nature slides.

An appreciation for fragile maiden hair fern fronds, sunshine sparkling on white birches bedecked with golden foliage, or the loon's haunting call in the dawn's mist continue to be her legacy for those touched by her love of nature.

In his 1972 piece, "Orra Phelps, An Appreciation" on her retirement as the Ranger-Naturalist, Dr. Ketchledge wrote:

> Orra Phelps has taught me various things these last eight years as I have visited her in the Ranger-Naturalist program and worked with her on our Natural History Committee. I have profited scientifically from her store of observations on the natural world. I have benefitted professionally from witnessing her skills working with people. Most importantly, I am continually enriched personally by the strength and beauty of her spirit and personality.[8]

Orra's impact on the study of nature in her role as the Adirondack Mountain Club Ranger-Naturalist is well illustrated by the opinion of Marvin E. Kirkland in an August 1973 letter to Grant Cole.

> The Forest Ecology course offered under the leadership of Dr. Orra Phelps and Virginia Phelps [Orra's cousin and replacement] was outstanding. My thanks to them. Dr. Phelps's enthusiasm, understanding, and intimate knowledge of the Adirondacks was transmitted to those who attended the course. To those who did not attend, especially members, I feel that they missed something.

Orra's friend, Douglas Ayres, gave voice to the loon's song and place in his poem, which he offered to be included in this book as a tribute to her love of the wild:

From Elk Lake Island Studded

Have you heard loon calls
— In the dark of the moon —
Rise from the gloom?

Have you heard loon calls
— At high noon —
Midday stillness break
From hidden corners
Of the lake?

Have you heard loon calls
From mist shrouded waters
— It's lands veiled and dim —
Just when eastern sky

Blooms over Mt. McComb
At Adirondack dawn?

Did you hear
Loud and clear
Primeval wilderness
Expressed?
Spirit of the wild
Released
In haunting
Yodel, wail or tremolo?

Then you know
Distillate of primordial
Time
Echoes of eons passed
Stabbing night
Greeting first light
Soaring to zenith sun.

Then you heard
Essence of all
Unspoiled outdoors
In the cry
Of a single bird!
Great Northern Diver,
— Gavia Immer —
Common loon,
Unique its utterance
To invoke
Embodiment
Of driftwood coves
Ripple lapped shores
Mountain girt

Silhouettes
Thrushs' songs
Conifer spires
Balsam fir and spruce
Uncommon attributes
Of a not too Common bird
— The Common loon —

Listen, then to
Yodel, hoot
Haunting wail and
Tremolo,

And fly on winged notes
To northern realms
Remote
Beyond the ken
Of undiscerning men.

— Douglas Ayres, Jr. [9]

—21—

At Home in Wilton
1972 to 1978

Wilton neighbors knew Orra Phelps as the friendly naturalist-physician-teacher who tended her flower and vegetable gardens, spun out Latin and common names of wildflowers, ferns, trees, and birds, and hiked in the Adirondacks as often as she could. Orra's neighbor, Wendy Best, recalled in her Chatham, New York gardening column Orra's manner of blending conservation with teaching as they toured Orra's garden:

> How's Mike doing these days? I saw him ride past my house yesterday on his new bike. That blue thing? Oh, that's Mertensia. Blooms in the very early spring and dies down completely by mid-summer, so it's hard to remember where you put it by autumn. A lot of people call it Virginia Bluebells. Want some? I'll dig you up a piece after it finishes blooming. Be sure to mark where you plant it. Look at that red-tailed hawk up there — He's looking for his dinner. I think there's a pair nesting nearby.[1]

When Orra said, "I'd like a spot of color and dark green for contrast out there in my hayfield," it was Dick and Wendy Best who found and transplanted a red maple and a cedar tree, now growing across from her modest gray house.[2] Wendy continued:

> It was so terrific to go out walking with her, even in the yard. . . . Dr. Phelps did not have a lot of conventional amenities of conversation, so she'd say what she had to say, but boy could you learn a lot. She would make observations about your garden: this plant would spread or that would grow tall. She had a sense of proportion in the gar-

251

den and knew exactly where to place things. She was one of my ten most intelligent acquaintances.[3]

Laura Snell, a Skidmore College student, shared Orra's vegetable garden. Laura recalls Orra's gardening savvy: space-saving pole beans, planting the outside three rows of sweet corn later to fool the raccoons into believing that the main crop wasn't ready, and keeping a five-gallon pail of water and a full watering can to give spot drinks to thirsty plants.

'Orra-isms' included: white flowering plants were still lovely in the twilight; and Russian olives, highbush cranberry, and mountain ash attracted the birds who, in turn, ate the mosquitoes. The magazine *Organic Gardener* was a regular part of her bathroom reading material and probably a source of handy tips.

Orra could tell by a slight mound and crack in her sandy soil where a fat potato swelled beneath the surface. She would thrust in her fingers and gleefully harvest part of her dinner.

Laura Snell recalled Orra's lying down on the lawn and relishing its softness, fragrance, and warmth.

> She's the only eighty-year-old I knew who'd kick off her shoes in my presence and lie down on her side in the grass. . . . When I was in college, she invited me to move in with her. I was very honored. It was extremely generous to offer her home and rides to college.[4]

Another of Orra Phelps's many botany students, Laura Meade, visited on September 10, 1979, Orra's 84th birthday, to have her wildflower slide identification verified. Encouraged by Orra, Laura gave inspired nature talks and slide shows and shared her love of alpine flora with yet a younger generation of naturalists such as Kathy Neal, an ADK Summit Steward.[5]

Neighbors Lorraine Westcott and her daughter, Jan, were frequent companions on Orra's walks. Lorraine shot excellent nature photographs while both absorbed Orra's love of nature. In high school young Jan was inspired to write an essay about Orra, quite a tribute both to her mentor and to their relationship.

On July 11, 1975, a small group of friends, neighbors, and family shared a woods walk, with Orra providing identification tips and tidbits.[6] The group (Orra Phelps; Walter and Alice Stroup; Marie and Rudolph Sturm, neighbors on the north and east; Wendy and Richard Best and daughter, Jan; Gloria MacMaster, owner of the old Phelps home on the southwest; Dee Dunn, a neighbor and Saratoga County historian; Lili and Sherene Aram, grand-nieces; and the author of this book) left through the back flower garden and took a newly trimmed trail northeast toward large birch and beech trees at the edge of the brook.

Using less "botanese" and more common names, Orra explained that of New York's approximately ninety ferns, thirty grew in these woods. Only nine ferns were introduced either by Orra or her mother: the Hart's tongue (grown from spores), glade, woodsia, Goldie's, walking, broad beech, polypody, bladder, and climbing (the last of which the author transplanted from Orra's nursery garden into the woods after Orra's death.)

The author tells of the "Orra Phelps" woods walk:

> We came to a point where we saw three large trees across the brook on a piece of Orra's land and a wire boundary line strung by her neighbor, Mr. Pippenbeck, in 1959. She also pointed to the approximate place where a large spring emerged from the west bank, flowed through a small channel about fifteen feet long, and entered the brook. She explained that the spring water surfaces because of the thick layer of clay beneath the glacial gravel.
>
> We turned and headed back along the western ridge trail, passing a hazelnut and a large oak near the spot where the family had dumped ashes for years. Old bottle-seekers had previously checked the site. Almost immediately behind the house we noted a clump of wood lilies which, Orra explained, bloom with an upright red cup, while the Canada lily has pendant bells.
>
> Farther along the trail Orra pointed to ladyslipper seed pods and foliage, wintergreen and pipsissewa leaves, both dark green and leathery looking. Below and to the left of the trail in a marshy area, Orra explained, were

the remains of the family's earlier attempt to make a stone dam and pool. Silt filled the pool and plants grew, creating an island. Here grow fragile bladder fern, arbutus, and water hyacinth. The latter was brought in 1948 from New Jersey by the Van Allers. Beside the trail we passed a sturdy picnic table, one of several hundred made and sold in the '60s by Dr. Adolf Dittmar and ADK Algonquin chapter crews to wipe out the Loj mortgage.[7]

As we viewed the confluence of the two streams over the left bank, Orra told how the bigger stream flowed east from Pratt's Pond, where beavers maintained a large dam. She taught that when beavers eat their food supply, they move upstream to where aspen and other food is more plentiful. The smaller stream to the south dries up in the summer.

We brushed by four-foot lacy royal ferns and crossed a small gully, where water seeped from a blind drain. Noting elderberry in bloom, Orra spoke of the elderberry fritters she cooked days before by dipping the flower heads in batter and frying them. Interspersed were stands of lady fern and glade fern, which is related to the silvery spleenwort. She contrasted Jack-in-the-pulpit with its two leaves across and a third at right angles with trillium leaves which are three equidistant. Along the trail we admired more ferns, woodsia, marsh or swamp; tall and graceful interrupted, sensitive, and silvery spleenwort, with its herringbone pattern of spore cases on the back of the frond. Before we crossed the stream, Orra indicated where yellow ladyslippers grow.

Nearby we saw broad beech fern with its flat top, and a little farther along Orra dug and we tasted Indian cucumber root, which has a crunchy flesh similar to water chestnut. Orra pointed out showy orchis and then ginseng. Next we passed the tract's only clump of oak fern, small and delicate with wiry, black stems resembling small brake ferns. Then Orra joked that the New York fern, which tapers toward both ends from the middle, resembles New Yorkers who burn the candle at both ends.

Soon we passed the property line onto Sturm's land, saw their old bridge, and then made a right turn up an old woods road past decomposing hemlock stumps and scads of seedlings. At the top of the hill, we turned right toward a sand pit and passed three large oaks, Phelps's boundary-line trees.

We then faced an open sandpit, from which Orra had sold sand and gravel when the state built the Wilton Developmental School. Her beloved fringed gentians bloom here each September. Our talk drifted to sweet fern, which is not really a fern, but a shrub of well-drained areas, with leathery leaves, a pungent smell, and edible seeds.

Slipping into the woods again south of the boundary-line oaks, we saw a large patch of pink lady slippers, pipsissewa, and creeping cedar (ground pine). We continued to the eastern ridge trail atop the brook bank and saw the evergreen, heart-shaped leaves of the galax once used by florists in violet nosegays and not native to New York State. Over the east bank, we saw rhododendron which had been introduced, and discussed why mountain laurel does not grow natively. Orra taught us that laurel needs acid soil and the Helderberg limestone below Albany formed a natural barrier to the laurel's spread north.

Looking down to the brook, Orra recalled spotting a green heron perched in an old willow tree overhanging the brook. Going down the bank trail, we examined rattlesnake fern. Amidst its three divided leaves rose a spore case spike from which spores would later fly out like dust. Then we saw white baneberry with its doll's eyes white fruit and thick flower stem (red baneberry has reddish fruit and a thinner stem). Stone steps, laid by Orra's brother, Leon, led to the brook where we saw Goldie's fern, one of the largest wood ferns, which Orra explained is differentiated by its golden-green color, large and coarse size, and backward-tilting blades.

The scent of new-mown hay drifted across Parkhurst Road, as we gathered on Orra's lawn for dessert and to discuss the future of her conservation land. Orra asked, "Is there anyone here who would not like to be on the Board of Governors of the conservation land?" All agreed they would like to be a part of it. Orra planned to set up an informal agreement so that the east side of the road would always be park land. She said she would especially like Wilton school children to use it and that an ecologi-

Charles and Bessie Haas and their grandchildren in a 1969 photo.

cally minded school person should be on the board. Around five, we parted, having had a day to treasure. [The land is now the Phelps Nature Preserve of The Land Trust of the Saratoga Region.]

Orra was very fond of her four nieces. When they were young, Orra came to the Haas farm to share their wonder at the three-foot-long wasps' nest on a bedroom window with the interior cells exposed and wasps working. She photographed the girls' May snowman with lilacs in its hair, pointed out bufflehead on the Haas creek, shared her love of wildflowers, and with the author, planted wild rice in the huge swamp just over the twin bridges from the Haas fields.

Orra related to family members differently. When she was driven to visit her niece, Phoebe Hunt, Orra would direct the driver (even family members) how to go, then how the table should be set, how to make the gravy, etc. "This is what we are going to do," she would say. She had a sergeant-like effect on some, yet she could sit on the floor when in her late eighties and put rollers in her grand-niece Kierstin Hunt's doll's hair. When the author was widowed, Orra came to Massachusetts and shared the first difficult winter.

Orra took pride in her appearance and had her hair dressed regularly. She would feel equally comfortable botanizing while wearing worn clothes, muddy boots, and an old hat with dirt under her nails. Once during her eighties, her hiking friend from the 1930's, Al West, visited and gave her some books. After he left, Orra turned to the author and said, "I'm so glad I had my hair done before Al came." Laura Snell recalled Orra's fondness for a leather jacket from the Deerskin Trading Post in Massachusetts and the way she looked in it. Laura also remembered Orra's pride showing once,

> . . . only because it was so rare. She was late getting to my apartment one day in 1978 and she was generally prompt. . . . When she did show up, she just made light of it. Years later, I found out she got a speeding ticket en route, didn't have her pocketbook, and had to go home to get it. So she was late and wouldn't tell me . . . that day. . . . She was smiling and pulled it off.[8]

Cooking and eating good wholesome food was basic fare. Wild plants that added zest to her menus included elderberry blossom fritters, fiddle heads, marsh marigolds, an occasional trout, and wild strawberry jam. Wendy Best recalled:

> Doc Phelps taught me how to use wild highbush cranberries for which we thank her every year. They smell kind of like old socks when they are cooking. We went into her kitchen one day and asked her what the smell was? Orra smiled, "Oh, it's highbush cranberry sauce." Then she gave us some and we liked it.
> Dr. Phelps liked to make bread. She's the one who taught me how to set a sponge for bread. She'd get the stuff about like pancake batter and then let it rise. Then you put more flour in — that's an Orra trick.
> She showed us about wild strawberries, about how good they could be and where to find some. She had the patience to pick several cups of those little berries and then make a sauce for ice cream. A very special treat.[9]

On rainy days Orra corresponded with far-flung friends and colleagues, working at her kitchen table, enjoying a fragrant rose bud or a few wild flowers in a vase. African violets, a gardenia, amaryllis, begonias, ferns, and a terrarium gave her an indoor garden even in the winter. Maps of the Adirondacks papered her hall and bookshelves groaned with well-worn Gray's botany manual, Peterson's bird and nature guides, family Bibles, her parents' books, and genealogical tomes. Other favorite pastimes were watching golf tournaments, the Olympics, and the news on television.

She arranged slide shows, sometimes for the ADK, sometimes for church, garden club, or nursing home groups. Evenings were her time to read biographies, historical fiction, especially of the North Country—books about pioneers and Native Americans—or to catch up on many natural history magazines and journals, usually with the cat in her lap.

Orra enjoyed her cat's company. She propped an eight-foot-long board along the back of her house and opened the window a few inches so her cat could go in and out easily. She also hung a glove with bells in the fingers inside her back door for the cat to ring to go out on frosty days. Her cat was pampered but earned its keep by controlling the rodent population. When asked how to keep moles from destroying one's bulbs, Orra replied, "Get a cat."

Orra was a whiz at jigsaw puzzles. Her Mount Holyoke classmate Mary Parker Firth[10] recalled Orra's marshaling how a puzzle was to be done in the living room at Adirondak Loj. First, you did the border, then any obvious islands such as a red schoolhouse, and then filled in the rest. Orra would ration her time at a puzzle or reading to save time for higher priorities. Hardly a clear night went by that Orra didn't scan the sky to glimpse Orion's belt or the Northern Cross before bedtime. With a window cracked for fresh air, she slept soundly.

During Orra's long life on the Phelps farm in Wilton, New York, she and her family unearthed many Native American artifacts. She shared this interest with Dr. Vincent Schaefer of Schenectady, and they surmised that one of the north-south Indian routes between Canada and the Mohawk River crossed Phelps land. From "Reminiscences of Saratoga," an article in *The Saratogian* compiled by Cornelius E. Durkee, we learn more of the Wilton branch:

The old "Indian Trail" started at the south end of Lake George near the present village of Lake George and continued to the Mohawk Castles on the Mohawk River, near Schenectady, a distance of forty miles. This trail led from Lake George on a southerly course to the great bend in the Hudson River, about ten miles west of Glens Falls. From the bend, it continued south through the towns of Wilton and Greenfield, about four to five miles from Saratoga Springs and through Galway to the lower castles of the Mohawk, about four or five miles west of what is now Amsterdam.[11]

Dr. Vincent Schaefer (left) and Douglas Ayres in a 1984 photo. Schaefer worked with Orra to examine Native American artifacts found on the Phelps farm in Wilton, N.Y.

The Phelps site in Wilton, typical for its level field, powerful spring, and good fishing made a favored camping spot. Orra's trout stream, the Little Snook Kill, is part of the drainage area of the Snook Kill of Wilton, an area which hosted major sites described as part of the Snook Kill Culture, circa 1400 BP (Before Present time) by Professor William A. Ritchie in *The Archeology of New York State.*[12]

At the author's request, Dr. Robert Funk, New York State Archeologist,[13] identified nineteen Native American artifacts found by Orra Phelps on the Phelps farm. Dr. Funk said the arrowheads were not from the Snook Kill Culture.

This is not surprising, apparently, because many different cultures are represented in the Hudson valley over the 11,000 years since the Ice Age and they traded widely. The Phelps farm site had apparently been occupied at various times between 4500 BP and 1470 BP (+/- 100 years).

The true Indian arrowheads were four Lamoka stem points, about one and one-half inches long, including one of pale brown and mottled flint, which he termed a variety of Onondaga flint, possibly from western New York bedrock. The others were definitely Onondaga because Lamoka stemmed points are of gray East Onondaga flint.

The largest of the points was a Susquehanna broad point, two and one-eighth inches long by one inch across. They have sloping shoulders and distinctive stems. This one with facial polish, perhaps from being bound with a lashing, represented a later culture, about 3200 BP by radio carbon dating.

The last one Dr. Funk identified was a little Normanskill point, from between the Stone Age and the "skill" points, with Orra's note "found while weeding potatoes." He said most of the artifacts seemed to have come from the plow zone. He does not know how important this site is, but said they all have a story to tell. He said the spring itself would have been an attraction. If one scraped off the "plow zone," one would find big hearths, burial sites, and remains of human bones.

All of these artifacts and the site are now registered with the New York State Department of Archaeology.[14] Though Dr. Phelps made hundreds of accessions to the New York State Museum Botany Department, there is no record that she shared the Phelps farm Native American artifacts with the Archeology Department.

In *Saratoga County Heritage*, Dr. Phelps left another legacy when she wrote the chapter on geologic history. She described fossil seaweed or stone cabbages (now believed to be *Cynobacteria*) in the Town of Milton; old Lake Albany sand beds; Stark's Knob, a volcanic remnant; the Saratoga Geysers; and Snake Hill at Saratoga Lake, among many other sites, as part of her rapid chronology of the 1.5 billion years of geology represented locally.[15]

Adirondack Mountain Club Member Emerita

Orra continued to hike the 132.2-mile Northville-Placid Trail into her late seventies. Yes, *late seventies*. She had covered six previous sections between 1928 and 1939, but had left the remainder untouched for decades.

The seventh stretch from Wakely Dam to Piseco was done in reverse, starting at the dam in the north and hiking 31.8 miles south to Piseco, camping out along the way, over the Labor Day weekend in 1972 with Dick Putnam and Alan Shepherd. Dick explained that the ranger station at Wakely Dam was informally called "headquarters" in the seventies, but at this writing is named Cedar River Station. Orra had already hiked the segment from Wakely Dam to Cedar Lakes once before in 1935.

Of the eighth section recalled in her completion report:

> . . . from Whitehouse to Piseco, a distance of 9.4 miles, I covered in a day trip in 1973. Whitehouse is so named because it once had a white house on the river where one shouted from the other side for a person to come by boat to row you across the

Dick Putnam and Alan Sheperd, Orra's Northville-Placid Trail hiking companions.

Sacandaga River. If no one came, you walked across the river on rocks, hoping not to get all your gear wet. In the high water of spring run-off it was especially hazardous.[1]

In 1973, Orra did not scamper across rocks as she might have in her thirties, but rather crossed on the suspension bridge over the West Branch of the Sacandaga River, again with Dick Putnam.

During a 1989 interview, Dick laughed when he thought back to Orra's hiking her final sections of the trail. At first, she told him she had just this one last section to go. Then there was one more to do and he believed there was perhaps still another. He felt she did not want to impose on other hikers to accompany a somewhat slower-paced hiker, but for the Putnams, it was a privilege.

Orra recorded her ninth section of coverage–the 12.2-mile portion from Wakely Dam north to Lake Durant–recalling:

> I did this in August 1973 with Dick Putnam camping at Stephens Pond, where I had also been in 1928, but then came in via Cascade Pond from Blue Mountain Lake.

When Orra and Mrs. Phelps camped at Stephens Pond in 1928, they took a census of the ferns and found nineteen species. Orra told interviewer Mary Brennan that when she returned in 1973, she recounted the ferns and found eighteen, but could not recall which fern was missing the second time.

Just before Orra's eightieth birthday in September 1975, she hiked her next-to-last piece of the Northville-Placid Trail. Her record of the tenth segment states:

> The portion from Lake Durant to Rt. 28, Long Lake, I did in two trips, both in 1973, one going north — one going south. I started at Lake Durant . . . and went north to the north lean-to at Tirrell Pond in August 1975.

On this ten-mile round trip Orra was again accompanied by Dick Putnam and his daughter, Tina.[2] Dick recalled insisting that they camp overnight rather than try to return the same day as eighty-year-old Orra had suggested.

Tirrell Pond at the foot of Blue Mountain must have been a favorite spot. Long after Orra had lost fluency of speech due to small strokes, at about age eighty-nine, when shown a slide of Tirrell Pond, she burst out with, "I know were Tirrell Pond is."

Today there is actually more wilderness along the trail than in the twenties, because most evidence of earlier logging — woodland clearings, tote roads, and burned-over acres — is hidden by regrown healthy forests. The ranger station at Shattuck Clearing has been removed in accordance with wilderness area guidelines. The New York State Land Master Plan explains:

> A wilderness area, in contrast with those areas where man and his own works dominate the landscape, is an area where the earth and its community of life are untrammeled by man — where man himself is a visitor who does not remain. A wilderness area is further defined to mean an area of state land or water having primeval character, without significant improvements or permanent human habitation.[3]

In 1978, Orra Phelps completed the last section of the Northville-Placid Trail, from Canary Pond to Whitehouse, left undone while somehow heading for other more imminently important places. Orra wrote in her Northville-Placid report:

> On September 2nd - 4th , 1978, I started at Whitehouse, walked in to Mud Pond lean-to, and on the 3rd continued the trail from Mud Pond to Canary Pond, the last stretch of my N-P coverage.

This octogenarian hiked the final section with Laura Snell. They carried packs, sleeping bags, food for three days, and slept one night in a lean-to and another on the ground. Her long-time friend and fellow ADK member Ruth Schottman recalled Orra's beaming smile when she told Ruth of her completion of the trail. Ruth saw "a glowing, excited, exultant Orra, coming to dinner, eighty-three years old, tired and proud, having just finished her final segment of the Northville-Placid Trail."

As Orra wrote to William White, N-P Trails record keeper, in her trail completion report, her random sequence of trips did not fit the prepared form but was done piece by piece over fifty years, the longest on record for any N-P Trail hiker. Her original record details the segments done

Orra at Mud Pond, at her completion of the Northville-Placid Trail in 1978.

from the southern terminus to the northern, but the author has rearranged them chronologically for this book. Orra hiked the trail in her typical way, enjoying the flora and fauna of each section, often teaching others as she went, and rediscovering old plant friends she had seen on some previous passes.

With the author, Orra relished going to Adirondack Loj, even for an overnight, and seemed to enjoy the attention she received as an honored guest. They would visit the nature museum, hike around the Kelsey Trail or out to Rocky Falls, birding and botanizing en route, or drive to South Meadow to check the sundew plants she remembered growing there.

Adirondack Loj at Heart Lake was even more familiar and loved than Johns Brook Lodge. She had first come in 1926 with her mother and

Ruth Schottman and Orra Phelps, naturalists, at Heart Lake.

Lawrence, been welcomed by Jed Rossman, and had first climbed MacIntyre, as Algonquin was then known. Through the years Orra, and often her mother or young friends, occupied lean-to number one, formerly at the edge of Heart Lake toward Mt. Jo.

Orra Phelps in the South Meadow with grand-niece Sherene Aram and the author.

She served many years on both the Natural History Committee and the Lodge Operating Committee, and during most of her ten years as Ranger-Naturalist, lived summers at the Loj. She had consequently come to know Heart Lake's flora and fauna like those of her own backyard.

An example of Orra's keen mind and understanding of plants is her 1976 article, "The Queen of Slippers" in the *New York Conservationist*, accompanied by one of her excellent photographs of the showy lady's slipper. Orra wrote:

> For beauty of form and color, the lady's-slipper of the queen (*Cypripedium reginae*) could well be the most outstanding of all the orchids native to the northeastern United States. . . . Not a roadside flower . . . the reginae grows best in a sphagnum bog often partly shaded by arborvitae and tamarack. Tall sedges, spice bush, and ferns may screen the bloom from sight. The moss underneath may be so wet that the orchid hunter may soon find himself in water over the ankles.
>
> The flower or "slipper" is globular in form, tinted a rose pink in broad streaks over white. The richness of the color varies from a pale pink to deep rose-purple. The slipper is framed by lateral petals and sepals of white of such substance as to give the appearance of crystalline sheen. A touch of yellow shows in the slipper's opening.

Well-established plants grow three feet tall bearing one or two blossoms. Many parallel-veined leaves, strongly plaited, clothe the stalk, giving the plant a robust look. The blooming season varies with the latitude but in New York State, the lady's slipper of the queen blooms between June 20 and July 1. . . . This flower, along with other native orchids, has been placed on the protected list of wild plants in New York.[4]

Orra, at eighty-five, continued to be vitally interested in the world around her, to contribute in diverse ways, and to be honored by other naturalists, the Adirondack Mountain Club, and the Nature Conservancy. In March 1982, Orra Phelps received a significant honor.

In March 1982 the E. New York Chapter of Nature Conservancy presented me with the Oak Leaf award for the work at the Loj [Museum and Kelsey Nature Trail] and for the work I did on the committee that made up the list of Protected Plants of New York State.[5]

The author's family in 1990: (left to right) Robbin Evans, Sherene Aram, Fred Arakelian, Mary Arakelian, Bill Mash, Lili Mash.

The Nature Conservancy was one of Orra's most admired organizations, one that is now responsible for the protection of 6.9 million acres in fifty states and Canada. The Nature Conservancy's success is due in part to local naturalists like Orra who did something about conservation wherever she could. A large part of Orra's core beliefs paralleled their mission "to preserve plants, animals, and natural communities that represent the diversity of life on Earth by protecting the lands and waters they need to survive."[6] She valued and was an active part of the Nature Conservancy's collective impact where the work and voice of one person is multiplied many times over. As long as she could see and write checks, she underwrote their efforts.

According to Dr. Eugene Odgen, former New York State Botanist, only one or two of these prestigious awards are given each year, and then only to the most worthy individuals. There were four major areas in which Orra Phelps excelled and gave notable service to the conservation of nature: field knowledge of eastern New York's flora, especially arctic-alpine plants; service in conservation education; accessions and service to the New York State Museum Department of Botany plus a considerable study of Stereums, a group of fungi; and development of New York's Protected Plant List. Orra's service in this fourth area, her committee work for the New York State Department of Environmental Conservation and the resulting revision and enlargement of the 1975 New York State Protected Plant List, was her most focused and most noted.

The selected activities mentioned above exemplify the range of her contributions to the protection of nature. It was the combination of these lifelong contributions, but especially the protected plant work and years of ranger-naturalist work in the Adirondacks, that brought Dr. Orra Phelps the Oak Leaf Award of the Eastern New York Nature Conservancy in 1982.

All her life, Dr. Phelps took great pride in her medical degree. In 1977 she returned to Johns Hopkins for their 50th reunion, where she received a commemorative bronze medallion on a stand. She proudly showed it to family and friends on her return and the family celebrated with a special brunch in her honor. She also maintained her New York State medical license for fifty years.

When in her eighties, friends still saw her as young at heart. Laura Snell recalled traits that were unusual in someone Orra's age.

> . . . her imagination hadn't solidified and she was also uninhibited. Instead of straight lectures on the glacial geology of Saratoga as we were driving along, she had no problem fantasizing that we were snorkeling under a glacial lake, which Laura felt unusual in someone her age.[7]

Ruth Schottman noticed that Orra smiled more as she aged, softening the lines in her weathered face.

The Fort Plain Girl Scout, Phyllis Brown, recalled the eighty-four-year-old Orra's faithfulness to the Browns' needs when their mother died. Doc arrived saying, "I just had to come." Phyllis continued, "She drove sixty miles out here and a lot of people who went to the funeral, my sister, brother, and everybody saw Doc. It was like a reunion. I'll never forget it."[8]

In October 1980, Orra had an auto accident that put an end to her remarkable independence. Her car had been her botanical foray van, log carrier, geological specimen carter, fisherman's lorry, hiker's truck, historian's wagon, and doctor's ambulance. Permanent equipment had included a foot-long digger made from an old car spring, ten power lenses, binoculars, maps, and black fly dope. The aged car had a hole in the driver's side floorboard through which one could see the pavement below and rust crept up the fenders.

Orra had long been prone to botanizing while driving. She would step on the gas, rush along, and then screech to a roadside stop for specimens. Friends and relatives worried about her safety. As her friend Lillian Hunt recalled, Orra had come to her house for an early dinner and they had enjoyed watching the 1980 Olympics from Lake Placid in color. Orra did not have color television.

> She left before dark because she didn't want to drive at night. I didn't hear from her, and I called and I called. I didn't know where she was because she knew every back road from here to home. Finally, at 8:30 p.m. she gave me a call. She had had an accident.[9]

It was believed that the eighty-five-year-old Orra had suffered a small stroke and blacked out. Her car ended hung down over a culvert on the Greenfield Road, not very far from home. She climbed out the passenger side window, a bit bruised and shaken, and walked to the nearest house to phone for help. Phoebe and Ronald Hunt came to take her home. After a few days she made what must have been a difficult decision: she donated her car to her young garden helper and reluctantly gave up driving.

As she aged, Orra became more stoic than ever. By the fall of 1983, she recognized she could no longer live alone and chose to live at the Home of the Good Shepherd in Saratoga Springs. She rented her house to Navy men to subsidize her expenses.

While living in Saratoga Springs, Orra hungered for nature and still loved adventure. She leapt at the chance to visit a clump of the locally rare *Hydrastis,* or Golden Seal, growing near Skidmore College. As Laura Snell, Orra's younger protegé, recalls:

> Taking her out from the nursing home, she asked to go to see her *Hydrastus.* We both knew that I knew nothing about taking care of an old lady and there was an extremely good chance that she was going to fall on the rocks. Well, she did fall . . . she wasn't exactly in good ambling condition . . . and I don't know if we ever confessed where we'd been and what had happened to her.[10]

Well beyond eighty-five, there remained something ageless about Orra. She related to people of all ages. She could walk with a little boy and find something of interest and explain it on a level that he could enjoy or go out with university professors speaking "botanese."

Dick and Wendy Best spoke of the admiration their son, Michael, had for Orra: "[She] was a real inspiration to him and largely responsible for his love of the out-of-doors and the mountains and the Adirondacks. He just really admired her so much."[11] They went on to tell of their shared, mutual ideals. When their daughter, Jan, worked a whole year to earn money for a new bicycle, Orra thought that was a great thing.

Orra believed in the value of working for something and seemed to epitomize the hard-working New Englander and upstate New Yorker, a person who had indomitable ethics. Maybe she was not very tolerant of people who did not feel that way, but she certainly knew what she thought was right, and went after what she wanted.

Orra never gave up the Adirondacks, even though she could no longer go there at will. As the Bests recalled:

She always had a slide projector set up in her room and would look at her slides of certain trips, primarily of Adirondack scenery and some of her favorite spots. That's how she kept in touch.

So we perceived that she would enjoy a day trip up there. . . We had never been to the Adirondacks, never driven through Keene Valley and were literally gawking out the windows. She rattled off the mountain names; knew them all.

We ate inside at Heart Lake, because it was a cool, but glorious October day. She enjoyed it so much. I remember speeding back down the Northway to get her back for dinner time.[12]

Just as Orra had inspired others to climb the Adirondacks, she moved the Bests to also become Forty-Sixers.

In August of 1975, when Orra Phelps hiked three and a half miles to Johns Brook Lodge (JBL) in the Keene Valley with the author and her family, she did so carrying a half-century's memories of the lodge, one of her favorite spots in the Adirondacks.

She had photographed the Great Range when the young trees around JBL allowed sweeping vistas and had argued to keep out a proposed road to the lodge, fearing it would spoil the wilderness character. She had witnessed the devoted supervision of Alice Waterhouse and Peggy Goodwin O'Brien, both Mother Superiors to JBL; the removal of the porch roof; Nubbins, the pack donkey; the discussions of the name, Johns Brook;[13] and countless meetings and overnights.

Nubbins, the cantankerous pack donkey at Johns Brook Lodge.

The author recalled, "That August 11th night we celebrated Orra's eightieth birthday, although it was actually her mother's birth date, to remember the many celebrations Orra and her mother had shared on that date. We marveled at the Perseid meteor showers, celestial fireworks so bright over the deep dark woods. Bats swooped and feasted on insects in the gathering darkness, then roosted along the high timbers of the lodge, while inside the fire in the great hearth drew us to its warmth.

Tired hikers soon shuffled to bed. Despite bear claw marks on the window screen, Orra chose to sleep in the big bed next to the open window and snored softly, content in her home away from home.

"The next day, Orra accompanied us along the Phelps Trail as our family[14] made our way toward Mt. Marcy. Orra pointed with her sturdy staff to flowers and ferns, naming them in her casual way. It was her plan to climb to the approximate 4,000-foot mark to keep her Forty-Sixer status current. There she stopped and rested on a nursery log, full of seedlings in moss. Another hiker came along and, after she bid us good luck, Orra shared with the newcomer more of her lore.

"After our hike, we refreshed ourselves in the cold water of Johns Brook as we shared our day's adventure and recalled the mountaintop plants we had seen. Orra visualized whatever we mentioned and was proud that she had done her 4,000-footer in her eightieth year."

Henry and Katie Germond also recalled being at JBL with Orra:

> One of Katie's most memorable days was spent in the Johns Brook Lodge kitchen as she helped Orra prepare lunch for a Board of Governors meeting [during a time when JBL had no regular staff for food preparation.] The main meat course and limited other supplies had been packed in, but much had to be improvised from items . . . in the storeroom. Katie will never forget all the ingenious methods that were used to produce a tasty and much-praised meal from meager resources.[15]

Orra checked to see if the roast was done by piercing it with a sharpened sapling stick and dipping a piece of bread to see how red the meat juice was. Hot peach cobbler was whipped together from canned peaches and a few other staples for dessert. The Germonds continued:

Their wide-ranging conversation added much to the day. The following morning Katie accompanied Orra as she improvised fishing tackle and sallied forth to catch a breakfast trout from Black Brook.

Orra often wrote of being at JBL in her letters, sharing her love of the region with friends and relatives. She often scooted back to Keene Valley over Lower Wolf Jaws, to take in one more High Peak view before she left for the valleys. Once, when the author returned from Cascade and Porter, Orra asked, "How was the blueberrying up there?" She never stopped wanting new information about the summits to update her store of data.

In an uncharacteristic reaction for her, Orra was piqued over writer and conservation consultant Anne LaBastille's 1976 book, *Woodswoman*.[16] Laura Snell recalled Orra's reaction:

One of the few times I have ever seen Dr. Phelps display a tinge of jealousy . . . was when Anne LaBastille was getting a lot of press . . . Orra said, "She hasn't done half the things I have done." This was unusual because she [OAP] was always so modest . . . She was bugged about that, she really was.[17]

In Orra's copy of *Woodswoman* she had penciled corrections and comments in the margin, noting LaBastille's confusion of similar species, inaccuracies, or differences in their versions of good conservation ideas. "Joe-pye-weed and boneset don't bloom in spring, the word 'canoe' was mixed with 'guideboat,' white-throated sparrow with white- crowned sparrows, and balsam with spruces." LaBastille had termed the Northville-Placid Trail a shorter version of the Appalachian Trail, to which Orra had penciled in, "not over mts. and length not 113 but 132+ miles."

Orra Phelps, a woman who knew so much about the vast Adirondack Park and who recognized it as largely wilderness, narrated a part of the Couchsachraga Association's 1980 documentary film, *The Adirondack: The Land Nobody Knows*.[18] Speaking in the film of the arctic/alpine mountaintop plant community she said:

The vegetation on the top of the mountains could be compared to a little low jungle, only ankle high. The grasses, plants, and the bushes all come up together. Walking on them breaks not only the branches, and knocks the leaves and the buds off, but also breaks the roots of these plants and they are attached in such shallow soil that they are in danger, always, of being lost.

Her final words, "They are in danger, always, of being lost" echoed her decades-long mission of protecting the Adirondacks and encouraging others to continue that mission beyond her lifetime.

Four books have been dedicated in honor of Orra and in recognition of her work. The first and third, in 1985 and 1992 respectively, were the eleventh and twelfth editions of *Guide to the Adirondack Trails, High Peak Region.* Dr. Edwin H. Ketchledge movingly wrote in the twelfth edition:

Dedication: Orra A. Phelps
September 10, 1895 - August 26, 1986

If it is possible for any one individual in her full life of achievement to personify the dual spirit and purpose of the Adirondack Mountain Club, Orra A. Phelps shines as our finest companion.

In her early seasons in the High Peaks, Orra explored the mountains and the trails, then edited the first edition of this trail guide, in order to lead others to the joys and satisfaction of the wilderness experience. In the subsequent years, Orra devoted her technical skills in botany and nature study to the development of our natural history program at Heart Lake, there for many years serving as Ranger-Naturalist and sharing her insights into the wondrous world around us as we climb. A whole generation of ADKers owes much of their understanding of the mountains to the educational programs presented by Orra and her associates. In the quality of her life and her service to others, Orra pioneered pathways that ever beckon others to follow, as they too explore and enjoy the many faces of the High Peaks.

In that first edition published in 1934, she proposed a series of guides to trails throughout the Adirondacks.

The eleventh edition was the first of the now-complete Forest Preserve Series and the twelfth edition is the continuation of that series. Thus, "better late than never," her dream has become an on-going reality; and it seems only appropriate that we should rededicate this twelfth edition to our dear friend, Orra A. Phelps.

— E.H. Ketchledge[19]

Chronologically, the second volume dedicated to Orra was by Howard W. and Elizabeth B. Jaffe in the *Geology of the Adirondack High Peaks Region, A Hiker's Guide*, published by the Adirondack Mountain Club, Inc. in 1986. They wrote, "This guidebook is dedicated to our friend, colleague, fellow hiker, and the inspiring first leader of the ADK Natural History Program, Orra A. Phelps, M.D."[20]

The Adirondack Forty-Sixers also honored Orra Phelps when they used a portion of her song, "Tahawus," for their 1991 book, *Of the Summits, of the Forests*.

Most recently, Dr. Nancy G. Slack and Allison W. Bell honored Orra Phelps in their book, *85 Acres, A Field Guide to the Adirondack Alpine Summits* published by the Adirondack Mountain Club, Inc. They wrote, "This book is dedicated to Adirondack explorers and botanists Jerome S. Kates and Orra A. Phelps, and to Norwegian ecologist Eilif Dahl."[21]

Reflecting on Orra Phelps's impact, James Goodwin mused that he and Orra Phelps had been so instrumental in opening the Adirondacks.

It's interesting that she wanted to make the mountains available to people and therefore brought many more people to the mountains than would have come otherwise [through her 1934 guidebook.] I was even a little guilty of the same thing. I wrote the description of how to climb the trailless peaks.[22]

As Grace Hudowalski wrote in the *Adirondac* article, "Orra Phelps Remembered":

The 1941 edition of Orra's guide carried a condensation of an article [James Goodwin wrote] for the 1939 *Highspots*. It sounds rather strange now, some forty-seven years later to read her comments on the trailless peaks:

"There are 21 trailless peaks with elevations of 4,000 feet or more. These are occasionally climbed by those who like adventure and arduous bushwhacking. With the help of the USGS maps of the region the ambitious hiker can map his own route for the ascent."

Little did she know—nor did we—how soon those "occasionally climbed" mountains would be invaded by a steady stream of hikers, hikers getting their first route information from the ADK Guide to the Adirondack Trails, 1941, edited by Orra A. Phelps![23]

Orra's medical degree from Johns Hopkins and fifty-year practice of medicine in New York State brought her academic recognition, financial security, and satisfaction in helping others. But as Douglas Ayres said, "She was so enthusiastic about the whole outdoors and the mountains, it's just too bad that she couldn't have devoted more time to it . . . It ought to have been her career." The author answered that it was a compromise she knowingly undertook.

In her school years, there were not many career opportunities in ecology, environmental protection, and earth sciences, especially for women. Ayres, a high school science teacher, similarly confined to a life indoors, reflected what must have been their common unfulfilled longing,

As many times as I went in the west door of the school—I'd look back at the sky and the trees and the wind and think, "Boy, how I'd like to be on top of Mt. Dix right now, or Marcy or MacIntyre."

Two ADK Guidebook editors, Dr. Orra Phelps at age 90 (1934 edition) and Tony Goodwin with son Morgan (1985 edition); and Neal S. Burdick (in back), series editor, at ADK Lodge, June 15, 1985. The eleventh and twelfth editions were dedicated to Orra.

When it came time to dedicate the eleventh edition of the guidebook on June 15, 1985, Dr. Mildred Faust, Orra's two nieces, Phoebe Hunt and the author, and grand-niece, Lili Aram, accompanied Orra to Heart Lake for the ADK reception. Tony Goodwin, editor of the eleventh edition, was very excited that both the original

Orra Phelps's much-decorated hat, which carries badges of the Northville-Placid Trail, the Wilderness Society, the ADK Forty-Sixers, and the Adirondack Mountain Club.

and the current editors, including Neal Burdick, were to be present. Both editors signed just six copies of the eleventh edition, a rarity for bibliophiles.

Sadly, by then a series of small strokes had left Orra with very limited speech and wheelchair-bound. Nevertheless, she was excited about the event and felt honored to have the eleventh edition dedicated to her. When the reception ended, she relished the familiar view across Heart Lake and rested on her many laurels.

Orra Phelps died in Glens Falls, New York on August 26, 1986, sixty years from the day she first saw Adirondak Loj. She is buried with her parents in Storrs, Connecticut, with an Adirondack anorthosite gravestone linking her to her beloved mountains.

— Epilogue —

Observations and Memories of the Author

Long before I had read the thousands of pages of Phelps letters and diaries, I was aware of the life-long symbiosis between Orra and her mother. By naming her first daughter after herself—a practice long done by fathers and first sons—Mrs. Phelps began the bonding between herself and her eldest daughter. They had the same vigor, intellectual curiosity, and independent nature.

In each other they had a kindred soul with whom to share all the scientific news of . . . botany, geology, ornithology, and astronomy, plus common interests in stamps, coin collecting and good books, especially those pertaining to the Adirondacks or New England history. These two female scientists made a most unusual duo, one of the earliest pairs of published mother/daughter botanists.

Through the Phelps letters, I have been privileged to share the intimate hopes and dreams, frus-

The author, Mary Arakelian.

trations and pains, pride and compromises of a most remarkable woman, Dr. Orra Phelps. In addition, during hundreds of hours of interviews with her former Girl Scouts, classmates, neighbors, relatives, hiking companions, Adirondack Mountain Club friends, botanical and other natural history colleagues I have shared their insights into her life, anecdotes, and words of admiration, respect, and humor.

This wealth of information has been added to my life-long loving relationship with Aunt Orra and my grandmother. As they nurtured me, we mutually shared our worlds, our love of nature, and our New England heritage. As if I were one of the Phelps children, I joined Orra and Mrs. Phelps for various Mt. Holyoke College reunions and witnessed their pride in their alma mater. For Mrs. Phelps's sixtieth and Orra's thirtieth reunions in 1948, I wore Mrs. Phelps's college dress in the reunion parade. Aunt Orra then took me to the science building where she showed me a model of the Dionne quintuplet embryos. The weekend was a heady experience, increasing my desire for a college education.

At the age of eighty-three, Orra gave the class address at their sixtieth reunion in 1978, which I was able to attend together with my daughter, Orra's grandniece, Sherene Aram. During Orra's last and sixty-fifth reunion in 1983, her class was housed in the college infirmary. She very proudly rode in the parade of classes and participated in all the events.

During childhood, I stayed with my grandparents and/or Aunt Orra many times for a week or two. We went birding, camping in the Adirondacks, and botanizing. When my grandmother was bedridden at the end of her life, I went to live with her and Aunt Orra in Wilton and, at fifteen, was entrusted with her well-being while Aunt Orra worked.

Aunt Orra asked for my high school valedictory speech to save, just as her mother had done when she was younger. Although the money for my education came from my parents, from scholarships, and from working while in college, the Bachelor's of Science degree I earned from the University of Rochester was due, in large part, to the influence of these two strong women. In my freshman year, I remember Aunt Orra saying, "Do take a course in geology with Dr. Harold Alling. Geology is so fascinating." Over dinner at his home, the silver-haired Professor Emeritus reminisced about the Adirondacks, his early days at St. Lawrence University, and his friendship with the two Phelps women.

Although, as an adult, I always lived a distance from Aunt Orra, we visited each other frequently and hiked together in the Adirondacks

Orra's nieces gathered for a recent photograph. (Left to right) Phoebe Hunt, Mary Arakelian, Dorothy Hanlon, and Rachel Kellogg.   *July 30, 2000 photo*

whenever we could. At times, when introducing me to her friends, she would slip and say "my daughter, Mary," in a manner which made me feel very special. Once when she came to visit me, she mused about not having married nor having her own family, but then said she had me and my sisters' families as "her family." Although she spent considerable time with my sisters and their families, they did not share as much of her world as I have.

She requested that I serve as her guardian and the executrix of her will, a role I have felt privileged to fill. I have been entrusted with her private papers, library, and residue and now hope, through this book, to inspire others to follow her example as stewards of our land, as friends to our fellow man, and as teachers, by example, to the next generation.

In Orra's formative years, her mother shared her broad scientific knowledge and Orra's sponge-like brain soaked in all she could. Orra always held her mother's botanical knowledge in the highest esteem, saying, "My mother is the real botanist in the family." Orra would write to Mamma describing an unfamiliar plant, fully expecting

Mrs. Phelps to either know it from field work or to find it in her Gray's *The Manual of Botany of Northeastern United States*, the bible for botanists, or other references.

By her teen years, Orra knew vast amounts of natural history and other basic sciences. Her formal education at Mount Holyoke College built upon this, plus her science teaching at New Hampshire College and continual learning from Mrs. Phelps and other scientists added to her fund of information.

Orra's interest in and knowledge of the rare plants of the Adirondacks began with fieldwork in 1913 with her mother. Interrupted only by Orra's years of schooling or work, Orra and her mother trekked into the mountains and through swamps looking for the unusual. Around Canton, on Mt. Marcy, in Indian Pass, up along Scott's Pond, along Mount McGregor's Lake Bonita, and in the Greenfield bog near their Wilton farm, the two botanists hunted for and relished finding in some spots orchids, gentians, pyrola, cassandra, cranberries, leatherleaf, and more.

Through the Phelps letters, I also learned that Orra applied for an honorary MA in Science degree for Mrs. Phelps on her 50th college anniversary in 1938. Orra solicited and received numerous letters attesting to Mrs. Phelps's lifelong service to science, especially to botany. Professors from Harvard, Syracuse University, Yale, and Cornell wrote of her many contributions to their herbaria, as did botanists from the New York and Brooklyn Botanical Gardens and the NYS Museum.

Mrs. Phelps was praised for finding two new species of plants, keeping abreast of new scientific information, preparing the huge Connecticut plant collection, and teaching science at the high school level and at camps and to other groups. Mrs. Phelps had also written numerous nature articles as well as a book about her childhood in Connecticut, *When I Was a Girl in the Martin Box*, published in 1949.

Although Mrs. Phelps's credentials and accomplishments were considerable, Mount Holyoke College did not award any honorary degrees that year. Mrs. Phelps felt quite honored with the many letters of testimony. Professor M.L. Fernald of Harvard, who edited Gray's botany manual, wrote in 1938:

My attention has been called to the very extensive fieldwork in botany which for many years was carried on by
Orra Parker Phelps . . . Beginning many years ago Mrs.
Phelps sent carefully collected and discriminatingly chosen plants of Connecticut and of northern New York to
the Gray Herbarium for comparison, and supplied us
with a large amount of very valuable material. At least
two plants she secured in northern New York proved to
be new to science and have been named in her honor. I
therefore feel that it would be an appropriate recognition if Mt. Holyoke were inclined to award her an honorary degree of Master of Arts at her fiftieth anniversary.
M.L. Fernald Director, Gray Herbarium, Harvard.
4/15/38

In a 1988 interview with Dr. Edwin Ketchledge, Syracuse University Professor Emeritus, he noted that the 1924 *Annotated List of Ferns
and Flowering Plants of New York State* by the then state botanist, Dr.
Homer D. House, was full of Mrs. Phelps's finds. She found many first
northern locations for rare plants in St. Lawrence County and surrounding areas. The book is a classic according to Ketchledge and is still in use.

As the younger Orra began her medical career, Mamma lived
even more through Orra, achieving goals vicariously that she had not
been able to achieve on her own. She increasingly depended on Orra
for interesting things to do and people to visit. She hungered for trips
with Orra and Orra's friends and rarely traveled on her own. They
traveled to Nova Scotia, the Gaspé, the Great Smokies, and to Florida.

Mamma wanted to know every scrap of information about
Orra's life and, at times, became intrusive on Orra's personal life,
her friendships, and her plans. Orra tactfully told her mother she
was capable of making her own plans, buying her own clothing,
and choosing her hair style.

The following excerpts show Orra's protests.

May 14, 1935
Dear Mamma,
Thanks for your suggestions. . . but I'm awfully good
at making plans myself. . . . Don't propose it to any folks
over there tho' for I may find someone myself.

September 11, 1939
Dear Mamma,

Don't think I don't understand how much you love the mountains, for I love them too — and the fragrance of balsam and streams and ferns and mossy logs. But we can't have such treats all the time — they'd lose their flavor if we did. But do get out roaming a little at home — just to drop the pressure of household affairs.

September 24, 1940
Dear Mamma,

You should not get such ideas — and build your hopes on them — because tho' I can always come when needed, it is not right for me to leave my place here and my job. It takes more than six hours a day in school to keep that job.

Orra, in turn, was emotionally tied to her mother, constantly fearing Mamma would have another depression. She listened to Mrs. Phelps's woes, encouraged her to vent her frustrations and bolstered her self-esteem, while at the same time allowing her mother to remain dependent. An example of Orra's encouragement is followed by Mamma's self-conscious reply. Orra wrote:

October 4, 1936
Dear M.

As for the Scotia party — just keep in mind that you're just as good as any of them and you know a darned sight more n' any of them.

Mamma's reply came flying back:

October 5, 1936
. . . As to Scotia meeting [talk on ferns at a garden club], when I am properly dressed I can face most anyone. It's only when my shoes are shabby or I haven't gloves or a fall hat that I feel worse than a shrinking violet. Thanks to my daughters this time I can hold my head high.

Had Orra been more free of family responsibility, she might well have established her own medical practice, married and had her own family, or traveled farther in her career. Should Orra have chosen a career in botany rather than medicine? Had she majored in botany at Mount Holyoke College, she might have remained there as a botany professor, but top positions were scarce in that field.

Her choice of medicine may have been an effort to separate herself from her mother. Medicine promised recognition, money, and service to her fellow man, which Orra felt she should give. Medicine also offered any number of jobs where the few positions in science teaching often went to men. In the end, Orra devoted perhaps as much time and energy to being a naturalist as she did to her medical career and gave quality service to both endeavors.

Why did Orra not have a private practice? I feel Orra chose public health in order to avoid the responsibility of a private case load. She was then free for hiking, traveling, or helping her family. She had the care of her parents and Francis on a regular and often urgent basis. Also there was the family's chronic shortage of cash which may have prevented Orra from starting a private practice, with its low initial income.

Why didn't Orra marry? After having read the Phelps letters, I recognize that Orra knew how stressful her parents' marriage was. Most likely she did not want to commit herself to anything similar. She was also responsible for Francis as his caretaker and for Mrs. Phelps until their deaths in 1949 and 1950, respectively.

From another perspective, many women scientists of that era chose between marriage and a career. Orra was a self-directed person and perhaps did not want to share her freedom or independence with a husband and children or to compromise her career by marriage. Throughout her life, she thought of Captain Coulter as the ideal man. Had her mother and her Aunt Bessie not been so interfering, and had Orra been able to disagree with their admonitions never to marry a Catholic and take an opposite position, she might have married him and had an entirely different life.

Likewise, had she been able to disentangle herself from her mother's interference with her friendship with Al West, they might have married.

I have included very little of this lamentable triangle, but the following excerpts give some insight.

> October 17, 1939
> Dear Mamma,
>   . . . Really, Al didn't say anything to me about himself, just talked about pictures. If he wrote you pages you'd still raise questions about something he didn't tell you. Don't expect him to tell anything, then what he does tell will seem like more. Why do you expect to know all the ins and outs of his life? Why do you keep some things of your doing and thinking to yourself? Because you don't want to be querried and cross examined. Maybe Al feels a bit like that too. Trust him — trust him even if you don't approve or agree.

There was also evidence that Mrs. Phelps liked being Al's friend, further complicating Orra's friendship.

> February 25, 1938
> Dear Orra,
>   . . . Al is fine, we both know it and feel his charm. He is one of the few whom I know whom I feel keenly appreciates things fine and beautiful — who knows the books I love and who rouses my desire to read those which have met with his approval. I know that I am out of date and that Al naturally seeks those his own age . . . he has aims, ambitions and friends to fill his life. That he has given me of his time and apparent interest is really more than I could expect. And I had hoped that my faith and interest in him might hearten him. He hasn't had any too much encouragement in the past. Possibly he is where he doesn't need it. I shall keep my interest in him [because] outlets for my great interest aren't too many.

The fact that the two Phelps women had many friends in common was both good and bad. It was natural that they enjoyed the same people with their mutual interests. They made a one-two punch in the affect they had on people, one having as much presence as the next and comparable scientific knowledge. Despite Mrs. Phelps's intrusions on Orra's personal life, it was Mrs. Phelps who had opened many doors for Orra through her education at Mount Holyoke College, her scientific friends in Connecticut and at St. Lawrence University, and with her early contacts with senior scientists at the New York State Museum.

The younger Orra was able to build on her mother's entrees and botanical knowledge through her extensive botanizing while hiking in the Adirondacks and in New England. She also joined other knowledgeable botanists in her explorations and associations such as Stanley Smith, Dr. Eugene Ogden, Dr. Richard Mitchell, Dr. Mildred Faust, Dr. Edwin Ketchledge, Dr. Nancy Slack, and Ruth Schottman.

Mrs. Phelps's letters contain many inspirational statements advocating the rights of women: higher education, financial independence, better mental health, and personal, political, and social equal rights. By her own example, she was a woman ahead of her times. Just as Mrs. Phelps had strong female role models, Orra also benefited from having her mother and other female role models. Orra advanced the causes of women even farther during her lifetime. She spoke on sex education for teenage women, led the senior Girl Scout troop and mentored her charges in the process, aided a friend with retarded children, and provided safe haven for battered women. At her home, she led college youth groups and counseled troubled youths.

Both Orra and her mother lived through much change, but they kept up with the times, a practice they both valued. They scoured the newspapers for scientific news, shared new books and journals, and corresponded with friends who did likewise. Orra lived from a childhood of the horse and buggy to men landing on the moon, a large span for one lifetime. In terms of environmental awareness, Orra was doing things about ecology before the word became popular.

To me, the biggest difference between Orra and her mother, and perhaps what was most remarkable about her, was personal. Orra was a self-actualized person who had fulfilled most of her personal goals, and who was comfortable with her being. Stable, mature, and independent, Orra was comfortable living alone because she related well to her many friends and to people around her. She reached out to them and took a personal interest in their lives.

With her remarkable good health and adequate income, she remained active well into her mid-eighties in organizations whose goals she admired. She was an outward-looking person, with vision, a healthy sense of priorities, and a strong religious faith.

Yes, she sometimes said she might have done more and that she missed family and friends who had passed on. But she didn't fret about this; she concentrated on broader interests, concerns, and service. She was a positive person who found joy in nature, stimulation in the work of younger scientists, and satisfaction in the memories of her full life.

Posthumously, Orra Phelps was further honored by being registered on October 16, 1997 with The Women in the Military Service Foundation.

Also, on October 24, 1998, The Phelps Nature Preserve in Wilton, New York was dedicated and has a New York State roadside marker at its entrance honoring Dr. Orra A. Phelps as a Distinguished Woman of Saratoga County.

Appendix A

MOUNTAINTOP FLORA

by Orra A. Phelps

Courtesy of the Adirondack Forty-Sixers, reprinted from *The Adirondack High Peaks and the Forty-Sixers*, 1970.

Among the scientists who made the first recorded ascent of Mount Marcy in 1837 there was one botanist, Professor John Torrey. It would be interesting to review any notes that he made then of the plants that he saw, their characteristics and manner of growth. The rocky top of the mountain hasn't changed much. The clouds, fog, rain, snow, the sunlight, temperature and wind are the same. But what of the plants? Has the invasion of man, increasing year by year, brought changes there?

Since the earliest ascents of the High Peaks of the Adirondack Mountains, those with their summits above the limit of stunted spruce and balsam, climbers have noticed the dwarf plant growth and certain species not found on lower mountains nor in the forest through which they had just come. Remarkable here is the tightly tangled mass of low shrubs with stiff branches and small leaves. Here and there are dense tufts of grass-like plants. Beneath the shrubs there is an almost continuous mat of lichens and moss. Walking over this jungle, barely ankle deep, is like walking on a springy cushion, with no sensation of the solid rock a few inches beneath.

The plant growth here is different from that in the valleys or on the forested slopes because the environment is so different. At these elevations the winters are long and the plants are buried in snow for months. The snow is their protection. It minimizes the extreme cold and shelters from the bitter winter winds. Wind is a dynamic factor for mountain vegetation. It is the wind rather than the cold that stunts the spruce and balsam. Only the low-growing, densely tufted grasses, sedges and tangled shrubs with roots intertwined can resist the wind's force.

Long winters mean short summers. Plants must burgeon, bud, bloom and set seed before the frosts of late August. The many hours of daylight between sunup and sundown in spring help the rapid growth. But these hours are not all bright with sunshine. Remember how often the mountain tops are wreathed in mists? All mountain top plants must tolerate this moisture. Most thrive on it.

The climatic conditions of 5,000-foot mountains in north eastern United States is similar to the climate of the arctic regions. It is not surprising then that there are interesting parallels between the flora of the arctic tundra and the flora of the highest Adirondacks, White Mountains and Katahdin. Plants common to both areas have been termed arctic-alpines. There are a few arctic-alpine plants in the Adirondacks. A somewhat larger group of plants, found on lesser mountains and south of the arctic circle may be classed as subarctic-subalpine.

Though the wind and snow make the mountain tops in winter seem like an arctic climate there are ways in which the plant environment on our mountains is different from tundra. Soil conditions may differ, also the amount of available water. Permafrost in the tundra means constant wetness in summer. There are very few places in the Adirondacks where there is permafrost. In the arctic there are the longer hours of daylight and the shorter growing season. It is not accurate to speak of the vegetative cover of our mountain as *tundra*, but in some places the soil, moisture, and plant growth show characteristics of tundra vegetation so can be called tundra-like.

Some mountaintop plants, like tundra plants, blossom almost as soon as the snow is off of them. The season for the arctic-alpines in the Adirondacks is the second week in June when there are still some patches of old snow around. These plants form their blossom buds the summer before. With protection of tight bud-scales, the buds survive the winter cold and are ready to burst with the first spring warmth. In July, the Leatherleaf buds are ready for next May and buds formed in August on the Labrador Tea blossom the following July. This feature helps plants survive in spite of the shortness of the growing season.

All climbers have noticed that elevation affects the time of blooming. As you ascend you move backward in the season. Plants in blossom at 2,000 feet are only budded at 3,000 feet and at 4,000 feet they are just unfolding their leaves. This has an advantage for us as often we can find at high elevations plants in flower that are past blooming elsewhere. This does not, however, apply to arctic-alpines. For them there is no elsewhere.

When climbing above the 4,500-foot elevation you have doubtless noticed that there are places where the footpath has been cut through the entire thickness of the spongy dark brown soil to the rock underneath. This soil is not glacial residual. It has been made, *in place*, over thousand of years by the accumulation of material from dead mosses, lichens, leaves, roots and stems of other plants with the addition of a small amount of mineral from the underlying rock. The chief characteristic of this soil is its sponginess, its ability to hold moisture and continuously supply the water requirements of the plants.

In the footpath, the boots of climbers break the twigs and roots of this intertwined, and interdependent, mat of vegetation. A slight depression forms where we tread. Seepage from the rock forms a rill, then a heavy rain cuts through the soil to the rock surface. In another storm, a chunk of soil, plants and all, is washed off the bedrock, soil without which there can be no rare arctic-alpines to bloom. On the mountains, nature is working against heavy odds and here one of the odds is boot traffic. We may well pause to wonder how long nature has worked to make the soil. How long will it take to replace the chunk, cut by boots and washed away?

Every Forty-Sixer and every aspiring Forty-Sixer should learn to recognize the plants and shrubs that are peculiar to the open high summits. We could also assume the responsibility of teaching other climbers. Next time you are on Algonquin, Mount Marcy, Haystack or Skylight and you stop for breath before racing to put your foot on the geodetic survey marker on the topmost rock, take a look at the plants at your feet that make up this unique tundra-like area.

BEARBERRY WILLOW or ARCTIC WILLOW, *Salix uva-ursi Pursh*, is a truly prostrate shrub, woody many-branched and seeming to creep vinelike out over open rock. The leaves are oval and a bright shiny green. Its pussies appear in early spring on the male plant. The seed catkin (female) appears at first as a bright red tip on the twig then turns brownish and elongates as the seeds develop. It is a true arctic-alpine and an important member of the tundra-like mountain vegetation.

LEATHER-LEAF, *Chamadaphne calyculata*, is one of the earliest blooming shrubs. The blossoms are a string of tiny white urn-shaped bells pendant on the slender arched twig. The shrub, barely a foot high on the mountaintops, holds its rusty green leaves over winter. This shrub is also found growing to a height of three feet in some sphagnum bogs or on the boggy shores of small ponds in the north. It is a plant that likes wetness so on the mountains will be found where there is continuous seepage.

LOW SWEET BLUEBERRY, *Vaccinium angustifolium*, is known from seashore to mountaintop and many hills and fields in between. The botanists consider the one found on our highest mountains a distinct variety. But I must say, parenthetically, its berries on Algonquin or Colden are twice as good as those from tamer sites! Its blossoms, a cluster of white or pink-tinged globular bells, appear in mid-June.

BILBERRY, *Vaccinium uliginosum*, is another blueberry but quite distinct in appearance. It is one of the important components of the tundra-like habitat. It grows tangled with the arctic willow and the sweet blueberry, but it is easily recognized by its oval blue-green leaf. Its flowers are similar to the former in size and shape, but tend to be pinker, almost red. The berry is blue, of course, and somewhat oval. It is edible but not quite as juicy and flavorful as the low sweet blueberry. The botanists distinguish a third blueberry but it takes a specialist to recognize it. You can enjoy eating its fruit without knowing its technical differences!

The PALE LAUREL, *Kalmia polifolia*, as well as the following species, grows both on the mountain summits and in cold bogs at lower elevations. This one is the earlier to blossom, a cluster of clear pink open cups with five tiny points on the brim. The blossom cluster is terminal, that is at the end of the twig. The leaf must be noted to make sure of the identity. It is a narrow, shiny green leaf, white at the base of the mid-rib on its upper surface and whitish over the entire under surface. It begins to bloom about June 15.

The SHEEP LAUREL or LAMBKILL, *Kalmia angustifolia*, has the same cup-shaped bloom but it is deeper pink, almost red. The blossom cluster is not terminal, but has a leaf cluster above it at the tip of the twig. The leaf is yellow-green above and beneath. This does not begin to bloom till the Pale Laurel is past its season, in early July.

These two laurels are not to be confused with another, the Mountain Laurel, *Kalmia latifolia*, found abundantly in the Berkshire and Catskill mountains and southward.

The LAPLAND ROSEBAY, *Rhododendron lapponicum*, when its cerise blossoms open in early June, is even more striking than the beautiful laurels. Its leaves are about an inch long, thick and appearing rusty. The individual flowers are an inch across and bright cerise in color. Flowering in terminal clusters makes the shrub more conspicuous and easily recognized. When not in bloom, it is difficult to find. Seeing it in its blooming season you may think it is abundant, but it is rare because it grows on only four or five summits where the environment meets its needs. It is a true arctic-alpine found in the tundra from Labrador to Alaska, also in Eurasia.

LABRADOR TEA, *Ledum groenlandicum*, grows in boggy areas at lower elevations in the north but is also found, often in dwarf form, in the peaty areas above 4,500 feet. The leaves, under an inch and a half long, appear rolled at the edges and the under surface is clothed in wooly felt, white when the leaf is young, becoming brown as the leaf matures. It holds its leaves over winter but these soon lose their rich green and become rusty. The flowers, small and white, occur in close spherical clusters about two inches across. Blooming time on the mountains is early July. There is an unusual stand of it on the way to Iroquois from Algonquin. This shrub illustrates particularly well the habit of bud formation in late summer for next summer's bloom.

The SMALL CRANBERRY, *Vaccimium Oxycoccos*, has been given the modifier wren's egg because of its small size and speckles on the unripe berry. This species is found in high mountain bogs and in the arctic tundra. It is not the large cranberry of lake shores, sphagnum bogs and Cape Cod! On the mountains, it may be found in bogs

292 *Appendix A*

but it is also found running through the matted tundra anywhere there is sufficient moisture. It is a creeping vine with tiny evergreen leaves. The half-inch blossom, a rich pink with four petals turned back on the stem, stands up about two inches above the vine. It looks like a miniature cyclamen with narrow petals. Once, I found a spot on the south side of Mount Marcy where the blooms were so thick that in spite of their tiny size, it could be described as a sheet of pink. The fruits can often be found when the snow goes off in the spring, having been in deep freeze all winter, very acid but quite edible. It is interesting to note that all the plants mentioned so far, except the first, the arctic willow, belong to the same family, the heaths, *Ericaceae.* Other members of this family found in the Adirondacks and in other parts of northeastern United States are huckleberry, wintergreen, snowberry, trailing arbutus and azaleas. Scotland's famous heathers also belong to this family. Most of the species are woody and many are evergreen.

Blooming conspicuously at the same time as the Rosebay is another rare arctic-alpine, *Diapensia lapponica.* There is no common name for it, but the Icelandic common name can be translated "Mountain Bride." This is not a shrub. The plant forms a low, dense leafy cushion which at blossom time is stuck full of two-inch stems each bearing a single pure white cup-like flower with a five-lobed margin. When past blooming the seed capsules, rising stiffly from the domed mat of the leaves, look like green pins in a leafy pincushion. About the middle of June, when you can see the clumps of white flowers near and far on the slopes of Algonquin, it may seem that this is a common plant. Not so! Like the Rosebay, it is rare because its habitat is so limited. Moreover, it is subject to the damaging effects of cloudbursts and wind and hikers boots!

MOUNTAIN SANDWORT, *Arenaria groenlandica,* is another tufted plant with white flowers, native on the open summits but sometimes found at lower levels where gravelly soil has washed off a peak. It is a seacoast plant in Maine and Nova Scotia. Its clumps of white blossoms are just as conspicuous as the *Diapensia,* but the two should not be confused, for the *Diapensia* is past blooming when the Sandwort is at its best in July. The tufted clump is composed of many slender stems with the tiny narrow leaves paired and close to the stem.

Each stem bears a five-petaled flower, but there may be dozens of flowers on the plant in bloom at the same time. It prefers to grow, not in the peaty humus like the members of the heath family, but in the pockets of gritty soil and in crevices. This preferred habitat makes it evident why it is also a seashore plant.

A third conspicuous white flowered plant is the THREE TOOTHED CINQUEFOIL, *Potentilla tridentata.* Its foliage and manner of growth are entirely different from the two previously described here so there should be no confusion. This plant has a three parted leaf (like clover) dark and shiny green, with each leaflet notched with three teeth. The stem is woody and subterranean. The flower stem is slender and branched, bearing several five-petalled white flowers. Like Sandwort it prefers the gravelly soil and is frequently found growing in rock crevices. Its range extends from Greenland to some areas in Georgia. In fall its foliage turns a lovely wine-red, making autumn color on the mountain tops.

Another plant, important but inconspicuous in the tundra on the mountains as well as the arctic tundra is the CROWBERRY, *Empetrum nigrum.* This is so prostrate that it appears like a many branched vine creeping out over the rocks, the runners closely covered with short needle-like evergreen leaves. The blossoms, hidden between the leaves and close to the ground are so small and appear so early after the snow melts that they are seldom seen. But the berries, first light green, later turning black, are often observed. It is the inky-black berry, the size of a small blueberry, that gives the name Crowberry. The fruit is eaten by the golden plover on the arctic tundra. It is said that the berry so colors the meat of the birds that this color is still evident after their migration to Patagonia, South America. The name *Empetrum* means "on rock" which is appropriate for the plant does spread out over rocks.

In its blooming season, late June, the NORTHERN COMANDRA, *Geocaulon lividum,* is so inconspicuous that it escapes notice. It sends up from a creeping rootstock a slender stem with simple alternate leaves. The tiny flowers are borne in the axils of the leaves, two to four together, only one of which will produce a fruit. It is in the fall when this fruit, bright red and a quarter of an inch in diameter, has matured that the otherwise obscure plant is usually discovered. In range it is an arctic plant but not truly an alpine, for it is more common in the peaty areas on lesser mountains.

One of the last flowers to bloom is the ALPINE GOLDENROD, *Solidago cutleri*. The plant is eight to ten inches in height, a single upright stem, thick and with but few stem leaves. It bears a few large flower heads, larger than in most goldenrods, with bright yellow flowers. It grows with the grasses and sedges in crevices or other spots where good soil has accumulated. This goldenrod, named for an early New England botanist, Reverend Manasseh Cutler, is found on the high mountains in New York and New England but not in the arctic.

There are a number of grasses, sedges and rushes on the mountain tops and in a few places these make a more or less continuous turf. The precise identification of these plants calls for technical training and skill with the hand lens, but some of them have characteristics by which we can recognize them "on sight."

The ALPINE HOLY GRASS, *Hierochloe alpina*, occurs as scattered plants about a foot high. As its other common name, Sweet Grass, suggests, it has a fragrant odor when crushed. It is a relative of the lowland Sweet Grass used by the Indians in basketry. Its European form was strewn on the ground at religious festivals, hence the name Holy Grass.

The most conspicuous of the grassy plants is not a grass but a bulrush called DEER'S HAIR, *Scirpus cespitosus*. It is conspicuous because there is so much of it. In favorable places it makes a lumpy turf with its dense tufts. In summer its green culms (stems) less than a foot high bend before the prevailing wind. In autumn, the green culms ripen to a bright straw color. The winter snows flatten and bleach them but they still cling to the tuft. In early spring, its new green spears rise from the clumps of last year's straw. The blossom and seed capsule are insignificant. It is its characteristic manner of growth that makes it a feature of the mountain tundra.

Another of the grass-like plants that gives character to the mountaintop wild garden is *Juncus trifidus*, the three-parted rush or HIGHLAND RUSH. It is densely tufted, the culms less than a foot high, each bearing at the tip three short leaves which, in season, enfold the tiny flower and later the seed. It does not form a turf as the Deer's Hair does, but grows in separate hummocks. This is a true arctic-alpine plant.

There is one plant in this group that in season is not only conspicuous but also is beautiful, the HARE'S TAIL COTTON GRASS, *Eriophorum spissum*. A clump of several, with their fluffy white tassels, can be seen from a distance. Close inspection reveals a number of slender stems, three-sided, topped by a head of bright white bristles. It grows from a foot to fifteen inches tall. This attractive plant is found in acid bogs from Baffin Island to Alaska and in favorable sites as far south as Pennsylvania. Once you see it the appropriateness of the common name, "Cotton Grass" is obvious although it is a sedge not a grass!

These nineteen plants are not the only ones that make up the characteristic mountaintop flora. There are numerous inconspicuous grasses and sedges and a few non-flowering plants, ferns and clubmosses or ground-pines. Shrubs that grow in the valleys survive on the summits in dwarfed form: Green Alder, or Mountain Alder, *Alnus crispa*, Bartram's Shad, *Amelanchier Bartramiana*, Mountain Ash, *Pyrus decora*, more shrub-like than tree at these heights; a shrub honeysuckle, *Lonerica villosa* and Meadow Sweet, *Spirea latifolia*. Flowering plants, more at home on the forested slopes, now and then find a favorable niche somewhere high on the open summit and flourish there. The total is well over one hundred.

As plant habitats, all of the forty-six peaks over 4,000 feet are different. There are the High Peaks naturally open where the few arctic-alpine plants are at home: Haystack, Marcy, Skylight, and Algonquin. There are the forest-clad summits such as the Sewards and "Couchy," Street and Nye. There are those summits bare as a result of fire: Cascade and Porter, Giant and Rocky Peak Ridge, South and East Dix. Some have only a small rocky open area, where occasional alpines may appear: Phelps, Nippletop, Santanoni and Panther Peak. Whiteface, floristically speaking, is in a class by itself in showing changes due to man's presence. Here tolerant lowland weeds have appeared and alpines are disappearing.

On the burned-over peaks, the plant environment has been radically changed. The soil has lost its depth of humus that once held plenty of moisture. What is left is a mineral soil, sandy, gritty or gravelly. Water drains quickly away. The plants that require moist, peaty soil are not here, only those plants that can tolerate the poor soil and the rugged climate.

As a generality, it may be said that the more nearly wooded the summit, the more likely the plants of the forested slopes and the trail-sides, will be found on top. Here the change in environment is minimal. Ferns and clubmosses are dominant.

Flowers that were seen along the trails where the roads end, are found usually two or three weeks later, blooming near or above the so-called tree-line. They grow among the fringe of dwarf trees below the summit where they find sufficient soil and some protection from the wind. These listed below are conspicuous and occur frequently.

GOLDTHREAD, *Coptis groenlandica*, a small creamy white bloom on a two-inch stem, above last year's stiff, shiny three-parted leaves. The new leaves appear after flowering.

BLUEBEAD LILY, or Clinton's Lily, *Clintonia borealis*, has three or four yellow-green bells atop an eight-inch stem which rises between a pair of large (7" x 3") smooth leaves. In the Fall, the fruits are blue, hence the name.

STARFLOWER, *Trientalis borealis*, well named for the starry white flower, usually seven-petaled, held on a slender stem above a whorl of narrow leaves. The plants are usually scattered and are conspicuous only when in bloom.

CANADA MAYFLOWER, *Maianthemum canadense*, is sometimes called Wild Lily-of-the-Valley. It bears a foamy cluster of tiny white blossoms on a four inch stem, with two leaves spaced on the stalk and appearing to clasp it. The plant also produces a great many single leaves from its widespread subterranean rhizomes.

BLUETS, *Houstonia caerulea*. Here is a plant that certainly looks out of place to those who know it in old pastures or on roadsides. Mistakenly called forget-me-nots the little bluish-white flowers with four points and a yellow eye, held up on three inch stems, grow from a mat of tiny leaves. Have you seen it on Mount Marcy? It is there.

NORTHERN WHITE VIOLET, *Viola pallens,* one of the commoner violets along the trail, flourishes also in boggy places on the summit and in dripping wet moss hanging over ledges.

ROSE TWISTED-STALK, *Streptopus roseus,* looks like a member of the lily family only to a botanist. It grows about a foot high, usually branching twice and arching over rather than standing erect. The leaves, parallel-veined, as a lily should be, are spaced alternately at regular intervals. The stem zigzags from leaf to leaf, hence the twisted stalk. The blossoms, one beneath each leaf, are tiny rosy bells that in fruit become a row of bright red berries. There is a less common member of this genus, a giant up to three feet tall, similar in appearance except the blossoms are greenish.

BUNCHBERRY, or DWARF CORNEL, *Cornus canadensis,* is the most conspicuous white-flowered straggler to reach the open tops. In flowering season, a ground cover of these plants with four broad white bracts appearing as petals surrounding a center of tiny flowers, makes a sheet of white. Close inspection reveals that each blossom rises from a whorl of six leaves, but all the other leaves are in fours. Its name, Bunchberry, is from its cluster of scarlet berries ripening in August.

TWINFLOWER, *Linnaea borealis.* This flower is named for the famous Swedish botanist, Carl von Linnaeus. It grows in Sweden, too, and from Labrador to Alaska and on the western United States mountains. The plant is twinned in the arrangement of its little leaves on long vine-like sprays, creeping over moss or rock. The flowers are also twinned, two pink bells atop a single slender stem that makes a Y branch at the tip. The flower has a fragile daintiness and a delicate fragrance.

COMMON WOOD SORREL, *Oxalis montana,* covers the ground with a carpet of leaves that look like shamrock. These leaves grow from a tangle of subterranean rhizomes. The flowers appear singly, just above the leaves, an open five-petaled white or pinkish blossom with red veining.

NARROW-LEAVED GENTIAN, or Mountain Gentian, *Gentiana linearis,* seems to have made a 2,000-foot jump for it is not a trailside flower. Left behind at the road's end it appears again above

4,000 feet. It blooms late, in mid-August, a cluster of intensely blue tubular flowers on a single leafy stem. However, they grow in clumps and are spectacular when they are in bloom, especially on Cascade Mountain.

Here are thirty of the most conspicuous and attractive plants which at blossoming time draw the eye of any mountain climber. These are the plants that we are tempted to take home, plant or branch to show off. Don't do it! These, and all plants on the lands of the state, are protected by state law. It is important that all climbers know this, but better still, that all know and respect the laws that affect the balance of nature in the mountaintop "tundra-like" environment.

We say we "love our mountains" when we really mean we enjoy the exhilaration of climbing and arriving where we feel on top of the world. If we love our mountains we should be willing to make every effort to preserve their beauty, the beauty of the rare flowers that bloom there. Our first responsibility is to respect the fragile habitat and do no harm to the plants.

If we love climbing mountains we are sure, sooner or later, to invite others to share our mountaintop adventures. Our second responsibility is to make sure that others, too, perceive that the mountains are not just a challenging pile of rocks, but are rock gardens, growing since glacial ages, and are to be treated with respect.

Appendix B

Genealogy of Orra Phelps and Orson Phelps, Descendants of William Phelps

William Phelps, b. Tewkbury, Eng. 1599, d. July 14, 1672

1st wife, Elizabeth, d.1635; 2nd wife, Mary Dover, d. Nov. 27, 1675

William and his brother George came on the ship, MARY and JOHN, from Plymouth, England. Arrived at Hull, Mass. May 30, 1630. Settled in Dorchester, Mass. In 1635 William and sixty others of same church moved to Windsor, Conn. He was active in local government and bought land from Indians. This William and his first wife, Elizabeth, were parents of Nathaniel, but William and his second wife, Mary Dover were the parents of Timothy. These two half brothers started the two lines from which Orra Phelps and Orson Phelps diverged.

Orra Phelps's Line

William Phelps m./1 Elizabeth _____

#22	Nathaniel Phelps, b. England 1627, m. Elizabeth Copley
#36	Dea. Nathaniel Phelps, b. June 2, 1653, Windsor, Ct.
	m. Grace Martin, August 11, 1676
#119	Samuel Phelps, b. Dec. 18, 1680, Northampton, Ma.
	m. Mary Edwards
#307	Samuel Phelps, b. Sept. 22, 1707
	m. Mindwell Fowler

#2340 Capt. Julius Phelps, b. May 8, 1780, Northampton, Ma.; d. Jan. 13, 1858
m./1 Phoebe Warner, June 8, 1809; b. Oct. 2, 1783, Northampton, Ma.; d. Mar. 8, 1834, Northampton, Ma.
      m./2 Jemima Wright, Dec. 30, 1835

#4992 Solomon Phelps, b. Jan. 24, 1814 (son of Julius and Phebe); d. Oct. 15, 1884
      m./1 Desire Hartwell, d. 1843
m./2 Nancy Leonard on June 16, 1845; b. Dec. 28, 1826; d. July 27, 1871

#8845 Charles Shepherd Phelps, b. Dec. 5, 1861, Northampton, Ma. (son of Solomon and Nancy); d. Apr. 12, 1941, Wilton, NY
m. Orra Almira Parker June 10, 1891, b. Aug. 11, 1867; d. July 16, 1950

Orra Almira Phelps, daughter of Charles and Orra A. Phelps, b. Sept. 10, 1895; d. Aug. 26, 1986
Charles Francis (1892-1949); Lawrence Hibbard (1893-1955); Orra Almira (1895-1986); Leon Stanley (1897-1965); Phoebe Elizabeth (1898-1968); Katharine DeWitt (1900-1975); and Sylvia Bessie (1903-1972).

Orson Phelps's Line

William Phelps m./2 Mary Dover

Timothy Phelps, b. Sept. 1, 1639 Windsor, Ct.; d. May 2, 1719
      m. Mary Griswold on Mar. 29, 1661; bapt. Oct. 13, 1644
William, b. Feb. 4, 1669 Windsor, Ct.; d. 1733
      m./1 Abigail Mudge, d. Apr. 24, 1705
      m./2 Ruth Barber on Apr. 18, 1706; b. July 24, 1683; d. Aug. 2, 1747

William (or Oliver), b. Mar. 16, 1702, Windsor, Ct. (son of William and Abigail); d. 1776 m./1 Ms. Moore, d. 1725

m./2 Diana Bishop, 1760; b. 1737; d. Jan. 19, 1813

#557   Orin (or Oren) b. Nov. 21, 1768, Windsor Ct.; d. Mar. 25, 1851

m. Ruth Schofield Nov. 1802; b. Jan. 13, 1784; d. Mar. 18, 1868

#1701   Orson Schofield Phelps, b. May 6, 1816, Weathersfield, Vt.; d.Apr. 13, 1905, Keene Valley, N.Y.

m. Lorinda Lamb, Dec. 20, 1845 at Wells, Vt.; b. Jan. 24, 1828; d. Mar. 9, 1917, Keene Valley, N.Y.

Information for Orson Phelps genealogy courtesy of the Keene Valley Library.

PARKER FAMILY GENEALOGY

John Howland, b. 1592 or 1593, d. Feb. 23, 1672 or 1673

Mayflower passenger, arrived Plymouth, Ma. 1620

m. Elizabeth Tilley, Mayflower passenger, b.1607. d. Dec 21, 1687

dau. Hope Howland, b. Aug. 30, 1629, d. Jan. 8, 1683

m. John Chipman, b. circa 1614, Dorchester, Eng.; d. Apr. 7, 1708

son John Chipman, b. Mar. 3, 1670, Barnstable, Ma.; d. Jan. 4, 1756

1st m. Mary Skiff, b. Nov. 13, 1671, Sandwich, Ma.; d. Mar. 12, 1711 or 1712

dau. Lydia Chipman, b. June 9, 1708, a twin, Barnstable, Ma.; d. June 23, 1790

m. Sept. 30, 1725 to Zephaniah Swift, b. Mar. 6, 1702 or 1703; d. May 9, 1781. (Wilmington, Vt. gravestone)

son Perez Swift, b. Feb. 14, 1725 or 1726, Sandwich, Ma.

m. Nov. 3, 1746 to Mary Fox, b. Oct. 7, 1722, Groton, Ct.

dau. Rebecca Swift, bapt. May 18, 1760, Lebanon, Ct.; d. June 17, 1831
m. Dec. 1, 1780 to Jonathan Nichols, b. Feb. 23, 1758, Mansfield, Ct., d. Feb. 13, 1829.

dau. Nancy Nichols, b. May 7, 1782 Woodstock, Vt.; d. Oct. 23, 1851
m. on Feb. 28, 1798 to Sylvester Stanley, b. Jan. 13, 1774, near Thompson, Ct.; d. Oct. 5, 1823.

dau. Almira Stanley Hibbard, b. Dec. 1, 1808; d. Feb. 28, 1887
m. Apr. 10, 1831 to Eliphaz Hibbard, b. Jan. 8, 1808; d. Nov. 14, 1880.

dau. Almira S. Hibbard, b. Jan. 25, 1846; d. Jan. 26, 1907
m. Nov. 23, 1864 to Martin Parker, b. Apr. 3, 1839; d. Oct. 27, 1898.

dau. Orra Almira Parker, b. Aug. 11, 1867; d. July 16, 1950
m. June 10, 1891 to Charles S. Phelps, b. Dec. 5, 1861; d. Apr. 12, 1941.

dau. Dr. Orra Almira Phelps, b. Sept. 10, 1895 at Storrs, Ct.; d. Aug. 26, 1986.
dau. Sylvia Bessie Phelps (Haas), (Orra's sister) b. Mar. 31, 1903; d. Apr. 18, 1972.

dau. Phoebe Louise Haas (Hunt), b. June 23, 1930.
dau. Mary Kay Haas (Aram, Arakelian), (author) b. Nov. 26, 1934.
dau. Dorothy Orra Haas (Busch, Hanlon) b. Dec. 3, 1937.
dau. Rachel Ann Haas (Rekow, Kellogg) b. Dec. 21, 1940.

Endnotes

Chapter 1

1 Orra A. Phelps, Handwritten explanation.
2 Tony Goodwin, ed. *Guide to the Adirondack Trails, High Peaks Region* (Lake George, NY: Adirondack Mountain Club, 1992). p. 142 (describes falls), OAP diary, Intercollegiate Outing Club roster, OAP slide tray with memoranda, and interview with Sid Wilson, IOCA hiker, 1990.
3 Bob Bebee, letter to M. Arakelian, 5 January 1989; Charles Russ's journal, September 1936; and phone interview with John Russ, August 1998.
4 Tony Goodwin, ed. *Guide to the Adirondack Trails, High Peaks Region* (Lake George, NY: Adirondack Mountain Club, 1992). p. 142, also OAP diary.
5 Orra Phelps, ed. *Guide to the Adirondack Trails, Northeastern Section* (Lake George, NY: Adirondack Mountain Club, 1934). p. 74 Hitch-Up-Matilda. This name goes back to an incident when Bill Nye, an old-time Adirondack guide, was leading a party of women through this pass and offered to carry a certain 'Matilda' so she would not get her long shirt wet. When she did not sit up high enough her skirt began to drag, prompting the others in the group to call out, 'Hitch up, Matilda.' The floating bridge was there after named for her.
6 Bob Beebe, letter to M. Arakelian, 5 January 1989. In this letter, he cites the accident as having happened in 1937, but Charles Russ recorded 09/06/36 in his journal.

Chapter 2

1 Phelps letters, OAPP to OAP, 19 November 1916.
2 Ibid. OAPP to OAP, 3 March 1917.
3 Charles Shepherd Phelps, *Rural Life in Litchfield County* (Norfolk, CT: Litchfield County University Club, 1917).
4 Mary P. Wells, *Boy Captive of Old Deerfield* (Boston, MA: Little, Brown 1904, 1929).
5 Phelps letters, OAPP to KP, 26 September 1917.
6 Orra Parker Phelps, *When I Was a Girl in the Martin Box* (New York: Island Press Cooperative, 1949).
7 Phelps letters, OAPP to OAP, 12 October 1916 and 19 October 1916.
8 Names, dates of birth and death of Phelps children: Charles Francis (1892-1949); Lawrence Hibbard (1893-1955); Orra Almira (1895-1986); Leon Stanley (1897-1965); Phoebe Elizabeth (1898-1968); Katharine DeWitt (1900-1975); and Sylvia Bessie (1903-1972).
9 Connecticut Geological and Natural History Survey, Bulletin 14, 1910.
10 Asa Gray, *Manual of Botany of the Northern United States* (New York: American Book Company, 1889).

11 Charles Phelps, letter to OAPP, 31 March 1904.
12 Dr. Mary Phylinda Dole, *A Doctor in Homespun,* 1941 (privately printed).
13 Dr. Phelps, interview by Mary Brennan, 1982.
14 OAPP diary 1910.
15 OAPP to OAP, 6 June 1917.
16 Ibid.
17 Phelps letters, OAPP to OAP, 3 January 1917.

Chapter 3

1 Orra Parker Phelps, *When I Was a Girl in the Martin Box* (New York: Island Press, 1949). p. 11.
2 Orra Phelps, interview by Mary Brennan, March 1982.
3 Ibid.
4 Ibid.
5 Ibid.
6 T. Gilbert Pearson, ed., *Birds of America* (New York: The American Garden Guild, Inc., 1917). Part II, 66.
7 Orra Phelps, interview by Mary Brennan, March 1982.
8 Orra Phelps, letter to Bessie Gammons, 1912.
9 Orra Phelps, interview by Mary Brennan, March 1982.
10 Lawrence Phelps to OAP, 1914.

Chapter 4

1 OAP, "Since Last Fall," English essay at St. Lawrence University, 23 May 1914.
2 OAP, letter to OAPP, 7 October, 1916. OAP's roommate was Elinor Laura Hodges, Winchester, MA.
3 OAPP, letter to OAP, 19 October 1916.
4 "Stone cabbages" refers to fossil *cyanobacteria* (blue-green algae), *Cryptozoon proliferum* and *C. undulatum,* Lester Park and Petrified Gardens, Saratoga Springs, NY. [Now illegal to collect.]
5 OAPP, letter to OAP, 30 October 1916 re: folio.
6 Orra Phelps, interview by Mary Brennan, 1982.
7 OAP, letter to OAPP, 24 October 1916.
8 OAP learned to dance in Salisbury and at MHC, Phelps letters, October 1917
9 OAP, letter to OAPP, 28 February 1917.
10 OAP, letter to OAPP, 25 March 1917.
11 Phelps letters, 4 November 1916.
12 Phelps letters, 10 March 1918.
13 Phelps letters, November 1918.
14 OAPP, letter to OAP, 5 February 1919, Kay and Phoebe Phelps both studied at MHC but graduated from Smith and Columbia, respectively.

15 OAPP, letter to OAP, 16 April, 1919.

16 OAPP, letter to OAP, 11 May, 1919.

Chapter 5

1 OAPP to OAP, 20 September 1919 (Peterson's *A Field Guide to Wildflowers*, 1968, p.282 lists *Liatris squarrosa* as rose purple, pointed, spreading flower bracts, one of eighteen species of *liatris* which often hybridize.)

2 OAP to OAPP, 19 October 1919.

3 OAP to OAPP, 2 November 1920.

4 OAPP to OAP, 20 November 1919.

5 OAP to OAPP, 25 November 1919.

6 OAP to OAPP, 24 January 1920.

7 "Shocks Cause Earth Cracks," *The Knickerbocker Press*, 20 January 1920.

8 Dr. Orra Phelps, "Geology of Saratoga County," *Saratoga County Heritage*, ed. Violet B. Dunn (Saratoga Springs, NY: Saratoga County, 1974). p. 36.

9 OAPP, to OAP, 28 September 1920.

10 OAP and Bessie Phelps, to OAPP, 20 September 1920.

Chapter 6

1 OAP, letter to OAPP, 16 July 1921.

2 OAP, letter to OAPP, 28 August 1921.

3 OAP, letter to OAPP, 24 September 1921.

4 OAP, letter to OAPP, 4 October 1921.

5 OAP, letter to OAPP, 31 October 1921.

6 OAP, letter to OAPP, 24 November 1921.

7 OAP, letter to OAPP, February 1922.

8 OAP, letter to OAPP, 5 November 1921.

9 OAP, letter to OAPP, 16 February 1922.

10 OAP, letter to OAPP, 13 April 1922.

11 OAP, letter to OAPP, 16 February 1922.

Chapter 7

1 E. Clark Worman, *The Silver Bay Story* (Buffalo, NY: Silver Bay Association, Win. J. Keller, Inc.). 1952.

2 OAP, letter to OAPP, 25 June 1922.

3 OAP, letter to OAPP, 1 August 1922.

4 OAP, letter to OAPP, 20 July 1922.

5 Carleton Coulter, letter to OAP, Spring 1924.

6 OAP, letter to OAPP, 24 March 1924.

7 Orra Phelps had several DAR ancestors.

8 Three of her children died in childhood, leaving Orra's father, Charles Phelps, who was ten when his mother died; plus six other siblings aged 6, 13, 15, 17, 19, and 21 … *Phelps Family of America and Their English Ancestry*, Vol. II, 1899, p. 858.
9 OAP, letter to OAPP, 1 May 1924.
10 OAP, letter to OAPP, 5 May 1924.

Chapter 8

1 Lee Miller to OAP, July 1924.
2 Orra A. Phelps, "My First Ascent of Marcy," 1924.
3 Tony Goodwin, ed. *Guide to the Adirondack Trails: High Peaks Region*, Twelfth Edition (Lake George, NY: Adirondack Mountain Club, 1992). p 245.
4 Laura and Guy Waterman, *Forest and Crag* (Boston: Appalachian Mountain Club, 1989). p. 175.
5 Lee Miller to OAP, 11 December 1924, 202 West 22nd St., Wilmington, DE.
6 Orra A. Phelps, M.D. Ed., *Guide to Adirondack Trails, Northeast Section* (Lake George, NY: Adirondack Mountain Club, 1934). p. 49 and Phelps's letters and diaries.
7 OAP, "My First Ascent of Marcy," 1924.

Chapter 9

1 Laura Snell, interview by the author, April 1988.
2 OAP, letter to OAPP, 3 February 1925.
3 OAP, letter to OAPP, 4 April 1925.
4 Gardiner Little, letter to OAP, 6 May 1925.
5 OAP, letter to OAPP, 27 April 1925.
6 OAPP, letter to OAP, 3 May 1925.
7 OAP, letter to OAPP, 28 May 1925.
8 OAP, letter to OAPP, 31 May 1925.
9 "30 DEGREE DROP IN TEMPERATURE; TREES DAMAGED," *The Saratogian*, 11 June 1925: 1.
10 "WILTON GIRL HOME AFTER LONG HIKE FROM BALTIMORE," *The Saratogian*, 17 June 1925.
11 OAP, letter to OAPP, 16 January 1926.
12 OAP, letter to OAPP, 25 October 1926.
13 OAP, letter to OAPP, 4 November 1925.
14 OAP, letter to OAPP, 19 November 1925.
15 OAP, letter to OAPP, 16 February 1926.
16 Florence, letter to OAP, 28 May 1926.
17 OAP, letter to OAPP, 22 November 1926.
18 OAP, letter to OAPP, 26 January 1927.
19 "DOCTOR'S DEGREE IN MEDICINE FOR SARATOGA GIRL," *The Saratogian*, 14 June 1927.

20 OAP, letter to OAPP, 22 March 1927.

Chapter 10

1 OAPP, Diary of 1925 Marcy Ascent.
2 Orra Phelps, ed., *Guide to Adirondack Trails, Northeastern Section* (Lake George, NY: The Adirondack Mountain Club, 1934). p. 78 and Alfred L. Donaldson, *A History of the Adirondacks* (Harrison, NY: Harbor Hill Books, 1977). Vol. 1: 144-146.
3 Alfred L. Donaldson, *A History of the Adirondacks* (Harrison, NY: Harbor Hill Books, 1977). vol. 1: 155.
4 OAP, letter to OAPP, 17 August 1926.
5 "Great Adirondack Guides," *High Spots* (Lake George, NY: The Adirondack Mountain Club: 1933). p. 15.
6 Ibid., 16.
7 Heart Lake also spelled Hart lake in simplified spelling by Harry W. Hicks and Melville Dewey, Lake Placid Club.
8 OAP, letter to OAPP, 11 October 1927.
9 OAP, letter to OAPP, undated 1927.
10 Grace L. Hudowalski, ed. *The Adirondack High Peaks and the Forty-Sixers* (Albany, N.Y.: The Peters Print, 1970).
11 OAP, letter to OAPP, 13 December 1927.
12 William G. Howard, *Northville-Placid Trail* (Lake George, NY: Adirondack Mountain Club, 1923).
13 OAP, letter to OAPP, 13 December 1927. [The proposed Santanoni trail from Cold River was never cut.]
14 Helena Pardee, *The Yaddo, Saratoga Springs*, NY, letter to OAP, July 1928.
15 OAP, letter to OAPP, 8 March 1928.
16 OAP, letter to OAPP, 14 June 1928.

Chapter 11

1 Complete plant list from Mrs. Phelps's 1928 diary in following endnotes.
2 OAPP diary, Location: en route to 13th Lake; also *Hypericum*, a St. Peterswort, and *Galium trifidum L.*, a type of bedstraw and *Senecio robbinsii*, a ragwort.
3 OAPP diary, Location: Thirteenth Lake: "and in a boggy area, a good deal of sedge, rush and various grasses as well as monkey flower and bristly buttercup." and information re: porcupine from *Encyclopedia Britannica*, (Chicago: Ency. Brit. Inc. 1966, Vol., 18). p. 246.
4 Asa Gray, *Manual of The Botany of the Northern United States* (New York: American Book Company, 1889).
5 OAPP diary, Location: Puffer Pond trail: and sheep's laurel, marsh speed well (*Veronica scutellata*), spiked loosestrife (*Lythrum salicaria L.*), twin flower in blossom and rafts of various sedges.

6 Red eft or newt in terrestrial stage.
7 Robert M. Pyle, *The Audubon Society Field Guide to North American Butterflies* (New York: Knopf, 1981). White bar may have been White Admiral, p. 635; Silver wing may have been Silver Spotted Skipper, p. 719.
8 Although Orra and Mrs. Phelps thought they might be too large for saw-whets, Beehler's *Birdlife of the Adirondack Park* (Lake George, NY: Adirondack Mountain Club, Inc., 1978). p. 115, lists the saw-whet owl as a permanent resident, very tame, habitat swamps, damper places; *National Geographic Field Guide to Birds of North America* (Washington, DC: National Geographic Society, 1983). p. 246 notes its raspy call, can be approached closely, size: 8".
9 Roger Tory Peterson and Margaret McKenny, *A Field Guide to Wildflowers* (Boston: Houghton Mifflin Co., 1968). p. 242.
10 OAPP diary, *Myosotis*, sky blue forget-me-not [see R.T. Peterson, *A Field Guide to Wildflowers* (Boston: Houghton Mifflin Company, 1968). p. 334 and in a little sag not far from Cedar River, eleven stalks of the large purple fringed orchid, *H. fimbriata*, as well as burnet and *Houstonias* still in bloom. White Cedar was first noted on a hill along road to Blue Mt. Lake and, where the trails head for Wakely, Orra found adder's tongue, *Ophioglossum*, as well as white flowered sand sperry.
11 Wherever "AMC" was used by Mrs. Phelps in her diary, it denoted the newly formed Adirondack Mountain Club.
12 OAPP diary, Location: Stephens Pond: "and white and yellow water lilies and water shield in the lake, Labrador tea, wintergreen berries, shad-bush, pipsissewa."
13 OAPP diary, Location: marsh near Stephens Pond, "On our return we saw one specimen of the green woodland orchid, *H. clavellata* as well as a colony of Goldie's fern. Saw Cor. – green, early, 6 in bunch. Saw Cor. Mat – one spec. on ret. trip. Along lake sheep's laurel was very vivid red, plus a few blooms of pale laurel and water lilies with slender stems. Leaves are thin with quite a wedge taken out."
14 Location: Nr. Stephens Pond: "plus *Habenaria orbiculata*. Further clarification from R.T. Peterson, *A Field Guide to Wildflowers* (Boston: Houghton Mifflin Company, 1968). p. 242 bract, coral root, Prince's pine in blossom, small stitchwort, pitcher plant, *Myriophyllum*, blackberry with dark green deep veined three parted leaves and blossoms, narrow petal reminding OAPP of clematis. Along the road Orra found *Microseris*.
15 Bruce Wadsworth, ed., *Guide to Adirondack Trails: Northville-Placid Trail*, (Lake George, NY: Adirondack Mountain Club, Inc., 1986). p. 108.
16 OAPP diary, Location: Long Lake: "and thistle blossoms, plenty of *H. tridentate*." Info for floating heart from Peterson, p. 6.

17 Dan Brenan, *The Adirondack Letters of George Washington Sears Whose Pen Name was Nessmuk* (Blue Mt. Lake, NY: The Adirondack Museum, 1962).
18 Information told the author by Kay Phelps many years later.
19 OAPP diary, Location: Cold River, "*Pyrola secunda*, much sheep laurel, rattlesnake plantain."

Chapter 12
1 Name changed to protect patient.
2 Dr. William Howe, Medical Inspector of State of New York, letter to OAP, 17 November 1931.
3 Adirondack Mountain Club (ADK) archives at New York State Library Manuscript/Special Collections, 29-17 December 1929. Hereafter referred to as ADK Archives at NYS Library.
4 John S. Littell to OAP, 30 December 1929.

Chapter 13
No Endnotes

Chapter 14
1 ADK Archives at NYS Library, pp. 30-193.
2 Ibid. pp. 30-53. Reference to the ATIS (a separate group from the Ausable Club but sharing many members) which maintains the trails in the Adirondack Mountain Reserve (AMR) privately owned by the Adirondack Mountain Reserve-Ausable Club.
3 Ibid., 1928, p. 11.
4 OAPP, letter to OAP, 27 June 1933.
5 OAPP, letter to OAP, 21 December 1932.
6 James Goodwin interview by the author, 1988.
7 ADK Archives at NYS Library, 1933 Annual Report.
8 William Toporcer, letter to M. Arakelian, 26 December 1988.
9 OAP to Howard Carlson, 15 October 1933.
10 OAP to Howard Carlson, 5 April 1934.
11 ADK Archives at NYS Library, Guidebook Contents, OAP to Committee, 7 April 1934.
12 OAP to OAPP, 6 April 1934.
13 ADK Archives at NYS Library, OAP letter to R. Mullarkey, 22 August 1934.
14 Simplified spelling was an attempt to reform spelling devised by Melvil Dewey, who for example, spelled Adirondack Lodge as Adrondak Loj, which has been perpetuated.
15 ADK Archives at NYS Library, H. Hicks to OAP, 22 September 1934.
16 ADK Archives at NYS Library, R. Carson to OAP, 25 September 1934.

17 ADK Archives at NYS Library, Henry G. Leach to OAP, 1934.
18 ADK Archives at NYS Library, ADK Treas. Bell to Pres. Andrews, 5 November 1934.

Chapter 15
1 Douglas Ayres, interview by the author, 30 August 1989.
2 OAP to OAPP, 2 December 1930.
3 Orra Phelps, interview by Mary Brennan, 1982.
4 Orra Phelps: Northville-Placid Trail Completion Report, 1978.
5 OAP to OAPP 13 November 1933.
6 OAP to OAPP, 9 April 1936.
7 OAP to OAPP, 14 February 1936.
8 OAP to OAPP, 9 April 1936.
9 Name changed to protect the patient.
10 "Tom," letter to OAP, 15 October 1936.
11 CSP to OAP, 24 May 1938.
12 Orra Almira Parker Phelps, LYGODIUM PALMATUM (Bernh.) SW IN NEW YORK. *American Fern Journal,* Vol. 29, No. 3, July-September, 1939.

Chapter 16
1 Phelps letters, 13 January, 22 January, and 2 February 1936.
2 Al West to OAP, 24 September 1936.
3 OAP to OAPP, 4 October 1936.
4 Orra A. Parker Phelps, "The University of State of New York Bulletin to the Schools," Vol. 24 No. 13, 15 March 1938.
5 Hal Burton, interview by the author, 2 September 1989 and Mary Dittmar, interview by the author, 25 August 1988.
6 Orra A. Phelps, "Marcy Centennial Hike," *High Spots* (Lake George, NY: Adirondack Mountain Club, December 1937).
7 Orra A. Phelps, "Tahawus," *High Spots* (Lake George, NY: Adirondack Mountain Club, December 1937). The Forty-Sixers are a hiking group whose members have climbed all 46 Adirondack High Peaks over 4,000 feet.
8 Maitland C. DeSormo, *Noah John Rondeau, Adirondack Hermit* (Utica, NY: North Country Books, Inc. Sixth Printing, April 1999).

Chapter 17
1 Maitland C. DeSormo, *Noah John Rondeau, Adirondack Hermit* (Utica, NY: North Country Books, Inc. Sixth Printing, April 1999).
2 OAPP, letter to OAP, July 1938.
3 Orra A. Phelps, *Cold River Country in 1938* (essay).
4 Probably OAPP's camp at Marcy Dam.

5   Morgan's wheel. Reference to L. Morgan Porter's trail measurement wheel.

6   Noah John Rondeau to OAP, 7 January 1939, Coreys, N.Y.

7   Orra also hiked to Cold River on 28 August 1941. See Phelps letters (Photos show Bob Fox, OAP, Sterno, Rondeau with words "When I walked from Corey's in and out to see Noah 41 or 42".)

8   Orra saved a receipt for marking the Kates trail maps and in their logs, now kept on microfilm by the Adirondack Museum at Blue Mountain Lake, are references to their meeting her on the trail as well as seeing her name on the trailless peak log books.

9   Herbert S. Kates, letter to OAP, 8 July 1938 (paper imprinted with Herbert S. Ka.es Illustrator, 48 West 48th Street, New York).

10 Bill, letter to OAP, 20 February 1938, Yale University, New Haven, CT.

11 ADK Yearbook 1939.

12 Al West, letter to OAP, 31 January 1939.

13 OAP, letter to OAPP, 24 July 1939 Marcy Dam.

14 OAP, letter to OAPP, 12 July 1939.

15 OAP, letter to Landon Rockwell, 4 July 1982, Wilton, NY.

16 OAP, letter to OAPP, 17 October 1939.

17 A.J. Renssing, letter to OAP, 11 August 1939 [He also included information about lean-tos in Piseco/West Canada Lake region.]

18 OAP to OAPP, 17 March 1940.

19 OAPP to OAP, 26 March 1940.

20 David Beetle, Trail Expert, *The Upstate Monthly*, Utica, NY. December 1941, p. 13.

21 OAP, letter to OAPP, 15 January 1941 and 21 January 1941.

22 "Charles S. Phelps," *The Saratogian* April 12, 1941.

Chapter 18

1   OAP to OAPP, letter, 2 February 1942.

2   Bob Owens to OAP, letter, 2 June 1942.

3   Lawrence Phelps to OAP, letter, 17 January 1944.

4   OAP to OAPP, letter, 18 January 1944.

5   OAP to OAPP, letter, 20 January 1944.

6   OAP to OAPP, letter, 3 March 1944.

7   OAP to OAPP, letter, 4 May 1944.

8   OAP to OAPP, letter, 22 April 1945.

9   OAP to OAPP, letter, 8 June 1944.

10 OAP to OAPP, letter, 2 August 1944.

11 OAP to OAPP, letter, 4 July 1944.

12 OAP to OAPP, letter, 2 July 1944.

13 OAP to OAPP, letter, 20 March 1944.

14 OAP to OAPP, letter, 2 July 1945.

15 Mary K. Haas to OAP, letter, 19 August 1945.
16 Name omitted to protect identity. Phelps letters, 3 February 1944.
17 Al West to OAPP, letter, June 1944.
18 John Haines, PH.D., interview by the author, October 1991.

Chapter 19
1 Elsa Jane Putnam Turmelle, interview by the author, 16 September 1989.
2 Ibid.
3 Ibid.
4 Ibid.
5 George Marshall, letter to Dr. Adolph Dittmar, 9 February 1981.
6 Orra A. Phelps, interview by Mary Brennan, p. 1 - 1 - 10, 1982.
7 Turmelle, interview by the author, September 1989.
8 Ibid.
9 See Phelps Genealogy.
10 Alton West, letter to OAP, 27 July 1934 (hike date either 7/22/34 or 7/15/34.)
11 Orra Phelps, letter to OAPP, 1 August 1934.
12 Orra Phelps interview by Mary Brennan, 1982.
13 Laura and Guy Waterman, *Forest and Crag* (Boston: Appalachian Mountain Club, 1989). p. 462.
14 Turmelle, interview by the author, 16 September 1989.
15 Richard Putnam, interview by the author, 16 September 1989.
16 Lillian Hunt, interview by the author, 12 September 1990.
17 Ibid.
18 William Endicott, interview by the author, 25 July 1988. Also Mark Nye, Jim Nye's son, verified that his father was a direct descendant of old Bill Nye, and that both Alexander Hamilton and Oliver Hazard Perry were also his forbears.
19 Marcella Bunke, interview by the author, undated.

Chapter 20
1 William O. Douglas, *Adirondac*, July-August 1962.
2 Landon Rockwell, "A New Friend for the Adirondacks," *Adirondac* (Lake George, NY: The Adirondack Mountain Club, July 1962). p. 56.
3 Ibid.
4 ADK Archives at NYS Library, pp. 30-38.
5 Dr. Orra A. Phelps, *The Kelsey Nature Trail at Adirondak Loj* (Lake George, NY: Adirondack Mountain Club, 1967).
6 Dr. Edmund H. Fulling, "Holiday Reminiscences in the Adirondacks," *The Garden Journal*, The New York Botanical Society, Vol. 13, No. 6, November-December 1963, p. 225.

7 E.H. Ketchledge, interview by the author, 1988.
8 E.H. Ketchledge, "Orra Phelps: An Appreciation," *Adirondac*. (Lake George, NY: Adirondack Mountain Club, January/February 1972). p. 13.
9 Douglas Ayres poem "From Elk Lake Studded" is printed here with the permission of the North American Loon Fund, Gilford, NH 03246.

Chapter 21

1 Wendy Best, "In Remembrance." *The Paper*, Chatham, NY. September 1993.
2 Wendy Best, interview, 31 March 1990.
3 Ibid.
4 Laura Snell, interview by the author, April 1988.
5 Laura Meade, interview by the author, August 1991.
6 Mary Arakelian, notes from Phelps woods walk, 11 July 1975.
7 Adolph and Mary Dittmar, interview by the author, 25 July 1988.
8 Laura Snell, interview by the author, April 1988.
9 Wendy Best, interview by the author, 31 March 1990.
10 Mary Parker Firth, interview by the author, 22 June 1990.
11 Cornelius E. Durkee, "Reminiscences of Saratoga," *The Saratogian* (Saratoga Springs, NY, 1927-28.) p. 251.
12 William A. Ritchie, *The Archeology of New York State* (Garden City, NY: Natural History Press, 1965).
13 Dr. Robert Funk, interview by the author, 26 August 1988.
14 See NYS Parks and Recreation regulations re: Native American sites.
15 Violet B. Dunn, Editor-in-Chief, *Saratoga County Heritage* (Saratoga Springs, N.Y.: Saratoga County, 1974) and taped interview of Orra Phelps by same.

Chapter 22

1 Orra A. Phelps, ADK Northville-Placid Trail completion report, September 1978.
2 Richard Putnam, interview by the author, September 1989.
3 Bruce Wadsworth, ed. *Guide to Northville-Placid Trail* (Lake George, NY: The Adirondack Mountain Club 1988). p.48.
4 Orra A. Phelps, "Queen of Slippers," *The Conservationist* (Albany, NY: State of New York, Department of Environmental Conservation, 1976). Vol. 30, No. 6/May-June, p.37.
5 Orra A. Phelps, undated hand-written notes. Phelps papers.
6 "Nature Conservancy," The Nature Conservancy, Arlington, VA.
7 Laura Snell, interview by the author, 1988.
8 Phyllis Brown, interview by the author, 30 August 1989.
9 Lillian Hunt, interview by the author, 12 September 1990.
10 Laura Snell, interview by the author, 1988.

11 Dick and Wendy Best, interview by the author, 31 March 1990.

12 Ibid.

13 Borden Mills, "Who Was John?" in *Cloud Splitter* (Lake George, NY: Adirondack Mountain Club, 1948). Information courtesy of The Adirondack Museum.

14 Author's hiking party: Dr. Orra Phelps, Dr. Ali M. Aram, daughters, Lili and Sherene Aram, Farhad Mohandessi, Mary Wright, the naturalist at that time, and the author, Mary Aram (Arakelian.)

15 Henry and Katherine Germond, "Orra Phelps Remembered," *Adirondac* (Lake George, NY: Adirondack Mountain Club, 1986) and personal interview by author.

16 Anne LaBastille, *Woodswoman* (New York: E.P. Dutton, 1976).

17 Laura Snell, interview by the author, 1988.

18 Paul Schaefer, Exec. Dir. *The Adirondacks: The Land Nobody Knows*, 16mm film (1980, Schenectady, NY: COUCH-SACH-RA-GA ASSOCIATION, The Association for the Protection of the Adirondacks, Inc., owner and distributor).

19 Tony Goodwin, ed. *Guide to Adirondack Trails, High Peaks Region* (Lake George, NY: The Adirondack Mountain Club, Inc. Eleventh edition, 1985 and Twelfth edition, 1992).

20 Howard W. Jaffe and Elizabeth B. Jaffe, *Geology of Adirondack High Peaks Region* (Lake George, NY: Adirondack Mountain Club, Inc. 1986). p. vi.

21 Nancy G. Slack and Allison W. Bell, *85 Acres, A Field Guide to the Adirondack Alpine Summits* (Lake George, NY: Adirondack Mountain Club, Inc. 1993).

22 James Goodwin, "Trailless Peaks," in *High Spots*, (Lake George, NY: Adirondack Mountain Club, 1939).

23 Grace Hudowalski, "Orra Phelps Remembered," *Adirondac* (Lake George, NY: Adirondack Mountain Club, 1986).

Bibliography

Orginal Sources (Unpublished)
Taped Personal Interviews by the Author

Ayres, Douglas
Best, Richard and Wendy
Brennan, Mary
Brown, Phyllis
Burton, Hal
Bunke, Marcella
Cole, Grant, Heidi, and Bruce
Cobane, Nellie
Dittmar, Adolf and Mary
Elliott, Carmen
Endicott, William
Firth, Mary Parker, MHC '18
Funk, Dr. Robert
Germond, Henry and Katherine
Geiser, Ralph
Goodwin, James
Haines, Dr. John
Hanmer, Rita
Herrick, Lynn
Hudowalski, Grace L.
Hunt, Phoebe

Hunt, Lillian
Ketchledge, Dr. Edwin H.
King, Maryde
LaPine, Madeline
MacMaster, Gloria
Meade, Laura
Menz, Helen
Newkirk, Dr. Arthur and Kay
Ogden, Dr. Eugene
Putnam, Richard
Schaefer, Paul
Shaw, Mildred
Slack, Dr. Nancy
Snell, Laura
Toporcer, Williarn
Tropasso, Joseph
Turmelle, Elsa Jane
Westcott, Lorraine
Wilson, Sidney
Wood, Mildred

Adirondack Mountain Club archival material
Interview of Orra Phelps by Mary Brennan
Johns Hopkins University archival material
New York State Museum, Education Department archival material
Orra A. Parker Phelps unpublished essays, poems, diaries, and notes
Orra Phelps unpublished essays, poems, diaries, notes and personal papers
Phelps and Parker family genealogical charts
Phelps family letters
Phelps letters received by Orra Phelps, not family
The Adirondack Museum microfilms
United States Military Academy at West Point Alumni archival material

Secondary Sources

PERIODICALS

Beetle, David. *Trail Expert*, The Upstate Monthly, Utica, N.Y., December 1941, p. 13.

Fulling, Dr. Edmund H. "Holiday Reminiscences in the Adirondacks," *The Garden Journal*, The New York Botanical Society, Vol. 13, No. 6 November-December 1963, p. 255.

Germond, Henry and Katherine, "Orra Phelps Remembered," *Adirondac* (Lake George, N.Y.: Adirondack Mountain Club, 1986).

Goodwin, James, "Trailless Peaks," in *High Spots* (Lake George, N.Y.: Adirondack Mountain Club, 1939).

Ketchledge, E.H., "Orra Phelps: An Appreciation," *Adirondac*, (Lake George, N.Y.: Adirondack Mountain Club, January-February 1972). p. 13.

MacMaster, Frederick, "Orra A. Phelps, M.D." *Adirondack Life,* Fall 1971, pp. 42-43.

Mills, Borden, "Who Was John?" in *Cloud Splitter* (Lake George, N.Y.: Adirondack Mountain Club, 1948). Information courtesy of The Adirondack Museum.

Phelps, Orra A., "Tahawus," *High Spots, Adirondac* (Lake George, N.Y.: Adirondack Mountain Club, December 1937).

Phelps, Orra A., "Marcy Centennial Hike," *High Spots* (Lake George, N.Y.: Adirondack Mountain Club, 1937). Information courtesy of The Adirondack Museum.

Phelps, Orra A., "Queen of Slippers," *The Conservationist* (State of New York, Department of Environmental Conservation, Albany, N.Y., Vol. 30, No. 6, May-June 1976). p. 37.

Phelps, Orra A. Parker, The University of State of New York Bulletin to the Schools, Vol. 24, No. 13, 15 March 1938.

Phelps, Orra A. Parker, *Lygodium Palmatum (Bernh.)* SW in New York (American Fern Journal, Vol. 29, No. 3, July-September 1939).

Rockwell, Landon, "A New Friend for the Adirondacks," *Adirondac* (Lake George, N.Y.: Adirondack Mountain Club, July 1962). P. 56.

Selected Books

Beehler, Bruce M., *Birdlife of the Adirondack Park*, (Lake George, N.Y.: Adirondack Mountain Club, Inc., 1978).

Brenan, Dan, *The Adirondack Letters of George Washington Sears Whose Pen Name was Nessmuk* (Blue Mountain Lake, N.Y.: The Adirondack Museum, 1962).

DeSormo, Maitland C., *Noah John Rondeau, Adirondack Hermit* (Utica, N.Y.: North Country Books, Inc. Sixth Printing, 1999).

Donaldson, Alfred L., *A History of the Adirondacks*, 2 Vol. (New York: The Century Co., 1921; reprint ed.: Harrison, N.Y.: Harbor Hill Books, 1977).

Dunn, Violet B., Editor-in-Chief, *Saratoga County Heritage*, 1974. p. 36.

Goodwin, Tony, ed. Neal Burdick, Series Editor, *Guide to the Adirondack Trails, High Peaks Region* (Lake George, N.Y.: The Adirondack Mountain Club, Inc. 11th ed. (1985) 12th ed. (1992).

Gray, Asa, *Manual of Botany of the Northern United States* (New York: American Book Company, 1889).

Howard, William G., Director of Lands and Forests, New York State Department of Conservation, *Northville-Placid Trail.* 1923.

Jaffe, Howard W. and Elizabeth B., *Geology of Adirondack High Peaks Region* (Lake George, N.Y.: The Adirondack Mountain Club, Inc. 1986). P. vi.

LaBastille, Anne, *Woodswoman* (New York: E.P. Dutton, 1976).

Longstreth, T. Morris, *The Lake Placid Country, Tramper's Guide* (Lake Placid, N.Y.: The Adirondack Camp and Trail Club, 1922).

Marshall, Robert, *High Peaks of the Adirondacks* (Lake George, N.Y.: Adirondack Mountain Club, 1922).

Mitchell, Richard S., *A Checklist of New York State Plants* (Albany, N.Y.: The University of the State of New York, The State Education Department, 1986).

O'Kane, Walter, *Trails and Summits of the Adirondacks*. 1928.

Pearson, T. Gilbert, ed. *Birds of America* (New York: The American Garden Guild, Inc., 1917). Part II. P. 66.

Peterson, Roger Tory and Margaret McKenny, *A Field Guide to Wildflowers* (Boston: Houghton Mifflin Co., 1968).

Phelps, Charles Shepherd, *Rural Life in Litchfield County* (Norfolk, CT: Litchfield County University Club, 1917).

Phelps, Oliver Seymour and Andrew T. Servin, compilers, *Phelps Family of America and Their English Ancestry,* Vols. I & II. (Pittsfield, MA: Eagle Publishing Co., 1899).

Phelps, Orra A., ed. *Guide to Adirondack Trails, Northeastern Section* (Lake George, N.Y.: Adirondack Mountain Club, 1934).

Phelps, Orra A., ed. *Guide to Adirondack Trails, Northeastern Section* (Lake George, N.Y.: Adirondack Mountain Club, 1941).

Phelps, Orra Parker, *When I Was a Girl in the Martin Box* (New York: Island Press Cooperative, 1949).

Pyle, Robert M., *The Audobon Society Field Guide to North American Butterflies* (New York: Knopf, 1981).

Ritchie, Prof. William A., *The Archaeology of New York State* (Garden City, N.Y.: Natural History Press, 1965).

Scott, Shirley L., ed., *National Geographic Field Guide to Birds of North America* (Washington, D.C.: National Geographic Society, 1983).

Slack, Nancy G., and Allison W. Bell, *85 Acres: A Field Guide to the Adirondack Alpine Summits* (Lake George, N.Y.: The Adirondack Mountain Club, Inc., 1993).

Tefft, Tim, ed., *Of the Summits, Of the Forests* (Morristown, N.Y.: The Adirondack Forty-Sixers, 1991).

Van Diver, Bradford B., *Roadside Geology of New York* (Missoula, MT: Mountain Press Publishing Co., 1985).

Wadsworth, Bruce, ed., *Guide to the Adirondack Trails, High Peaks Region and Northville-Placid Trail* (Lake George, N.Y.: Adirondack Mountain Club, 1972).

Wadsworth, Bruce, ed., *Guide to the Adirondack Trails: Northville-Placid Trail* (Lake George, N.Y.: Adirondack Mountain Club, 1986).

Waterman, Laura and Guy, *Forest and Crag* (Boston: Appalachian Mountain Club, 1989). P. 175.

Wells, Mary P., *Boy Captive of Old Deerfield* (Boston: Little, Brown, 1904 & 1929).

Worman, E. Clark, *The Silver Bay Story* (Buffalo, N.Y.: Silver Bay Association, Wm. J. Keller, Inc., 1952).

Index of Names and Places